VERNACULAR ARCHITECTURE AND REGIONAL DESIGN:
CULTURAL PROCESS AND ENVIRONMENTAL RESPONSE

VERNACULAR ARCHITECTURE AND REGIONAL DESIGN:
CULTURAL PROCESS AND ENVIRONMENTAL RESPONSE

KINGSTON WM. HEATH

AMSTERDAM · BOSTON · HEIDELBERG · LONDON · NEW YORK · OXFORD
PARIS · SAN DIEGO · SAN FRANCISCO · SYDNEY · TOKYO

Architectural Press is an imprint of Elsevier
Linacre House, Jordan Hill, Oxford OX2 8DP, UK
30 Corporate Drive, Suite 400, Burlington, MA 01803, USA

First edition 2009

Copyright © 2009, Elsevier Ltd. Published by Elsevier Ltd. All rights reserved

No part of this publication may be reproduced, stored in a retrieval system or transmitted in any form or by any means electronic, mechanical, photocopying, recording or otherwise without the prior written permission of the publisher

Permission may be sought directly from Elsevier's Science & Technology Rights Department in Oxford, UK: phone (+44) (0) 1865 843830; fax (+44) (0) 1865 853333; email: permissions@elsevier.com. Alternatively you can submit your request online by visiting the Elsevier website at http://elsevier.com/locate/permissions, and selecting *Obtaining permission to use Elsevier material*

Notice
No responsibility is assumed by the publisher for any injury and/or damage to persons or property as a matter of products liability, negligence or otherwise, or from any use of operation of any methods, products, instructions or ideas contained in the material herein. Because of rapid advances in the medical sciences, in particular, independent verification of diagnoses and drug dosages should be made

British Library Cataloging in Publication Data
Heath, Kingston Wm
  Vernacular architecture and regional design: cultural
  process and environmental response
  1. Vernacular architecture 2. Sustainable architecture
  I. Title
  720.1'03

Library of Congress Cataloging-in-Publication Data
A catalogue record for this book is available from the Library of Congress

Library of Congress Control Number: 2008940779
ISBN-13: 978-0-7506-5933-8

For information on all Architectural Press publications
visit our website at www.architecturalpress.com

Typeset by TnQ, Chennai, India
www.tnq.co.in

Printed and bound in Great Britain

09 10 11 12 13 10 9 8 7 6 5 4 3 2 1

Working together to grow
libraries in developing countries

www.elsevier.com | www.bookaid.org | www.sabre.org

ELSEVIER   BOOK AID International   Sabre Foundation

Contents

Dedication vii
Acknowledgements ix
Foreword: on the study of 'regional architecture' xi
Preface – Regionalism reconsidered xiii
List of illustrations xvii

Section One   Exploring the Nature of Place 1
   1 An interpretive model for assessing regional identity amidst change 3
   2 Architecture as cultural production 22

Section Two   From Regional Theory to a Situated Regional Response 37
   3 Introduction 39

Part One   People – Improving the Human Condition Through Design 49
   4 Finding patterns within the local building culture, and preserving the continuity of
      tradition through participatory housing and community development 51
   5 Facing the challenge of a framework approach 61
   6 Rewriting history through architecture 75

Part Two   Locale – Interpreting and Accommodating Characteristics of an Evolving Landscape 91
   7 Embracing the urban contradictions of a border zone 93
   8 Overpainting sprawl as a sustainable landscape 108

Part Three   Environment – Appropriate Technologies and Design Tied to the Dynamics of Place 125
   9 A poverty of resources/a richness of expression 127
  10 Celebrating and safeguarding the environment through residential design 146
  11 Architecture of response rather than imposition 159

Index 179

To my wife, Randall May Heath. You invest my life with meaning, joy and wonder.

Acknowledgements

This topic, which explores the bridge between vernacular architecture theory and contemporary regional design, has been a central concern of mine since the mid-1980s. I, therefore, have many intellectual debts to pay for the development of my ideas in this text.

While at the University of North Carolina, Charlotte (UNCC) I organized a symposium in 1988 entitled 'Regionalism, Contextualism, and the Search for a "New" Vernacular.' Speakers included E. Fay Jones, Steven Izenour, Rob Quigley, Dell Upton, and Robert Craig. Subsequent guest speakers to UNCC graciously provided time for interviews. These interviews included wonderful discussions with Sam Mockbee, Joseph Esherick, and James Cutler. Those discussions led to a manuscript draft entitled 'Context as Text' that was presented to MIT Press in 1995, but was not published. Instead, some of the theoretical content was developed into conference presentations and articles for the Vernacular Architecture Forum and the Association of Collegiate Schools of Architecture. One of the case studies from the 1995 manuscript – an application model of the regional theory offered in the original draft – became the *Patina of Place: The Cultural Weathering of a New England Industrial Landscape* published by the University of Tennessee Press in 2001. While the theoretical model presented in the earlier manuscript was refined in this study, much of the original manuscript written in 1995, six chapters in all, was never published and all the case studies herein are the product of the past few years.

I would like to thank the School of Architecture at UNCC for granting sabbatical leave to develop the present manuscript. Also, as in the *Patina of Place*, my colleague Gregor Weiss provided evocative drawings of the mobile home transformations that we discussed together at length. Countless hours were spent typing early drafts and discussing concepts with my very talented thesis students and teaching assistants Todd Williams, Donia D. Schauble, and Matt Draughn. Their loyalty and friendship mean much to me. I hope this work does justice to their collective efforts.

At the University of Oregon, several colleagues were generous with their time. Howard Davis read the prospectus and made helpful comments at various points of the manuscript development. Tom Hubka and Robert Melnick responded to selected chapters on vernacular theory. Those chapters benefited, as well, from the editorial review by Camille Wells and Pamela Simpson for the journal entry of 'Assessing Regional Identity Amidst Change: The Role of Vernacular Studies' published in *Perspectives in Vernacular Architecture*, volume 13 (2), 2006/2007. Michael Fifield provided background on the tsunami recovery efforts in Sri Lanka and provided me with images. Also, University of Oregon architecture professors Brook Muller, John Reynolds, Alison Kwok, and Nico Larco lent commentary on an earlier draft of the case study on Glenn Murcutt that led to the clarification of key design issues for the author. Natalie Perrin, my graduate assistant, helped in many ways to keep the book manuscript on schedule.

Of course, many thanks are due the architects whose case studies are chronicled in this text. Their willingness to expand upon concepts in their respective chapter entries, provide original drawings to clarify design responses, and provide me with high-quality images to represent their work was much appreciated.

Finally, a thank you is insufficient to recognize the many contributions of my wife, Randall. She listened to me read the various versions of chapter entries (and their revisions); provided many insightful comments in the process; offered editorial suggestions; and (as a research librarian) made certain that all my citations were accurate. She has my unwavering gratitude and love – she is a partner in every sense of the word.

Eugene, Oregon
2008

Foreword: on the study of 'regional architecture'

Regionalism is a concept that has different meanings in different disciplines. In geography, it refers to a geographic territory that shows specific identifiable characteristics. In politics, regionalism is an ideology which focuses on using this unique geography to advance specific political goals like autonomy or separatism. In art, regionalism has been a realist modern movement that flourished in America during the 1930s, shunning urban life and focusing on rural heartland practices and imaginaries. In architecture, regionalism has been an approach that attempted to understand buildings using the contextual forces that surround their production. Critical regionalism designated a form of architectural practice that embraces modern architecture critically for its universal unifying qualities while simultaneously responding to social, cultural, and climatic contexts of the region in which it is built.

Not since the pioneering theorizing of regional design, by such figures as Alexander Tzonis and Liane Lefaivre and later Kenneth Frampton, have we in the discipline of architecture returned to probe these ideas more thoroughly. Kingston Heath, however, does exactly this for us in this important book. Unlike these earlier important studies and the many intermediate contributions in the interim, this book attempts to communicate to three very different groups of people: scholars of vernacularism and regionalism in all their spatial manifestations, architects who pursue a critical practice stance that is based on a specific understanding of regionalism, and architectural educators who are interested in learning from the vernacular and applying knowledge of cultural processes in responsive and responsible design. It is this interesting mix of concerns and the use of a wide range of case study types that make this book unique.

The terms vernacular, regional, indigenous, and traditional are often used interchangeably but they have to be dealt with here with a degree of care particularly in the current era of globalization. Today, there are many vernacular forms that are not indigenous to a particular region or even place-bound. There are also vernacular forms that emerge in the crucible of specific building traditions but that quickly move outside of these traditions. Indeed in today's world, tradition can no longer be thought of as the static legacy of a past that is handed down from one generation to another. Instead it is and must be always understood as a dynamic project for the reinterpretation of this past in light of the needs of a current present and a future. Traditions are also ever changing but they somehow do not die easily. However, I have argued elsewhere that the built environments of the new global order exhibit a sense of placelessness resulting possibly from the fact that tradition and the practices of the vernacular are increasingly becoming less place rooted and more informationally based. I went on to suggest that we have not come to the end of tradition, but that our conception of tradition as a repository of authentic and valuable ideas that are handed down from one generation to another has lost its utility. I believe that the notions of isolation and rootedness and the implications of these notions fostered by early work on the practices of the vernacular within the geography of regions have already been significantly challenged.

Heath's book is a very good demonstration of what comes next. His multi-scaled case studies nicely show modernity's complicity in locating and defining the vernacular as a situated regional response that restores the centrality of place in the current discourse. Also, unlike previous books on this subject, this book clearly illustrates both how certain scholars have attempted to interpret the new emerging landscape so that designers can better respond to it, and how architects have attempted to improve the human condition through design that is tied to the dynamics of place.

In an era where the space of flows has often overwhelmed the space of places, it remains to be seen whether this dichotomy of place versus flow can indeed be broken by the mere practices of the vernacular. Only time will tell.

Nezar AlSayyad
University of California, V.C. Berkley

Preface
Regionalism reconsidered

Regionalism is more than a stylistic category. It is an attitude toward design that endeavors to bring about positive change through the introduction of appropriate technologies. Or, it strives to sustain and refine successful design strategies that are culturally embedded within a region, that emanate from the landscape, and/or that speak to the values, customs, and needs of its inhabitants. Or, it chooses to be deferential – that is, ecocentric rather than egocentric – in its response to the changing social circumstances of a locale without sacrificing design integrity or invention.

The intent of this study is not to politicize the debate over the most appropriate methods for addressing various regional conditions. Instead, the work reconsiders regionalism from the point of view of the social process of place making, the multiplicity of cultural identities, issues of climatic response, and the effects of dramatic social change. It is a situated regionalism, one that looks at improving the present human condition through design. Many of the case studies focus on locales abandoned by corporate capital; that are marginalized politically; that have been dramatically altered by natural disasters or human imposition; or that have been transformed into bland oblivion by insensitive development.

These are the cultural domains where few design professionals and regional scholars choose to venture. The places often lack social harmony, economic stability, conceptual clarity, or physical uniformity (except perhaps in the scale of transformation). The issues are frustratingly complex and only able to be addressed incrementally in most cases. But some try. This book draws attention to a few that ventured into forgotten landscapes, or that drew attention to the need to reform critically important aspects of their disciplines. In this regard, this is a book aimed at the next generation of architects, urban designers, and regional scholars that are looking to different avenues of inquiry for understanding and addressing the dynamics that shape Place – not just to the images that signify it.

Often, the design efforts discussed in the following chapters yield a revised definition of local distinctiveness, and apply methods of analysis that are not typically part of standard design inquiry. For example, some practitioners study the built environment through a culture concept, whereby regional landscapes become sources for exploring the manner in which human populations around the globe create, adapt, and transform their environments in response to personal beliefs, human interactions, situational opportunities and constraints, traditional and evolving technologies, and forces of the natural environment.[1] Given this construct, the relevance of architecture resides no longer solely in understanding the details of specific sets of design decisions by professionals in the field, but also in the recognition that architecture is inevitably a collective social act.[2] Hence, by reading the human reinscriptions on the land that reflect the manner in which the built environment has evolved over time through human intervention, a more socially engaged understanding of regional factors may be found.

One may think of such evidence of collective adjustment within a locale as patterns of contradiction. Such expressions within a landscape can offer architects the specifics of regional adjustment that the users of the built environment have felt compelled to express. These evolving architectural tactics within today's cultural landscapes can offer architects the opportunity to probe changing social and environmental conditions for sensitive and meaningful responses that are critically engaged in the current human situation.

Frederick Jameson argues in the introduction of his text *The Political Unconsciousness* (1982) that one should address a building not as *object* but as *effect*; without the full consciousness of the ways individuals adapt to their environment, we seek to understand what produces the *effect* manifested in the building. Often, an observer is limited to isolating regional response to patterns of effect, since *cause* remains absent because consciousness is limited by the changing nature of place itself that has many variables. Because the insider is often immersed in the phenomena of place (what Relph refers to as the *existential insider* in *Place and Placelessness*) and responds to his/her locale generally, with the unconscious awareness born of familiarity, the local builder is sometimes unaware of the multiple dynamics at play in shaping built form within its regional setting. The attuned outsider (what Relph calls the *empathetic outsider*), on the other hand, by virtue of his/her separateness from the locale, is more apt to see not only patterns of consistency within a landscape but critical points of *contradiction* (Jameson's term). The conclusion I reach is that in the awkward synthesis of old and new patterns of effect that emerge in response to dynamic forces of regional change, lies evidence of an *evolving vernacular* within a landscape. These contradictions call out for accommodation and offer opportunities for the architect to produce an empathetic response that will be at one with the people and the emerging situational context.

This stance (of responding to the patterns of contradiction within a locale) is in stark contrast to some architectural scholars who believe that it is essential to study only the historic precedent of unaltered building types as source material for authentic regional insights. But, by seeking to limit our awareness of the built environment to issues of original design intent, we ignore significant insights into the current regional and subregional forces that constitute the evolving history and identity of a locale and the changing priorities of its people.

In an effort to examine the social process of place making, Section One of the study puts forth an argument to broaden the scope of regional issues addressed in architectural education, and it offers a theoretical exploration into the nature of vernacular forms as expressions of evolving regional patterns. This section of the book supports the notion that vernacular architecture is a dynamic process of development over time by the collective actions of individuals. In the end, it is *people* who individually address the challenges and opportunities of a locale and act on the basis of local knowledge that is collectively shared; together, they develop an identifiable regional architecture. The effort is made throughout the text to illuminate such phenomena and to stress the importance of discerning the manifestation of these collective regional forces and human responses in our own built environments that can lead to effective place-based design.

Attention shifts in Section Two from a theoretical model that addresses building forms and practices undertaken by individuals outside of the architectural profession to various application models represented in current professional practice. This section of the study explores recent design efforts by architects, urban designers, and planning professionals that address an array of highly particularized forces at play within a locale. The case studies go beyond an examination of the work itself to explore how design decisions were prioritized in light of the regional situation. For that reason each case study clarifies the 'regional filter' that shaped each work and guided the resultant design intent and process. Emphasis is placed on residential and public works that are anchored, principally, in socially and/or environmentally responsive concerns. While not all the professionals and the sites selected are well known to the public at large, the regional strategies and social/environmental priorities addressed in the work are broadly relevant and applicable.

This approach to bridging the vernacular research methods of the anthropologist/social historian, and the regional design investigations of the architectural educator, is the product of having developed field studies and building analyses of various regional forms within the framework of teaching vernacular architecture in design schools over many years. This book, therefore, may be valuable to students of architecture who are seeking to address the particularities of place in their design investigations by offering a broad range of interrelated issues to consider in the reading of a landscape before moving to the actual generation of form and the manipulation of space. To aid in the interpretation process, a series of original drawings and photographs parallel the text to enhance the understanding of textual details. Figure captions in Section One, for example, outline the main points of the theoretical argument, while the illustrations are selected to assist in the reading of regional or cultural indicators.

The goal is not to make design professionals quasi-anthropologists. Instead, it is to move the designer beyond an outsider's view of place, whereby *a priori* decisions or aesthetic imperatives alone guide design. The responsibility for positive social and environmental accommodation should not reside at the feet of professionals exclusively, however. It needs to be a collective enterprise in order to be embraced in an enduring and socially relevant way. Through partnerships among community groups, non-governmental organizations, local governments, enlightened developers, academic programs, and architectural firms, a genuine engagement with the locale is more likely to produce a design response that is rooted in an understanding of the needs, mind, and spirit of another society. Such a design approach that seeks to address a locale from the vantage point of the concerns and values of its local citizens and the critical dynamics of place is what is referred to in this study as *situated regionalism*. By seeing the built environment as more than a composite of isolated form-types, plan-types, or design features, and exploring, instead, built forms and spaces as part of human and environmental systems, buildings and their contexts can offer insights into a series of regionally appropriate practices and improve the current social and environmental situation through design.

Notes

1. For a leading study that applies the method of ecological history to uncover long-term changes and modes of production that shaped colonial New England habitats, see William Cronon, *Changes in the Land: Indians, Colonists, and the Ecology of New England*, New York: Hill and Wang, 1983. See Bernard L. Herman, *Architecture and Rural Life in Central Delaware, 1700–1900*, Knoxville, TN: University of Tennessee Press, 1987, for a demonstration model of how buildings speak eloquently both of generations of gradual change and of radical transformations. For a significant study about how even a noted landmark, like Olmsted's Central Park, is used and changed and thus offers a shifting definition of its identity and social meaning that moves well beyond its primacy as an art object, see Roy Rosenzweig and Elizabeth Blackmar's *The Park and the People*, Ithaca, NY: Cornell University Press, 1992. For a discussion of the physical weathering of buildings as a result of natural forces, see Mohsen Mostafavi and David Leatherbarrow, *On Weathering: The Life of Buildings in Time*, Cambridge, MA: MIT Press, 1993. For a broad overview of how buildings change over time through human intervention, see Stewart Brand, *How Buildings Learn: What Happens After They're Built*, Middlesex: Penguin Books, 1994. In his discussion of the changing role and purpose of cities in Western society, and the processes used to create and transform the physical fabric of those cities, James Vance uses the term *urban morphogenesis*. See James E. Vance Jr, *The Continuing City: Urban Morphology in Western Civilization*, Baltimore, MD: Johns Hopkins University Press, 1990.

2. While creative intent is a critical determinant of built form, architectural historian Kurt Forster reminds us that architecture is seldom a one-person affair; rather architecture is a collective enterprise. Through a collective matrix with many other individuals who will use or construct a particular work, a social meditation of ideas shapes, and will continue to shape, a given work through the full term of its usable life. Architecture, then, is a direct end product of the cultural and environmental milieu out of which it came. See Shaking the Getty Tree: Kurt Forster talks about historical research, *Design Book Review* (Fall 1986), 8–12.

List of illustrations

Chapter 1

1.1 Mount Airy Plantation, Richmond County, Virginia (circa 1760). 4
1.2 Sung Tak Buddhist Temple, formerly Pike Street Synagogue (1903–1904), New York City. 5
1.3 1879 statue of Sergeant William Jasper, Revolutionary War hero, Savannah, Georgia. 6
1.4 The Poyas-Mordecai House, an elite version of a Charleston, South Carolina, single house. 7
1.5 A modest single house duplex, Charleston, South Carolina. 7
1.6 A woven reed mat covering is renewed approximately every five years on a traditional residence, Luang Prabang, Laos. 8
1.7 Structural model 1. 9
1.8 Peter Eisenman's Falk House (Cardboard Architecture House II, 1969–1970), Hardwick, Vermont. 10
1.9 Mobile homes sold as commodities off the sales lot in Charlotte, North Carolina. 10
1.10 The Kluge House (circa 1873), Helena, Montana. 11
1.11 Northern California home transformed into a personal fantasy of the American home as one's own castle. 11
1.12 Las Trampas, New Mexico, Spanish mission. 12
1.13 Garden façade, John Ridout House (1764–1765), Annapolis, Maryland. 13
1.14 William Boardman home built in 1687 with later additions, Saugus, Massachusetts. 13
1.15 A three-dimensional exchange model, 'Dynamics that shape vernacular form.' 14
1.16 Asian decorative features overlaid onto a 1913 classically inspired commercial structure, San Francisco's China Town. 15
1.17 Prayer beads and makeshift altar amidst temporary housing, Sri Lanka. 15
1.18 Two Appalachian outbuildings reflecting enduring traditions. 16
1.19 A circa 1830s log house with 1860s addition, Middlebrook, Virginia. 17
1.20 A classic Shenandoah Valley home, called an 'I-house.' 17
1.21 The 1930s El Vado Motor Court on Route 66, Albuquerque, New Mexico. 17
1.22 The Route 70 Twin drive-in theater in Burlington, North Carolina, 'for sale.' 18
1.23 A German-style log crib barn circa late 1700s, Rowan County, North Carolina. 18

Chapter 2

2.1 An Oregon mobile home decorated for the winter holidays. 23
2.2 Locations for Gallatin County, Montana, and Cabarrus County, North Carolina. 23
2.3 A mobile home situated in a ranch setting in Gallatin County, Montana. 24
2.4 A Gallatin County, Montana, mobile home responding to various regional climatic factors. 24
2.5 A Gallatin County, Montana, mobile home with a weather baffle as a climatic response. 25
2.6 Selected regional responses of a mobile home in southwestern Montana based on photographic field data. 26
2.7 Regionally adjusted southwestern Montana mobile home. 27
2.8 Regionally specific design accommodations for a mobile home located in southwestern North Carolina. 28
2.9 Ladder back oak rocking chairs on a mobile home porch, Cabarrus County, North Carolina. 29

xviii   List of illustrations

2.10 An entrance portico added to a North Carolina mobile home evoking associations of a Southern plantation house. 29
2.11 Furring strips and foam insulation added over the metal cladding of this Gallatin County, Montana, mobile home. 30
2.12 Regionally adjusted southwest North Carolina mobile home. 31
2.13 Woodlawn Plantation, Assumption Parish, Louisiana, 1937 HABS drawing. 31
2.14 Members of the Vernacular Architecture Forum (VAF) photodocumenting the ruins of an eighteenth-century plantation, Tidewater region of Virginia, 2002. 32
2.15 and 2.16 The 1916 Goodhue Company Cooperative Department Store in Red Wing, Minnesota, as seen in the 1960s and since restoration to its 1916 likeness. 33
2.17 An exterior view of the 1892 Armory, Portland, Oregon. 34
2.18 Portland Armory adaptively reused as a performing arts facility, the Gerding Theater. 34

Chapter 3

3.1 San Francisco De Assisi adobe mission (1813–1815), Rancho De Taos, New Mexico. 40
3.2 Design schemes drawn from Texas history for the Austin Museum of Art by Robert Venturi, Denise Scott-Brown, and Steven Izenour. *Center Magazine*'s 'New Regionalism Issue,' volume 3, 1987. 41
3.3 Eric Moss's Petal House for Brad and Maritza Culbertson, Los Angeles, California (1981–1983). 42
3.4 Michael Graves' Regional Library, San Juan Capistrano, California, 1983. 43
3.5 and 3.6 Detail of Michael Graves' Regional Library, San Juan Capistrano, California. Detail of San Francisco De Assisi adobe mission built 1813–1815, Rancho De Taos, New Mexico. 44
3.7 Villa Maria, Little Italy district of San Diego, California, 1999. 45
3.8 Villa Maria apartment unit designed by Rob Wellington Quigley. 45
3.9 Hult Center for the Performing Arts in Eugene, Oregon, of 1979–1982 designed by Hardy, Holzman, Pfieffer Associates of New York. 46
3.10 Seaside, Florida, planned and designed by Andres Duany, Elizabeth Plater-Zyberk, and Robert Davis. 46

Chapter 4

4.1 Detail of a bicycle rickshaw and driver in Vellore, India. 52
4.2 Location of the site. 52
4.3 'Always a temple' – this pattern element is a small temple located in its traditional position within the community. The layout is recorded by camera. 53
4.4 Observations of the various temple's spatial relationships and physical features were recorded in field notes by Kerr and Moses. 54
4.5 Site locations (top), street sections, and field notations (below) by Kerr and Moses. These social and spatial patterns are related to collecting water in the village. 54
4.6 A site-marking ceremony at the start of the house construction. Each lot was exactly 13.5 square meters. 55
4.7 Existing housing in Tamil Nadu, where bicycle-rickshaw drivers and their families lived prior to the completion of the new project in Vellore. 55
4.8 Vellore community members walking the perimeter of the site. 56
4.9 Community members in Vellore being asked to contribute their ideas about what they wanted in a home. 56
4.10 The first two experimental houses in Vellore. 57
4.11 Annamalais house plan. 58

4.12 View of the experimental house during construction. 58
4.13 A Vellore family and rickshaw shortly after their home was completed. 59
4.14 A Vellore home culturally weathered with ceremonial rice flour threshold art, pottery, and a raffia shading device added in the months following occupation. 59

Chapter 5
5.1 Pre-existing site condition of a Mahaweli Dam site. 62
5.2 Map with the town sites located. Dehiattakandiya, the subject village, is denoted by the red circle. 64
5.3 Various design schemes of the initial state towns of Dehiattakandiya and Girandurukotte. 66
5.4 An affected site in the planned reservoir bed at Randenigale. 67
5.5 Opening of the completed Victoria Dam, flooding down river village sites. 67
5.6 Mahaweli town: structure and relationship chart to serve the new irrigation settlements in downstream and upstream areas. 68
5.7 Hierarchy of service centers. 69
5.8 Structural shells under construction in the village center of the town of Teldiniya. 70
5.9 Drawing of one of the three plan types for stores with living spaces above that lined the main streets of the town center of Dehiattakandiya. 71
5.10 Three-quarter view of the salt box form's structural shell shortly after construction. ...71
5.11 Three-quarter view of the double-story post office in the new town center of Teldeniya after storeowners and clients reclaimed the building and foreground spaces. 72
5.12 Simple structures with fixed windows at the higher level were designed with the façades facing the square to maximize the view of the foreground space. 72
5.13 Rear courtyard of the Mahaweli office in Dehiattakandiya, designed as a multipurpose space for parking and outdoor activities. 73

Chapter 6
6.1 Entrance view of the Museum at Red Location, Port Elizabeth, South Africa. 76
6.2 and 6.3 Map of South Africa with the location of the site in Port Elizabeth marked. 76
6.4 Unplanned urban habitats built during apartheid. 77
6.5 A British concentration camp built during the Anglo-Boer war, circa 1900. 78
6.6 Former concentration camps today. 79
6.7 View from the former barracks toward the museum. 80
6.8 and 6.9 Two faces: (public face) houses are closed to the street, while (private face) of the houses offer a socially inviting interior rooms. 81
6.10 View of the new government-built housing with the former barracks in the foreground. 82
6.11 Plan view of the entire museum complex as presently envisioned. 82
6.12 Council of the South African Trade Union poster (1980). 83
6.13 The saw-tooth factory becomes a symbolically loaded feature in this museum section. 83
6.14 Memory boxes as repositories for objects of cultural value in the home. They serve as a metaphor for preserving cultural memory related to the struggle against apartheid. 84
6.15 A single figure sits in contemplation at the foot of the memory box. 84
6.16 The pedestrian traffic flow through the museum grounds stresses the notion of permeability built into the museum design. 85
6.17 Wattle posts are visible in the pavilion to the rear of the image. 86
6.18 Storyteller mural, center left. 86
6.19 Portrait exhibit of those who fought against political oppression in this region of South Africa. 88

6.20 A memory box with the haunting reminder of political abuses. 88
6.21 The installation (within a memory box) of a kitchen space resembling one in a relocation shack. 89
6.22 Sectional views of the Post-Apartheid Museum at Red Location. 89

Chapter 7

7.1 and 7.2 View from the Mexican side of the ten-foot steel border wall separating Tijuana, Mexico, from San Diego, California, in the USA. 94
7.3 Architect's global reference map of converging economic influences in the border zone between the USA and Mexico. 95
7.4 *Improvisation*: A dwelling made out of discarded packing crates and corrugated sheet metal erected on the eastern edge of Tijuana. 96
7.5 A habitat in Tijuana made from found objects, such as an old garage door used as an end wall. Note the illegal tapping into an electrical power source – what Cruz refers to as *an architecture of insurgency*. 96
7.6 California bungalows scheduled for demolition by San Diego builders are moved across the border, and placed on a row of steel superstructures for appropriation by the new owners. 97
7.7 *Densification*: An *ad hoc* use of space to support one of the California bungalows moved across the border. 97
7.8 Cruz's manipulated images serve as visual tools for stressing the paradoxes that exist on either side of the ten-foot-high steel wall separating San Diego and Tijuana. 98
7.9 *Simultaneity*: An example of 'unofficial centers of community and commerce.' The addition to the right serves as a repair shop – one of several 'non-conforming business practices' found in Tijuana. 99
7.10 Illegal energy use in Tijuana. 99
7.11 'Two urbanisms:' *an urbanism of difference and contrast* (Tijuana to the left) versus an *urbanism of sameness* (a San Diego subdivision on the right). 100
7.12 Site of 'Bedrooms at the Border' prior to construction. The 1927 church is located in the bottom right of the highlighted square. 101
7.13 Perspective sketch of remodeled 1927 church, 'urban room' arcades for informal markets with affordable housing above, and its context. 101
7.14 Living Rooms at the Border for Casa Familia, San Ysidro, San Diego: sketches of the three phases of development. 102
7.15 and 7.16 Drawing from Cruz's field observations on recycled housing. 102
7.17 One of a series of slender building blocks and linear gardens proposed by Cruz in the 'Senior Gardens' scheme. 103
7.18 View of the angular rhythm of rooflines alternating with large open spaces, designed to strengthen the spatial flow among housing units, to provide a flexible climate response of sunlight and shade, and to enhance community-oriented activities like the street market to the left. 103
7.19 View of the public garden space and living units at 'Senior Gardens' designed to accommodate positive social interaction and supervision by grandparents who are caring for their grandchildren. 104
7.20 Teddy Cruz feels that a sustained engagement with local communities can only be accomplished through collaborations involving multiple stakeholders. 104
7.21 Small projects that acknowledge the histories and identities of culturally specific communities spring from collaborative efforts involving architects, non-profit developers, city planners, and other agencies. 105

List of illustrations xxi

7.22 Juxtaposed images of conformity and non-conformity/aesthetic blandness and ethnic texture. 105
7.23 Cruz's vision for overlaying planning strategies of hybridity, simultaneity, improvisation, and flexibility onto a landscape of sameness. 106

Chapter 8

8.1 New graphics speak to the neighborhood's revitalized image. 109
8.2 and 8.3 A *before* view of a section of 7th Avenue (left) as a consequence of car-dominant, barren strip development. On the right, the same view after green infill, pedestrian pathways, and climatically and socially responsive *outdoor rooms* are layered onto the streetscape. 109
8.4 Location of Phoenix, Arizona, in the context of the contiguous forty-eight US states. 110
8.5. Detail map of Phoenix's 7th Avenue *stripscape demonstration project* located at the intersection of 7th Avenue and Glenrosa. 111
8.6 and 8.7 Comparative images of urban commercial use patterns along 7th Avenue are recorded and translated into *emergent typologies*: an ad hoc sidewalk space (left) for additional customer seating is photographed and labeled *found*; a rummage sale condition on vacated space (right) is also *found*. These urban situations of appropriated, underutilized, spaces later informed the concept of outdoor rooms. 112
8.8 and 8.9 Billboard Theater as *found* (left) and (right) public art display *staged*. 113
8.10 and 8.11 Photographic documentation translated into spatial constructs: *emergent typology* 'retail garage sale' condition (left) and the 'private court' condition (right) are translated into localized urban environments. 114
8.12 An axonometric blowup of the *programmatically indeterminate* housing volume constructed over the pedestrian path. 114
8.13 A computer model illustrating the hybrid construction principle as applied to the *Garage Sale Retail typology*. 115
8.14 Drawing of the scheme for layer one *bands* of streetscape development. 116
8.15 Illustration of the composite LampShade function: *vertical shade screen + monument sign + public art program = art/sign-shadescreen*. 116
8.16 Drawing of the scheme for layer two of streetscape development – *bands + vertical elements + canopies (LampShades)*. 117
8.17 Drawing of the scheme for layer three of streetscape development – *bands + vertical elements + canopies (LampShades)*. 117
8.18 and 8.19 Illustrations of the various LampShade functions: *consumptive/productive, sign-shade*. 118
8.20 Illustration of the various LampShade strategies in use. 119
8.21 Post-construction evening view of the LampShade urban strategy implemented as a bus stop and ad-hoc marketplace for local artists. 120
8.22 Drawing of the scheme for layer four of streetscape development. 120
8.23 Plan view of the layer four redevelopment scheme for 7th Avenue and Glenrosa. 121
8.24 and 8.25 Before and proposed neighborhood redevelopment schemes for Melrose Street at 7th Avenue. 121
8.26 Image of the contextual color palette. 122
8.27 Graphic design logo for M7 'Melrose on Seventh Avenue' by Andrew Weed. 122
8.28 Night scene of Misty's Bar urban context as completed. 122
8.29 Daytime site condition as built. 123
8.30 Nighttime site condition utilizing the security lighting canopy, illuminated art/sign-shadescreen panel, and Greenscreen climate control area. 123

Chapter 9

9.1 and 9.2 The layering of meanings in art, the play of natural light, and an emphasis on sensory perception are all considerations of this display space made from recycled materials for the Rock Art Visitors' Centre. 128

9.3 and 9.4 Global representation of Namibia's place in the universe. 130

9.5 In this view of the HRDC Building clerestory, light is softened by the roof infill matting that is made from invasive *prosopis* (mesquite) branches. 131

9.6 Forty-gallon (150 liter) oil drum lids appropriated as light screens and space separators. 131

9.7 A restroom sign made from a forty-gallon (150 liter) oil drum lid at the Northwest Rock Art Visitors' Centre rests against a gabion basket wall. 132

9.8 Original roof detail indicating pop riveted convex drums, sealed to prevent leakage during rain. 132

9.9 Construction photograph showing roofing tiles made from quartering recycled 200 liter oil drums. 132

9.10 and 9.11 Flattened kerosene cans (see detail), embellished with sponge painting, are used as cladding material on a dwelling. 133

9.12 Corporate metal signage is hung on a steel pole frame to enclose domestic space in a Namibian town context. 134

9.13 Both indigenous traditional dwellings and those utilizing hybridized features gleaned from recycled materials serve as design generators for the architect. 134

9.14 and 9.15 Renderings of the second location of the Northwest Rock Art Visitors' Centre overlaid onto the site. 136

9.16 A sectional drawing through the toilet cubicle (dry toilets). 137

9.17 Detail of the visitors' toilet washbasin made from a halved Leadwood tree trunk salvaged from a nearby riverbed. 137

9.18 and 9.19 The original observation platform with a view of rock cut art below. 138

9.20 During stage one of the trance ritual, images are induced by the shaman through sensory deprivation. The second stage is called *association*; visual patterns often appear at this time. 139

9.21 The third trance stage is *transformation* wherein the artist transforms and becomes the animal itself. Here, the 'dancing kudu' (part man, part animal) appears. 139

9.22 The transmutation of the four-toed lion into the five-fingered captured lion spirit is now possessed by the hunter during the *transformation* stage. 140

9.23 View of the defaced rock artwork. 140

9.24 and 9.25 Landscape features such as the San People's natural shelters serve as form generators for the Visitors' Centre. The section drawing shows the information display area on the right with the craft shop on the left. 141

9.26 View of gabion wall baskets hand made on the site. 142

9.27 The materials, building form, coloration, and rhythms are consciously selected to camouflage the building in its desert context. 143

Chapter 10

10.1 A writer's studio in Maine, one of four recipients of an Honor Award for Excellence in Architecture from the American Institute of Architects, New England Chapter. 147

10.2 Mount Desert Island, Maine, USA, context map of Somes Sound. 147

10.3 View of the south-facing aspect of the Writer's Studio amidst the tree cover. 148

10.4 View of the studio footprint from below. 148

10.5 View of the entrance of the Writer's Studio, facing southeast. 149

10.6 Diagram on the left is of a typical New England house with an equal number of windows on all sides. Diagram on the right indicates the circuit of December sunlight for the Writer's Studio. 150
10.7 View of the Writer's Studio illustrating reduced northern exposure. 150
10.8 House One, Falmouth, Maine, was designed as a prototype for improved modular housing by Carol Wilson and Susan Ruch and built by Burlington Homes of New England in 1994. 151
10.9 Plan view of the Writer's Studio. 151
10.10 View looking east along the passageway to the studio area. 152
10.11 Photo of screenwriter Jay Cocks at his desk in the recessed work area. 152
10.12 Interior view from the writer's desk looking east toward the window seat/day bed. 153
10.13 Interior view of the Writer's Studio looking west toward the writer's desk from the sleeping alcove. 153
10.14 Interior view of the Writer's Studio looking west toward the living room. 154
10.15 Interior view looking west, showing the steel columns running through the interior space 154
10.16 and 10.17 Template designed by Wilson for a joist/rafter connection. 155
10.18 Demonstration model of the modular units as viewed from behind House One looking toward the architect's studio. 156
10.19 Plan view of House One with later additions. 156
10.20 View of House One on site, looking from the studio deck space toward the interlocking cube of the bedroom/living room. 157
10.21 View from House One looking toward the architect's detached studio. 158

Chapter 11

11.1 View of the east façade of the House in Kangaroo Valley. 160
11.2 Australia's regional divisions. 161
11.3 Marika-Alderton house in Yirrkala Community Eastern Arnhem Land, Northern Territory, Australia. 161
11.4 The house in Kangaroo Valley in its setting. 162
11.5 Detail of Kangaroo Valley within its environmental context. 162
11.6 View of the 360-degree composite photo of the site context. 163
11.7 The House at Kangaroo Valley on a north-facing hillside. 164
11.8 Drawing of sun angles related to the site's topography. 164
11.9 Preliminary sketch of the view angle facing north. 164
11.10 Plan showing detail contours and Murcutt's landform adjustments with comments. 165
11.11 Sketch of plans 1:100 Alternatives with notations. 165
11.12 Refined plan solution with annotations by Murcutt for the client explaining the quality and flexibility of various spaces. 166
11.13 Refinement sketch dated February 25, 2002. 166
11.14 The Kangaroo Valley house's northern elevation maximizes its exposure to the sun, while the ten-degree shed or *skillion* roof slope facilitates rain encashment in several storage tanks fed by two large roof gutters. 167
11.15 Augmented construction plan (dated 2003) with room designations highlighted by the author on the final scheme. 167
11.16 Detail sketch of the gutter/roof connection for the bed and writing desk bays clearly reflecting the architect's concern for how design features are precisely detailed to function efficiently. 168

11.17 1:5 section through the kitchen window showing an oversized gutter connected to the wide-mouth drain spouts to facilitate the water tank encashment system. 168
11.18 Analytical sketch of the internal insulating operable blinds and the external aluminum blinds with fixed blades. 169
11.19 Drawing of the clerestory window. 169
11.20 Sectional drawing showing the sun angle during equinox. 170
11.21 Drawing of the wall section. 171
11.22 Sectional detail of the steel and rock fireplace with heat exchange. 171
11.23 A section workup of a sliding slatted timber screen assembly unit. 172
11.24 Note the light reflecting from the lily pond onto the ceiling. 173
11.25 Natural lighting illuminates the writing table looking west from the dining/kitchen/desk area, past the foyer, and terminating at Bed 1. 173
11.26 View of clerestory, light louvers, and sliding screens. 175
11.27 View of the completed house at Kangaroo Valley amidst its natural setting. 176

Section One

Exploring the nature of place

1

An interpretive model for assessing regional identity amidst change[1]

Tradition is the illusion of permanence.

Woody Allen in the movie *Deconstructing Harry*.

Often, in architecture circles today, discussions about regional identity turn quickly to terms and phrases like authenticity, a sense of place, or *genius loci*.[2] Somehow, it is assumed that an authentic landscape is a *fixed* entity, a fragment of the past that has endured the ravages of nature and human action (Figure 1.1). As such, these salvaged settings can become the seat of memories, capable of providing inner richness to later generations through their evocative presence. Implicit, too, is the notion that not only has the historical site survived untouched, but the original concepts that shaped it have survived as well. Hence, by preserving such iconic forms and features, the meanings that such works originally held can be bequeathed, intact, to later generations. Seemingly suspended in time, such works trigger our historical imagination and serve as referents for heritage tourism; provide evocative imagery for contemporary design; and once decoded for formal strategies and design vocabulary, may be reconstituted elsewhere as a means of manufacturing imagined heritage.

Place, however, is more than a geographically definable entity accentuated by historical and visual landmarks; and heritage is not the aesthetic replication of a selected past. On an emotional level, place is a mental construct different for each of us, and, in the case of childhood dwelling places, tied from youth to personal experience. Obviously, there are some recurring points of congruence that tie long-time inhabitants of a locale to a place in a collective way. This collective heritage is often the product of shared work and recreational patterns, common ethnic and economic bonds, shared social and spiritual values, actual or invented historical identities, and even broadly shared experiences of human struggle and natural disaster. These regionally situated commonalities, in turn, produce shared mental attitudes, sensibilities, and associations.

Of course, no culture is monolithic, and such a construct as presented above assumes constancy. For example: (1) is it possible for long-standing regional elements to maintain their vibrancy amidst an influx of new cultural influences? (2) Are such regional characteristics equally authentic to new arrivals that bring different priorities and preferences with them from elsewhere? (3) As these old and new traditions interface in built form, is this new vernacular just as authentic? (4) And might we see such hybridized forms resulting from such encounters between local and outside forces offering a different dimension of regional identity?[3]

Note, for example, the Sung Tak Buddhist Temple, formerly Pike Street Synagogue, designed by Alfred E. Badt (1903–1904), located at 13–15 Pike Street, New York City. This synagogue was built at a time when New York's Lower East Side was the heart of Jewish immigration – 200,000 Jews lived in this area by the 1890s served by 60 synagogues. By the 1930s, the Orthodox population dwindled in this section of the city as families moved to newer

Copyright © 2009 Elsevier Ltd. All rights reserved.

FIGURE 1.1
Mount Airy Plantation, Richmond County, Virginia (circa 1760), viewed from the park. While some sites such as this are often interpreted as static entities created at a single moment in time by a single mind, vernacular scholars like Dell Upton have demonstrated that sites 'seem to take on varying colorations according to the angle from which one views them [e.g. white and black landscape perspectives].' These multiple readings can provide a broader range of historical narratives that define a site's collective meaning. (Photograph by the author.)

apartments in Brooklyn and the Bronx. By 1980, this synagogue stood vacant. It has recently been rehabilitated as a Buddhist temple on the main level, apartments above, and commercial space below reflecting the building's ability to reflect and accommodate the social changes within its neighborhood context (Figure 1.2).[4] Cultural transformations in built form, then, may compromise the aesthetic character of a resource (Criterion C on the United States National Register for Historic Places), but at the same time may serve to transmit a more complex story of the evolving character of an urban setting that has historical value (Criterion A).

Similarly, the Residential Hotel served the Japanese–American population in Stockton, California, until the World War II internment policy (the 1942 Executive Order 9066) went into effect. The Filipino–American community that replaced the Japanese as agricultural workers in the region subsequently occupied the property. Today, it is celebrated as part of Stockton's 'Little Manila' Filipino American Heritage, rather than part of the layered ethnic identity of the locale with an equally important historical narrative to relate.

It is certainly appropriate to continue to document and preserve the forms and features connecting a place to its *official* past. But, since historic preservation and regional design are also concerned with cultural identity as a determinant of Place, shouldn't we be concerned, as well, with how buildings and their adjacencies are transformed over time in response to changing regional criteria? If we are to understand the nature of a locale, the record of ongoing change is as relevant as episodic moments of isolated achievement. Change informs us about who we are as eloquently as our past deeds and accomplishments reflect who we were (Figure 1.3). (For an application model of accommodating the changing ethnic identity of Place, see the case study on Teddy Cruz in later in this text.)

Perhaps, as Nezar Al Sayyad suggests, we should try to understand *tradition* in light of a changing world, and begin to move away from an enduring or fixed concept of cultural heritage. 'Instead,' Al Sayyad argues, 'we should embrace multiple and transformative states of identity – an *immediate present* that is a constantly moving target.'[5] Doreen Massey, in her insightful book, *A Global Sense of Place*, suggests that the uncertainty of what we mean by the 'particularity of local places, and how we relate to them' amidst the reality of the 'time–space compression' of today, establishes a state of social anxiety. The current concerns about fragmentation and disruption brought on by

FIGURE 1.2
Sung Tak Buddhist Temple, formerly Pike Street Synagogue, designed by Alfred E. Badt (1903–1904), located at 13–15 Pike Street, New York City. (Photograph by the author, 2006.)

participation in the global village as well as shifting migration patterns have provoked a yearning on the part of maker and user alike for 'an (idealized) era where places were (supposedly) inhabited by coherent and homogeneous communities.' In retaliation against the geographic fragmentation of our times we engage, occasionally, in defensive, reactionary responses, Massey contends, that take the form of nationalism, sanitized heritage, and outright antagonism to newcomers.[6] See, for example, Union Station, a recent Civil War themed subdivision in rural LaGrange, Ohio, designed by developer Calvin Smith. The 'blue and gray' site plan includes simulated cemetery markers for opposing American Civil War generals Ulysses S. Grant and Robert E. Lee in this built expression of manufactured history.

How, then, can the notion of the *authenticity of place* be reconciled within this framework of transformative states of identity and multiple sources of local and global influence? The challenge before us is to conceptualize regional expression as a broadly conceived and dynamic cultural *process*.

The recognition that regional settings are linked inextricably to cultural process strikes at the heart of much of vernacular architecture studies today, just as the desire to preserve distinctive ways of life – past and present – is part of the emerging cultural conservation movement.[7] Increasingly, programs in historic preservation (benefiting from the field of cultural landscape studies) are recognizing that *both* relatively intact historic settings *and* reconstituted cultural traditions need to be addressed, and that consideration should be given to seeing a landscape as the product of ever evolving human and environmental factors.[8] (For a demonstration model of how evolving attitudes about locale – in this instant toward strip development in Phoenix, Arizona – shape a landscape, see the case study on Darren Petrucci later in this text.)

In addition, by focusing the interpretive context of regional design and its related fields on issues of cultural process and environmental response, it is hoped that every human setting may be considered worthy of study and accommodation. To that

6 Vernacular Architecture and Regional Design

FIGURE 1.3
1879 statue of Sergeant William Jasper, hero of the Revolutionary War, located in Madison Square, Savannah, Georgia. This work illustrates how cities, through commemoration, strive to construct enduring – though often eventually challenged – identities and memories. (Photograph by the author, 2003.)

end this chapter addresses the issue of regional identity through an inquiry into the dynamic processes that generate vernacular or regional aspects of design. It turns to methods currently used in vernacular studies and puts forth a threshold proposition that focuses attention on various states or conditions of evolving places and spaces instead of applying the term *vernacular* to certain building types, periods of construction, or settings shaped by non-professionals.

What does vernacular mean?

Historically, the terms *regional* and *vernacular* are virtually interchangeable. The linguistic root of the term vernacular, from the Latin root *vernaculus*, refers to a native language or dialect, especially its normal spoken form. It denotes commonly used, recognized, and understood speech patterns characteristic of a specific locale. This is what sociolinguist Dell Hymes refers to as the 'ethnography of speaking.'[9] As such, it stands in contrast to the formal literary language of a society that is oriented toward global academic discourse. By and large, this distinction applies to vernacular buildings and vernacular landscapes as well. Vernacular buildings and settings are regionally distinctive, regionally representative, and regionally understood.

How, why, to what extent, and by what means such spaces, forms, and features occur is determined by a particularized set of local as well as external influences. Over time, these elements become part of the predictable pattern of use and expression within a region or subregion and are carried out on both a conscious and subliminal level, as well as being embraced across broad socioeconomic barriers (Figures 1.4 and 1.5). This blending of pre-existing and imported elements assembled into distinctive localized expressions has been characterized variously as *cultural weathering*, *creolization*, or *hybridity*.

The first notion, *cultural weathering*, views regional settings as the product of layers of collective change over time, whereas the last (*hybridity*) stresses the amalgamation of two fixed entities into a third, identifiable thing.[10] Nezar Al Sayyad argues that all cultural experiences are hybridized, and that all vernacular forms are transitional. This author contends that while hybridized cultural expressions are the norm, particularly among colonized cultures, there are discernible patterns of human adjustment within these hybridized constructions of identity that define regional or subregional distinctiveness.[11] When people share an awareness of the locale, adjust to its regional circumstances, and collectively apply adaptive strategies – the regional distinctiveness of Place emerges. People almost invariably alter objects, buildings, spaces, and settings in accordance with prevailing opportunities, constraints, and sensibilities. Observing and documenting such strategies of accommodation can assist regional scholars in understanding cultural identity both in the past and in the immediate present.

Jukka Jokilehto takes the discussion of the sociopolitical complexities that define Place a step further. He states, 'the recent prevalence of terms such as *vernacular*, *ethnicity*, and *intangible heritage* in preservation theory, signals the move towards the

FIGURE 1.4
The Poyas-Mordecai House, an elite version of a Charleston, South Carolina, single house – a subregional building type in the Tidewater South. Its hall-and-parlor plan is oriented toward a side-yard condition and makes use of the porch or piazza as a circulation path, surveillance point, and climate response. (Photograph by the author, 1994.)

recognition of the localized phenomena as having global importance.' His aim is not simply to 'revel in the glorification of the local,' but to advance new global standards for external funding to address local realities. An internal tension arises, Jokilehto admits, between the ideology that all historic preservation is locally defined, and the desire to create global standards of heritage policy through doctrinal charters.[12]

The particular nature of cultural practices in Thailand is a notable example of this uneasy fit of global versus local preservation policies. Dr Thada Sutthitham, Dean of the Faculty of Architecture at Khon Kaen University, Thailand, brings her training in the fields of architecture, historic preservation, and environmental studies to bear in her observations on the mismatch between Southeast Asian and Western approaches to preservation. The traditional reed housing of Thailand and Laos, she notes, is highly vulnerable to the tropical conditions, lasting only about five years; thus the frequent replacement of building elements challenges the Western preservation precept of *integrity* (Figure 1.6). Further,

FIGURE 1.5
A modest single house duplex located west of Charleston's city center. (Photograph by the author, 1994.)

FIGURE 1.6
A woven reed mat covering is renewed approximately every five years on a traditional residence in Luang Prabang, Laos. (Photograph by the author, 2007.)

there is a cultural practice in Thailand of burning a house and most of its contents when the head of the family dies to rid the dwelling of bad spirits. The property is then divided among family members, at which time the cultural patterns on the land are renewed. On occasion, agreements are made with family members to give the house to a Buddhist temple. The family dwelling is relocated and reused as a monk's residence or as a school, challenging standard Western conventions of preserving a resource's original context. In such instances local attitudes maintain that 'it is more important to preserve the continuing *life ways* than the houses themselves.' But, such intangible heritage does not conform easily to global preservation policies like the Venice Charter. According to Sutthitham, 'Those standards do not work for Thailand. The Burra Charter in Australia [the ICOMOS Charter for Places of Cultural Significance], that addresses cultural landscapes, comes closer.' A Thailand Charter for 'Cultural Routes' is being discussed, but the Thai framers want no authority embedded in it that prescribes rules on intentions for heritage conservation. 'It is not our cultural way,' says Dr Sutthitham.[13]

Intangible heritage is defined in the UNESCO Convention for the safeguarding of the intangible heritage as:

> ... the practices, representations, expressions, knowledge, skills – as well as the instruments, objects, artifacts and cultural spaces associated therewith – that communities, groups and, in some cases, individuals recognized as part of their cultural heritage. This intangible cultural heritage, transmitted from generation to generation, is constantly recreated by communities and groups in response to their environment, their interaction with nature and their history, and provides them with a sense of identity and continuity ...[14]

(For a demonstration model of designing in accordance with intangible cultural values at a World Heritage site, see the case study on Nina Maritz later in this text.)

In an effort to understand the local in global terms, the study of vernacular environments, therefore, leads inevitably to the need to acknowledge the range of forces acting on a particular society that prompts regional building patterns, spatial adjustments, and meaning. On the structural model that follows, these collective forces are described as the *regional filter* (Figure 1.7). Among these forces are climatic, cultural, social, racial, historical, political, economic, and religious factors. Located above the regional filter are the categories of *high style*, *popular* and *folk*. These categories are represented as separate conceptual frameworks, because they constitute distinct disciplines. They are shaded, however, to represent overlapping spheres of influence. This condition of overlapping cultural intentions better represents the manner in which most built environments today are determined given global commercial and communication systems. Connecting the spheres of cultural influence to regional factors on the chart is the individual as conveyor of knowledge and as an agent of change. (For an illustration of how an architect addresses the inconvenient truth of a regional heritage of racial and political oppression within a museum context, see the case study on Jo Noero later in this study.)

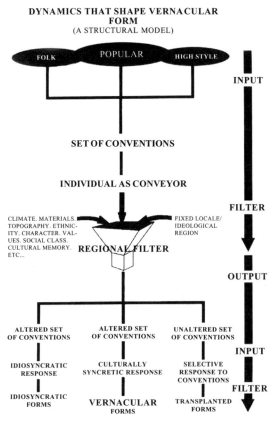

FIGURE 1.7
Structural model 1. (Diagram by the author.)

Individual versus collective cultural expressions

The following distinctions are motivated by a desire to assess the regional dimension of a landscape, building, or object. Some resources (as shaped by their makers) will respond little to pronounced regional dynamics within their own setting except in minor ways that are inevitable, and will maintain the original set of ideas that governed them prior to their entering the region (see the right column of the structural model in Figure 1.7). Peter Eisenman's Cardboard Architecture House II (Falk House, 1969–1970, Hardwick, Vermont) is a built manifesto of progressive design theory placed on its site with little regard to contextual issues (Figure 1.8); mobile homes on a sales lot are, in essence, dwellings sold as commodities (Figure 1.9); and the Kluge House, 1870s, built in Helena, Montana, is a rare example within the Rocky Mountain region of the USA of *Pachwerbau* construction transferred directly from Germany to the gold mining camp of Last Chance Gulch, Montana, with no regional adaptation or architectural following (Figure 1.10). These resources provide examples of relatively intact conceptual frameworks customarily characterized as high style, popular, and folk.[15]

In other cases, buildings will change in singular ways (see the left column of the structural model in Figure 1.7). For example, if a building project within a particular locale is limited to a personal gesture or a statement of personal belief, then the end product is an act of idiosyncrasy and not a vernacular impulse. Consider eccentric works by visionaries, now known as *outsider art*, such as Watts Towers (1921–1954) by Simon Rodia. Rodia was an Italian immigrant who built two concrete and iron-framed structures in Los Angeles, California, out of discarded materials such as green 7-UP bottles, broken china, and shells embedded in cement. Another example is a bicycle that Mississippi native John Martin equipped with any number of non-traditional accessories so that it could be 'ridden to heaven,' or a standard tract house in northern California, transformed by the owner(s) into a real-life 'castle' (Figure 1.11). Some expressions of human behavior, then, may remain elusive as they relate to the manipulation of the physical environment and function on a level of scattered individual responsiveness that may, or may not, form their own continuities elsewhere. Sheer whimsy, as well as highly individualistic artistic or practical expression, often guides design.[16]

Still other buildings and objects will be conceived in ways that may be considered vernacular – that is, regionally distinct (see the center column of the model, Figure 1.7). Perhaps structures like an eighteenth-century Spanish mission in New Mexico fit the image of vernacular architecture that many hold (Figure 1.12). Its adobe construction and characteristic tower massing speak to the unique union of local Pueblo craft traditions and transplanted Spanish colonial belief systems and aesthetic formulas when looked at from the perspective of architectural history. It also represents to some scholars like folklorist Deana Darrt-Newton 'by far the most devastating blow to the fabric of Indian life and culture … because it was the first wave of colonization, [whereby] Spain's motivation [was] to obliterate Indian cultures to effectively harness a labor force in service to the Crown.' A single aesthetic interpretation of this resource, Darrt-Newton argues, presents 'racialized regimes of representation [that] erase[s] or radically

FIGURE 1.8
Peter Eisenman's Falk House (Cardboard Architecture House II, 1969–1970), Hardwick, Vermont. (Modeled by Robert Beelen for architect Peter Eisenman; image courtesy of the Lava Research Team.)

minimize[s] slavery and abuses of Native people, framing them as the faceless workforce necessary to the inevitable progress of European civilization.'[17] Hence, vernacular resources are those that express not only traditional building elements common to a locale, but the political, social, and environmentally particular forces at play as well.

Many buildings and settings – not just those designed by non-architects – hold the same potential of becoming vernacular expressions depending upon the degree to which they respond to the regionally specific forces acting upon them. For example, gentry townhouses in Annapolis, Maryland, built during the late colonial period, may appear at first to be anything but vernacular (Figure 1.13). As Orlando Ridout has demonstrated, wealthy, often politically prominent, Annapolitans collectively launched a competitive building

FIGURE 1.9
Mobile homes sold as commodities off the sales lot in Charlotte, North Carolina. (Photograph by the author.)

FIGURE 1.10
The Kluge House (circa 1873), a folk housing form culturally transferred from Germany into a mining camp context in Helena, Montana. It is the sole example of this traditional housing type in the state. (Photograph by the author.)

campaign. Though contemporary building practice in England and eighteenth-century pattern book designs influenced these houses, such outside influences were adapted gradually to local traditions. Building vocabulary, material usage, and craft techniques were disseminated among builders and users alike until early experimentation yielded to a fully developed pattern of local building practice. This coalesced building culture was in place by 1760 and lasted until the political turmoil of the mid-1770s. These local practices included the use of slab chimneys, all header bond masonry – often combined with *galleting* (small pebbles placed in the mortar), and the Annapolis plan that afforded better visual access to the formal garden at the rear of the house than did the standard Georgian plan. As Gretchen Buggelin astutely observes, style is not merely fashion; it is a statement of personality and purpose.[18]

Crossing the vernacular threshold

At what point might we consider a work as being regionally expressive? The vernacular threshold is crossed when there is a discernible and consistent variation of previous rules of thought and behavior conducted simultaneously by regional inhabitants in

FIGURE 1.11
Originally built in northern California as a common building type, this home was transformed into a personal fantasy of the American home as one's own castle. (Photograph by the author, 2007.)

FIGURE 1.12
Las Trampas, New Mexico Spanish mission, 1760. (Photograph by the author.)

direct response to new or changing forces within a locale. Indeed, in addition to broad patterns of influence, the vernacular may be prompted by the act of an individual as an agent of change. However, when representative numbers of people within a region embrace aspects of a unique building response in a collective and consistent manner, they produce something that is no longer idiosyncratic – it is *culturally syncretic.* It is vernacular.

Sometimes, a vernacular resource is the result of the reworking of pre-existing elements that have been transplanted from elsewhere and are adapted to a new environment and new social circumstances. Similar to Darwinian theory, some forms may be culturally and/or environmentally pre-adapted to a new setting. Take, for example, the English center-chimney, hall-and-parlor house with a rear lean-to that was transplanted to the New England landscape during the seventeenth century. In the East Anglia region of England, where the majority of Plymouth Colony settlers had lived, this form represented less than five percent of the building stock. As historical archeologist James Deetz observed, when imported to New England where abundant old growth timbers made extended lean-tos possible and the thermal mass of the centrally placed chimney addressed the harsh climatic factors, this house form became increasingly popular. By the last quarter of the seventeenth century, the so-called Cape Cod house had grown into the most representative of all New England residential building types (Figure 1.14).[19]

On other occasions, regionally distinct patterns are the result of an innovative application or exploration of new technologies or materials brought into a region. Such was the case in the Caribbean Islands. After World War II, the US military operations there left thousands of empty fifty-five gallon steel oil drums. What once was an eyesore of discarded material became found objects for some of the local residents. The cans were cut in half, burned to remove paint and oil residue, and the lids pounded repeatedly until they were concave and produced the desired notes when struck. The result was a new regional art form: *pon* drums used by so-called steel bands. Here, individuals took objects that originated in one aspect of culture and operated under one set of conventions, and modified or altered those conventions and created something distinctive to a particular geographic region and period of time. We see a similar process taking place again in the following case studies when Nina Maritz recycles oil drums as building materials for the Visitors' Interpretation Centre for Prehistoric Rock-cut Art in Namibia and Glenn Murcutt responds to the *culture of components* by adapting the standardized tripartite window to new sustainable demands. Though one is creatively reusing discarded materials and the other is augmenting standard industrial components, both are transforming materials beyond their original capabilities into a sophisticated aesthetic and environmental response that is capable of being embraced widely within the locale.

An interpretive model for assessing regional identity amidst change **13**

FIGURE 1.13
Garden façade, John Ridout House (1764–1765), Annapolis, Maryland. (Photograph by M. E. Warren, courtesy of the Historic Annapolis Foundation.)

Many of us who view buildings archaeologically see them, in essence, as cultural cocoons – layers of adaptive response infused with human values.[20] Several vernacular scholars assert that regionalism has a chronological dimension whereby forms, building technology, and decorative details are shaped by a variety of social, economic, and cultural factors working at different levels and at different speeds on local building practice. Their work illustrates that some ideas are readily accepted or assimilated while others fail to take root. Additionally, immigrants from different cultures move into an area, often bringing new ingredients to the cultural mix. Sometimes this new mixture changes local practices dramatically, and sometimes it has very little influence.

On occasion, new arrivals to a locale will recast the identity of place by restructuring foreign or existing elements in accordance with their particularized view of the universe. Over time, the changes evident in the building's form, plan, structure, or use reflect the choices people have made in adapting elements in their built environment in response to new regional realities; *new vernacular* forms result (Figures 1.15 and 1.16). This new vernacular condition is the end product of a collective and cohesive framing of ideas as processed over time through a different regional filter. The new filter is the result of social, political, economic, technological, and/or environmental flux affecting the locale. In the end, it is the particularized set of regional influences that defines the uniqueness of our habitats in their global context.[21]

FIGURE 1.14
William Boardman, a successful joiner, constructed his home in 1687 in Saugus, Massachusetts. By 1696, a lean-to or 'out-shot' and fireplace flue were added to the rear of this New England hall-and-parlor traditional form, creating a separate room for cooking. This five-room plan is referred to in New England as a Cape Cod house. (Photograph by the author, 1978.)

14 Vernacular Architecture and Regional Design

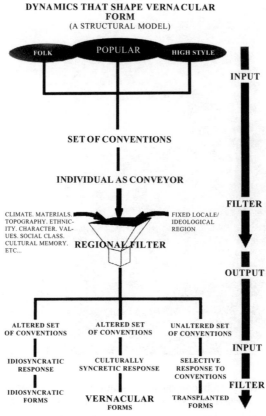

FIGURE 1.15
A three-dimensional exchange model, 'Dynamics that shape vernacular form.' (Diagram by the author.)

Often, there may be many vernacular impulses present within a region from different points in time; or groups of buildings may represent the sweep of history embodied in one place. While we may feel uneasy with the visible tension of competing cultural values as expressed in built form (and it should be said that such evident alterations to the pre-existing social and architectural fabric are often steadfastly resisted by long-time residents), this threshold of change is a most meaningful informant for understanding the level of accommodation or resistance between older and newer traditions. (Again, Teddy Cruz's case study is relevant here with regard to acknowledging hybridized cultural resources as a basis for what he terms *temporal urbanism*.)

Vernacular architecture, then, represents a localized response to broad cultural systems, historical events, and environmentally determined regional forces. As such, vernacular architecture often points to an observable condition of dynamic cultural and environmental *change*; it speaks of transition rather than stasis. It marks a liminal period, a threshold of conscious change and accommodation expressed in built form, whereby simultaneous identities result.[22]

Consider for a moment the catastrophic effect of the 2004 tsunami on the traditional communities of Southeast and South Asia where entire communities and regions lost their homes, family, friends, and livelihoods. This environmental disaster not only dramatically altered the lives and living environments of the storm victims, but these communities faced an infusion of outside influence and resources that, while desperately needed, produced a very different cultural landscape than was previously familiar to them. In order to address the critical immediate needs for housing, prefabricated building forms and building systems from outside the region were introduced to the native populations, such as concrete shell housing designed to resist cyclones that offered shelter in Sumatra, or the sudden transition from mud walls and thatched rural residential forms – might we think of these stabilized vernacular forms as *folk*? Folk, akin to traditional, indicates a later, fully evolved, stabilized, and embedded building response that embodies a very slow rate of change within its distinctive locale or within its transplanted setting. Folk artisans repeat themes, forms, and building technologies, but these elements are also allowed to grow, change, and evolve as needs, opportunities, and constraints present themselves (Figure 1.18).

Traditional craft responses may be so culturally engrained among local inhabitants that the original motivations behind certain acts proceed largely with unspoken familiarity. Conscious acts of creativity continue, often involving different materials and technologies. The basic structure of traditional practice, having been worked out by previous generations of settlers, however, is now replicated and continually refined by later folk builders.[24] No longer having to confront cultural and climatic issues anew as initial occupants, these acculturated folk builders are now free to move on to stages of formal articulation, elemental refinement, aesthetic elaboration, or simple adjustment to the complexities (or aspirations) of prevailing social conditions.[25]

FIGURE 1.16
Asian decorative features are overlaid onto this 1913 classically inspired commercial structure in San Francisco's China Town as a means of projecting a new cultural identity than previously existed in this section of the city. (Photograph by the author.)

roofs to concrete housing in villages like Tamil Nadu, India.[23] This building response may seem like yet another illustration of the loss of regional identity to the forces of cultural globalization – a principal concern of the proponents of critical regionalism. Yet, the resilience of cultural tradition should be given more credence for maintaining its vitality. Cultural patterns and preferences simply reemerge in different combinations or in awkward synthesis with the new. This is the hopeful side of the *new vernacular* (Figure 1.17).

Stabilized vernacular or folk

On the other hand, when a building practice becomes entrenched – this is particularly true of

FIGURE 1.17
Prayer beads and a makeshift altar are placed among temporary housing in Sri Lanka eight months after the tsunami – reflecting the desire for cultural persistence amidst change. (Photograph courtesy of Michael Fifield.)

FIGURE 1.18
Two nearly identical Appalachian outbuildings reflect enduring traditions, while employing technologies and materials from different eras of construction. (Photograph courtesy of Tennessee Historical Commission, 1979.)

For example, the house in Figure 1.19 began as a rectangular log house with an offset entry of Scottish–Irish origin. It was built in Middlebrook, Virginia, about 1830. Around 1860, it was given a balanced massing by an addition to the right of the original structure, marking a transitional phase that was broadly embraced in the area's building practice – what folklorist Henry Glassie has referred to as a 'mental event' that occurred in many places simultaneously – as was the practice of covering the entire structure with clapboard siding to disguise its incremental construction. As historian Ann McCleary explains, this notable change reflects a shift in housing preference in the region away from earlier ethnically linked building types. By 1850, regional ideas and popular pattern book designs coalesced to produce the classic Shenandoah Valley home as the dominant building form – a brick or frame, central-passage plan, often called an 'I-house.' This stabilized vernacular form endured into the early twentieth century with various stylistic overlays (Figure 1.20).[26]

Points of transition and stasis within a landscape are experienced generally as a matter of degree, however, for change is constant and adaptation is always possible. Howard Davis has suggested to the author that the 'vernacular–folk' dichotomy always exists; that there are elements of both, as people may be both conservative and inventive; and that at different times, different degrees of these attributes are more or less dominant. While there may be points in a community's development where there is marked continuity in building practice, there will be other moments when there is an evident shift from traditional ways to new applications. Ultimately, *vernacular* and *folk* responses may follow each other within a particular community or particular building tradition.

Extinct vernacular

Beyond acknowledging the presence of stabilized vernacular forms, there is another condition through which Place is constructed by its inhabitants: the rejection of outmoded forms often leading to an *extinct vernacular*. The concept of a *usable life* may be applied to architectural forms. This is most evident, perhaps, among artifacts of popular culture: works designed to capture the momentary trends, cultural urges, and marketable ideas of mass culture. Examples come to mind of auto camps and motor courts

FIGURE 1.19
A one-room deep, rectangular log house of Scottish–Irish origin built in Middlebrook, Virginia (circa 1830). The balanced massing was added to the right circa 1860 transforming its outward appearance to that of the newly popular and socially progressive I-house. This is an example of an evolving vernacular form. (Photograph courtesy of Ann McCleary.)

built by local entrepreneurs between the 1920s and 1940s, such as the El Vado Motor Court along Albuquerque's Route 66 (Figure 1.21), that have been superseded by Motel-8's and similar hotel chains; filling stations replaced by Kwik Stops; *drive-in* restaurants (that began to emerge in the USA during the 1920s) replaced by *drive-thru* restaurants; and drive-in movie theaters rendered obsolete by home entertainment centers and various forms of computerized entertainment (Figure 1.22). The

FIGURE 1.20
The stabilized vernacular plan type of a 'Shenandoah Valley home' – a brick or frame central-passage, one-room deep I-house. (Photograph courtesy of Ann McCleary.)

FIGURE 1.21
The El Vado Motor Court, built in 1937 along Albuquerque, New Mexico's, once-famed Route 66 was recently threatened by demolition. (Photograph by the author.)

FIGURE 1.22
The Route 70 twin drive-in theater in Burlington, North Carolina, 'for sale' – an extinct vernacular. (Photograph by the author.)

same is true of traditional building forms such as North Carolina German crib barns, which have given way to pole barns and prefabricated Butler buildings (Figure 1.23). Similarly, nations with long-standing colonial influences that have since gained political independence are consciously destroying visible

FIGURE 1.23
A German-style log crib barn built in the late 1700s by the Miller family in Rowan County, North Carolina, with one-ton hay bales sitting outside the barn. The increased scale that is demanded by modern farming practices precludes accommodation by some traditional structures leading to an extinct vernacular. (Photograph by the author, 1988.)

references to that part of their nation's heritage and rebuilding in a manner that represents their current post-colonial political identity. (See the case study on Nihal Perera.)

Rather than viewing vernacular forms and settings as fixed entities in time, they may be better differentiated according to a three-dimensional exchange model (Refer to Figure 1.15). A vernacular form may reach a point of relative stasis within its environment (*stabilized vernacular* or *folk*); be in a transitional or liminal phase (*evolving vernacular*); or reach a point at which its functional vitality, symbolic power, and cultural value is rejected or maintained largely through memory (*extinct vernacular*). Placing the emphasis on such thresholds of change draws attention to the form-types and plan-types that emerge during an era in light of *patterns of effect* critical to their contextual relevance today.

Notes

1. Previously published, in part, under the title: Assessing regional identity amidst change: the role of vernacular studies, in *Perspectives in Vernacular Architecture: The Journal of the Vernacular Architecture Forum*, 13 (2006/2007), 76–94. I would like to thank Thomas Hubka and Howard Davis for their comments on this chapter.
2. For discussions on regional philosophy and architecture see C. Norberg-Schulz (1980), *Genius Loci: Towards a Phenomenology of Architecture*, Rizzoli; M. Heidegger (1975), Building, dwelling, thinking, in his *Poetry, Language, Thought*, Harper & Row. On cultural geography and place making see C. Sauer (1925), The morphology of landscape, in *Geography*, 2, no. 2 (12 October), 19–25; Yi-Fu Tuan (1977), *Space and Place: The Perspective of Experience*, University of Minnesota Press; P. Adams, S. Hoelscher and K. Till, editors (2001), Place in context: rethinking humanist geographies, in their *Textures of Place: Exploring Humanist Geographies*, University of Minnesota Press. For place-studies see: T. Creswell (2004), *Place: A Short Introduction*, Blackwell; L. Buell (2001), The place of place, in his *Writing for an Endangered World*, Belknap Press of Harvard University Press; W. Berry (1990), The work of local culture, in his *What Are People For?*, North Point Press; and E. C. Relph's (1976), *Place and Placelessness*, Pion.
3. For arguments in support of 'expanding the preservation footprint ... for an enhanced understanding of cultural diversity,' as defined by the general historic preservation 'template,' see A. J. Lee (2004), From historic architecture to cultural heritage: a journey through diversity, identity, and community, *Future Anterior*, 1 (Fall), 15–23.

    In the same volume, Lauren Weiss Bricker uses the failed efforts to save the 1957 Holiday Bowl as a 'unique expression of the rich cultural and social history of the Japanese–American community in Los Angeles' to point out the 'need to develop more effective ways to protect places associated with ethnic and cultural groups, whose significant historical roles have only recently been recognized.' The fact that the 'Googie'-style coffee shop, designed by architects Armet and Davis (with interiors by Helen Fong), was saved on the basis of stylistic significance over the attached Holiday Bowl, which was expressive of local ethnic and cultural history, demonstrates the need, Bricker contends, to 'set guidelines for the treatment of these examples of recent history., L. Bricker (2004), History in motion: a glance at preservation in California, *Future Anterior*, 1 (Fall), 5–13.
4. City Building (Field Site #55), New York, New York, Vernacular City: Field Guide for the Vernacular Architecture Forum's Annual Meeting, June 14–17, 2006.
5. N. Al Sayyad (2006), Consuming tradition and the end of regionalism – keynote address for the 4th Savannah Symposium, 'Architecture and regionalism,' Savannah, Georgia, February 24, 2006. See also his (2001) *Consuming Tradition, Manufacturing Heritage: Global Norms and Urban Forms in the Age of Tourism*, Routledge.
6. D. Massey (1994), *Space, Place, and Gender*, University of Minnesota Press, 232–233.
7. For an introduction to the development of the cultural conservation movement see O. Loomis (1983), *Cultural Conservation: The Protection of Cultural Heritage in the United States: A Study*, Library of Congress; R. E. Stipe and A. J. Lee, editors (1987), *The American Mosaic: Preserving a Nation's Heritage*, Wayne State University Press; M. Hufford, editor (1994), *Conserving Culture: A New Discourse on Heritage*, University of Illinois Press.
8. In this regard, three recent collections not only offer studies of landscape heritage, but also raise relevant questions regarding the social and political forces that shape preservation designations. See C. A. Birnbaum and M. V. Hughes, editors (2005), *Design with Culture: Claiming America's Landscape Heritage*, University Press of Virginia; J. F. Donnelly, editor (2002), *Interpreting Historic House Museums*, Rowman Altamira; and G. L. Dubrow and J. B. Goodman, editors (2003), *Restoring Women's History through Historic Preservation*, Johns Hopkins University.
9. D. Hymes (1981), 'In vain I tried to tell you': Essays in Native American ethnopoetics, University of Nebraska Press.
10. D. Upton (2001), 'Authentic' anxieties, in *Consuming Tradition, Manufacturing Heritage: Global Norms and Urban Forms in the Age of Tourism*, N. Al Sayyad, editor, Routledge, 300. 'Hybridity' is often used to illustrate the effects of immigration on built form and cultural practice; it represents the redefined cultural identity of both the immigrant population and, ultimately, that of the host setting. For use of the term 'creolization' see the work of J. D. Edwards and N. Kariouk Pecquet du Bellay de Verton (2004), *A Creole Lexicon: Architecture, Landscape, People*, Louisiana State University Press, 77. The authors state that 'In anthropological literature, creolization has come to refer to a process of open-ended cultural syncretism which characterizes all colonized places throughout the world, particularly those colonized after ca. 1450.'

11. J. Nardone (2003), Roomful of blues: jukejoints and cultural landscapes of the Mississippi Delta, in *Constructing Image, Identity, and Place: Perspectives in Vernacular Architecture IX*, K. Breisch and A. K. Hoagland, editors, University of Tennessee Press, 166–175. Views from abroad: conservation practices in Thailand, Lecture to the International Preservation Policy and Practice class, the University of Oregon by Thada Sutthitham, May 23, 2006.
12. J. Jokilehto (2006), Preservation theory unfolding, *Future Anterior*, 3 (Summer), 1–9. Some statements above were excerpted from M. Jorjani (2006), Forces beyond our control: examining the political edge in preservation, *Future Anterior*, 3 (Summer), viii–xi.
13. Interview between Dr. Sutthitham and the author during the ICOMOS: Thailand Conference, Udon Thani, Thailand, November 17–18, 2006.
14. UNESCO, Convention for the Safeguarding of the Intangible Heritage (Paris, October 17, 2003), Section I, Article 2.1. Available at: http://www.unesco.org/culture/ich/index.php?pg=00006
15. For early efforts to distinguish among these three aspects of culture, see Kingston Heath: Removing the cultural scotoma in architectural education, in *Proceedings of the 77th Annual Meeting of the Association of Collegiate Schools of Architecture* (1989), and Returning to the American grain: the vernacular as regional expression and source for high style, Aesthetics of the rural renaissance, *Proceedings of the 1987 Conference* (1987), 108–121.

    For a recent call for a 'shared nomenclature and a shared strategy of classification,' see T. Hubka (2007), Nomenclature and the classification of American (vernacular) housing, *Vernacular Architecture Newsletter*, No. 111 (Spring), 1–8.
16. Works that reflect isolated attitudes of personal vision or belief within a geographic region are now being referred to as 'outsider art.' For earliest work, see Roger Cardinal's *Outsider Art* (Praeger, 1972) and Roger Manley's *Signs and Wonders: Outsider Art Inside North Carolina* (North Carolina Museum of Art, 1989). Additionally, some cases of individual response are not linked solely to geographically defined factors such as climate, economic base, or political boundaries; instead, they are part of a broader, less discernible, network of belief or practice. This is what I refer to as the 'ideological region' on the structural diagram. In certain instances an interest, for example, in national popular trends such as 'wood-butcher architecture' that was perpetuated by such publications as the *Whole Earth Catalogue* during the 1960s and 1970s, established a network of belief and practice among a widely dispersed generation of counterculture builders. These often highly individualistic responses to the locale were tied not only to local forces but to the broader, national, social, and aesthetic movement defined by counterculture embedded organizations. In such instances, the patterns of behavior are so widely practiced among a particular group as to be said to define an 'American vernacular.'

    With regard to the issue of seeking a 'logical symmetry' for individual behavior within a region, Chris Abel argues that 'things become more realistic, and manageable, if it allowed that the sought-for continuities are not the all-or-nothing relations of identity, but more tolerant connections of some sort between different forms or states of existence, most usefully described in the terms of relations of analogy.' See his: The language analogy in architectural theory and criticism: some remarks in the light of Wittgenstein's linguistic relativism, *Architectural Association Quarterly* (December 1980). The source for the above quote is his article, Regional transformation, in *Architectural Review*, No. 1077 (November 1986), 37–43.
17. D. Dartt-Newton (2008), Nostalgia as epistemology: mission museums and the Indian/Mestizo community of the California coast, a paper presented at the Anthropology Colloquium, March 7, 2008, University of Oregon. The vernacular scholar today generally acknowledges that a particular historic resource, as well as broad cultural landscapes, will be perceived differently by different cultural groups, this factor demands that the researcher devise readings of a resource to ascertain the multiple layers of meaning that constitute the full range of 'authentic' identities within a locale.
18. M. M. Miller and O. Ridout V, editors (1998), *Architecture in Annapolis*. Vernacular Architecture Forum and Maryland Historical Trust, 81–84, 115–117, 131–135; G. Buggelin (2003), *Temples of Grace: The Material Transformation of Connecticut's Churches 1790 to 1840*, University Press of New England, 72.
19. J. Deetz (1977), *In Small Things Forgotten*, Anchor Press/Doubleday, 99.
20. The author is indebted to the work of these scholars, some of whom include James Deetz, Dell Upton, Henry Glassie, Bernard Herman, Edward Chappell, Gabrielle Lanier, Howard Davis, and Tom Hubka.
21. For an application model of this phenomenon, see K. Heath (2001), *The Patina of Place: The Cultural Weathering of a New England Industrial Landscape*, University of Tennessee Press, Chapter 6.
22. 'Liminality' is a term borrowed from Arnold van Gennep's formulation of *rites de passage*, 'transition rites.' *Limen* is the Latin for threshold. According to Victor Turner (1974), 'during the intervening liminal period the state of the ritual subject (the "passenger," or "laminar") becomes ambiguous, neither here nor there, betwixt and between all fixed points of classification; he passes through a symbolic domain that has few or none of the attributes of his past or coming state.' *Dramas, Fields, and Metaphors*, Cornell University Press, 231–232.

    As this concept relates to my structural model, I see the liminal stage as a juncture of cultural ambiguity and contradiction. In a process I refer to as 'cultural weathering,' information, aspects of social practice, or design elements are dissociated from the original source. They are then reconstituted through the collective processing of ideas that are operational within a region to meet the particular needs of a new culture. This syncretistic blend of past and current identities can result in a 'new vernacular' which, in turn, can distinguish the uniqueness of a region or subregion. See K. Heath (2001), *The Patina of Place:*

The Cultural Weathering of a New England Industrial Landscape, 177.
23. Special thanks to Deepti Murali, who served as a volunteer during the relief efforts in Tamil Nadu, one of the hardest hit areas of India. Personal correspondence with the author, March 5, 2008.
24. H. Glassie (1975), *Folk Housing in Middle Virginia*, University of Tennessee Press.
25. In Kent, England, for example, the three-unit house plan (between 1300 and 1650) stayed the same in plan and formal configuration but took on such sequential exterior refinements as braced framing, close-studding, and tile covering. Service rooms such as kitchens came later as an adjustment to the basic house plan, but the core structure was always identifiable. However, the room functions of the three-unit house of the late medieval period were turned around during the early modern period with the insertion of stacks and the flooring over of the hall. Service rooms and the parlor changed places, and the high end and the low end of the house flipped. In the second half of the seventeenth century, service rooms began to appear in rear outshots or lean-tos.
26. See A. E. McCleary (2004), Forging a regional identity: development of rural vernacular architecture in the central Shenandoah Valley, 1790–1850, in *After the Back Country: Rural Life in the Great Valley of Virginia, 1800–1900*, K. E. Koons and W. Hofstra, editors. University of Tennessee Press, 92–110.

2

Architecture as cultural production

To apply the conceptual model offered in the previous chapter and to add specificity to the notion of regional dynamism, the mobile/manufactured home is selected as a standardized, mass-produced type. This form type is explored in two regionally distinct contexts in the USA: southwestern Montana and southwestern North Carolina. Constituting ten to twenty percent of new housing production in the USA, according to Dolores Hayden, manufactured homes tend to be more popular in southern and mountain states – hence, the applicability of these two case studies.[1]

Cultural weathering

Though manufactured homes are the number one means of unsubsidized housing in the USA (according to *Building Tomorrow: The Mobile/Manufactured Housing Industry*), outside the USA, the mobile home does not enjoy the same popularity, nor does it hold the same iconic status (Figure 2.1). However, the mobile home's fundamental simplicity allows for a discussion about how individuals in an extremely harsh climate, for example, collectively shape and modify their living environments to address regional design issues and broadly shared cultural values. The aim is to demonstrate how a critical understanding of the nature of place stems from a grasp of the forces propelling regional adjustment.

A first reading of a mobile home placed in the Rocky Mountain region of the American West, for example, involves functionally dominant responses. In such an environment as Montana, where climatic factors are particularly critical, seasonal demands for basic survival are most evident. Functional imperatives related to pure environmental design, therefore, can often outweigh aesthetics in some regions.

The North Carolina mobile homes, by contrast, provide a different scale of visible and invisible interactions involving practical, social and aesthetic responses that establish a middle ground that is more common. This is primarily because weather conditions, while influential in design, do not dominate the North Carolina lifestyle to the extent that they do in Montana. As a result, mobile home alterations in North Carolina tend to reflect social as well as functional concerns (among just a few of the issues embodied in the transformation of the type) in a more evident manner (Figure 2.2).

Case study one – Gallatin County, Montana

The owner of a mobile home, regardless of where it is located – alongside others in a small urban mobile home park, or isolated in a Western ranch setting on the outskirts of town – confronts the regional filter from the moment the mobile home is put into place. A mobile home introduced into the northern regional climate of Montana and set up in a mobile home park unaltered remains, for the purposes of interpretation, a product of popular consumer culture and the broad network of corporate logic that shaped it originally. Here, we might consider the mobile home as an *architectural blank*, because up until recently mobile homes were aesthetically neutral, regionally indistinct, and perfect for adaptation (Figure 2.3).

If the owners of such mobile homes respond to the climatic factors of heavy snow loads and to energy demands that accompany severe cold temperatures, they are addressing the regional filter. They may choose to build a shed roof or pitched roof superstructure similar to pole barns for hay storage common to the area over the factory-made dwelling to counter the heavy snow loads (Figure 2.4), or place small rectangular hay bales around the base of the trailer for skirting to counter heat loss under the house, or build a wooden entrance portico mimicking similar structures in the

Copyright © 2009 Elsevier Ltd. All rights reserved.

Architecture as cultural production   **23**

FIGURE 2.1
An Oregon mobile home decorated for the winter holidays. (Photograph courtesy of Dennis Galloway.)

area to serve as a weather baffle and wood storage area (Figure 2.5). While not all the design responses will be the same, consistent elements reappear. Within the infinite varieties of mobile home adaptations that can exist, the particularities of place begin to narrow the range of variations to the point that regional design biases are represented in identifiable configurations.

A weather baffle is an adapted response that directs snow away from the door; additionally, interior and exterior door alignments generally are placed in such a manner as to cut down on direct drafts when a door is opened. The weather baffle, therefore, is a key pragmatic design feature; it stores firewood, holds boots, catches snow and mud, and protects against heat loss. The degree to which this feature is developed in the Gallatin Valley of Montana depends generally on long- or short-term living arrangements and the financial resources of the mobile home occupants.

One of the regional design strategies that springs from local knowledge relates to the building site.

FIGURE 2.2
Locations for Gallatin County, Montana, and Cabarrus County, North Carolina. (Map courtesy of US Central Intelligence Agency, *World Fact Book*, 2008.)

24 Vernacular Architecture and Regional Design

FIGURE 2.3
A mobile home situated in a ranch setting in Gallatin County, Montana. (Photograph by the author.)

Because of the severe winters along the Northern Rocky Mountain Range, placing dwellings close to a maintained road reduces the need to plow one's access route, reducing loss of time and money (refer to Figure 2.4). Because many mobile home owners have limited resources or their residences are temporary, long extension cords lead from the trailer's power source to a vehicle's engine block, where a head-bolt heater heats either the water lines or oil during temperatures that can reach forty below zero-degree Fahrenheit. Such tactics are used when garages are not affordable.

Further, facing nine months of fuel expenses during the winter, residents often install propane tanks near the mobile home rather than rely on expensive electric heat. Generally, there is also a wood-burning stove located inside the manufactured home, augmented by an overhead fan that forces the heated air downward.

Seen from the perspective of cultural weathering (that is, architecture as a collective response over time to regional conditions), the adapted mobile home can be a regionally responsive, regionally appropriate, and regionally distinguishable product within its context in southwestern Montana. It is of a place, of a people, and, inevitably, of a time (Figures 2.6 and 2.7).

FIGURE 2.4
A Gallatin County, Montana, mobile home responding to various regional climatic factors. Note its location near a paved road, weather baffle at its entrance, shed roof wooden superstructure to protect the thin metal envelope, and hay bales to reduce drafts below the structure. (Photograph by the author.)

Case study two – Cabarrus County, North Carolina

The southwestern region of North Carolina occasionally receives four to five times the annual precipitation of Montana. It has high humidity, a great deal of direct sunlight, and high summer temperatures. Here, the mobile home receives

FIGURE 2.5
A Gallatin County, Montana, mobile home with a weather baffle as a climatic response. This mobile home, at the time of the photograph, was used as rental housing for college students living off-campus. (Photograph by the author, c. 1986.)

a protective covering in the form of a pitched roof, as does its Montana counterpart, but the roof pitch is lower since it is more likely to shed rain than snow, and the roof supports on Carolina mobile homes do not have to be placed below a three-foot frost line (Figure 2.8). In this region, the roof forms tend to be extended, forming an open porch to the front for shade and air circulation, and often a carport off to the west side to absorb the heat of the day (much like the long narrow house forms architect Glenn Murcutt designs to address similar climatic demands in New South Wales, Australia, discussed in Section Two).

In southwestern North Carolina, the environmental dictates that determine the need for a front porch blend with, and are reinforced by, the cultural traditions related to the use of the front porch for evening and Sunday socials. The piazza, as the porch was originally called, appeared as early as the eighteenth century on the North Carolina coast as an essential weather barrier and intermediate social zone. It is not uncommon to see the regionally distinct ladder back oak rocking chair on the mobile home porches of this locale as often as on the porches of the ubiquitous Southern I-house as an expression of cultural persistence (Figure 2.9).[2]

While the housing form of a mobile home tends to be understated because of economic constraints, it is not without pretensions. On occasion, projected status, related to both the historic and mythic past, asserts itself in these trailer adaptations. Portico-shaped entries, recalling the symbol of established agrarian wealth, prestige, and power embedded in the Southern plantation house, are occasionally added to Carolina mobile homes to reaffirm – through iconographic reference – their regional links as part of the 'Old South' (Figure 2.10). Similarly, Montanans along the Rocky Mountain chain, fond of log structures reminiscent of the 'Old West,' have been known to screw furring strips into the mobile home's metal cladding, insert rigid foam insulation between the wooden spacers, and encase their dwelling's metal skin with inexpensive slabs from the lumber yard to approximate a log structure (Figure 2.11).

These mobile home adaptations represent culturally, economically, and environmentally acceptable solutions within a region, yet such user-limited choices are not exclusively the product of local influence. Other individually modifying factors can be national or global in scope. These may include ideas generated by do-it-yourself magazines, or alterations inspired by television makeover programs, or household accessories made available by large-scale building supply stores. These components of extra-local influence are, in turn, limited by such factors as accessibility and means, which affect the selection and use of items ranging from building technologies to building materials. Thus, while there might be a vision of improved living shaped by mass culture, limited resources and regional realities adjust that vision in such a way as

26 Vernacular Architecture and Regional Design

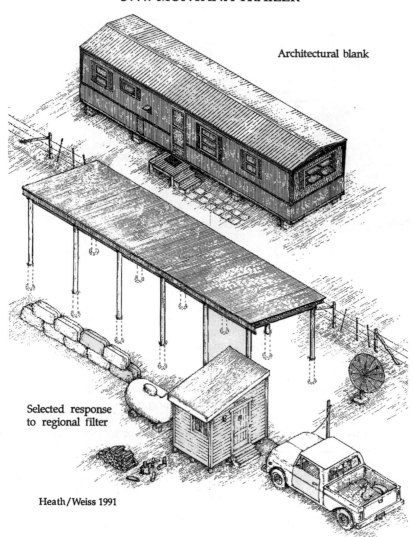

FIGURE 2.6
Selected regional responses of a mobile home in southwestern Montana based on photographic field data. (Drawing by the author and Gregor Weiss.)

to simultaneously contribute to and detract from the outside source of influence. As these regional conditions change, so too will the building patterns.

While it is possible to isolate the specifics of regional adjustment that separate one locale from another as basic typologies, these elements are merely the effective response to regional dynamics. What is of central importance in vernacular studies is to understand the cultural process behind such collective social acts. The case studies above are not intended to be an endorsement of manufactured homes as a living environment *per se*. The exercise is simply a means by which one can extract the prefabricated container from layers of adaptive response (its cultural cocoon, if you will) and begin to understand – at the most pragmatic level – programmatic priorities, environmental strategies, material preferences, and social practices that begin to reflect the subregional preferences of one socio-economic group. Collectively, these mobile home conversions when placed within the context of other factors offer a range of distinctive elements that provide an environmental, cultural, and symbolic statement of Place (Figure 2.12).

FIGURE 2.7
Regionally adjusted southwestern Montana mobile home. (Drawing by the author and Gregor Weiss.)

Place, change, and heritage conservation

Perhaps in the end it is too easy for us to be emotionally disinvested when discussions of environmental and cultural transformations are limited to the spare architectural trappings of a manufactured home. Are the lessons less relevant when extended to forms we traditionally refer to as historic structures or even contemporary design? (See the discussion of *House One*, the sustainable manufactured home prototype, discussed in the Carol A. Wilson case study.) As part of our training in architecture, urban design, architectural history, or historic preservation, we have been taught to look for cohesive patterns of stylistic or formal development within a region. This information allows us to point to the *key distinguishing features* that characterize a regional form as originally conceived by its designer/builder. In light of this training, how can adaptive changes to existing buildings, which may, in turn, contribute to *lack of integrity* according to some, assist us in assessing regional identity?

Traditional preservation policy tends to value *product* over *process*.[3] There is good reason for this stance. The earliest preservation efforts in the USA, such as those at Mount Vernon and the Hermitage, came out of an initiative to rescue the product-buildings critical to defining nationhood. Without such efforts much would have been lost (Figure 2.13). But the organizational development of the field of historic preservation is at a point where it is ready to reinvent itself to better reflect the needs and realities of the times: a *new* historic preservation agenda. As others have suggested, there is a need to reach a middle ground through revising the National Register of Historic Places and National Historic Landmark criteria for *significance* and *integrity* to acknowledge not only cohesive patterns of aesthetic, technological, historical, and craft expressions, but also significant patterns of change and cultural development that have emerged, particularly in vernacular and ethnographic settings that delineate the local and regional distinctiveness that has evolved.[4]

Entire academic disciplines are structured around the principle of understanding the nature of

28 Vernacular Architecture and Regional Design

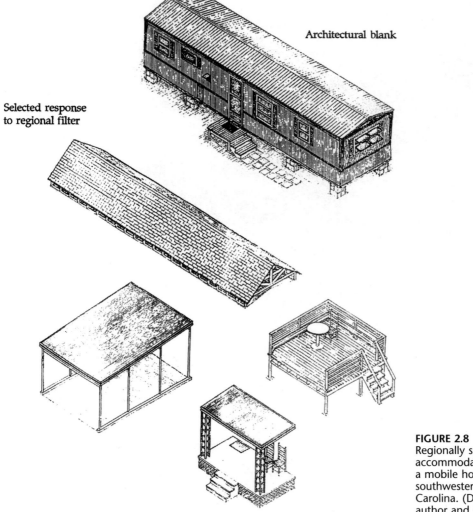

FIGURE 2.8
Regionally specific design accommodations for a mobile home located in southwestern North Carolina. (Drawing by the author and Gregor Weiss.)

buildings and their adjacencies solely as a product of original design intention. Exploring the critical evidence of a building's initial phase of construction allows us, as researchers, to get in touch with *our* past, and to attempt to unlock the meanings and motivations these buildings once held for our forebears (Figure 2.14). But, exploring how buildings and settings are transformed in response to the individual and collective forces acting upon them at various points in time also tells us much about the nature of the cultural setting that has evolved. By reading buildings and objects as being linked inextricably to landscape forces, a story begins to unfold about what tools people employed to physically shape and socially produce their living environments, and what meanings those changes hold for us today.

To that end, design schools, architectural history programs, and preservation policy may find it fruitful to emphasize the interrelated roles that cultural and environmental systems, changing historical and social circumstances, and ordinary people play as designers of the regional settings they inhabit. Preservation, in particular, is dedicated not only to stewardship, but to education. Perhaps, instead of viewing adaptive accretions to a building and its setting as loss of integrity, we may see such collective adjustments simply as a redefinition of

FIGURE 2.9
Ladder back oak rocking chairs, barely visible in the shade of the adapted front porch of a Cabarrus County, North Carolina, mobile home. (Photograph by the author.)

a locale's cultural heritage that speaks of a different record of habitation and a new collective identity of Place.

Programs such as the National Trust's Main Street Project have done much to resurrect histories that were in danger of being lost, and engender pride in local communities through the stewardship of its built environment.[5] When combined with the financial support offered by the state as a certified local government, assistance from federal and state tax incentives for certified rehabilitations of buildings located within National Historic Districts, the National Trust Loan Fund, the Main Street Loan Program, and public and private partnerships, many

FIGURE 2.10
An entrance portico added to a North Carolina mobile home evoking associations of a Southern plantation house. (Photograph by the author.)

FIGURE 2.11
Furring strips and foam insulation added over the metal cladding of this Gallatin County, Montana, mobile home enable its owner to add sawn slabs from the nearby lumberyard so that his home takes on the bearing of a log cabin and, simultaneously, addresses the locale's environmental demands. (Photograph by the author.)

city planning offices have successfully revitalized their old urban centers – at least physically.

But, buildings and settings, alone, do not make Place; *people*, in their interrelationship with the natural and built environment, make Place. Simply returning a 'blighted' commercial district to the outward expression of its former 'glory' may work for certain communities, but generally it is not the whole story.

In the frustration that accompanies declining populations and the loss of a community's economic base, it is natural to yearn for rapid and dramatic solutions to complex social problems. How often have we witnessed during the 1950s and 1960s in America the other extreme of placing modern facelifts (or so-called *slipcovers*) on older structures as a salve for economic stagnation (Figures 2.15 and 2.16). As long-time residents face the wrenching reality that the vitality of their community – that once seemed to be the physical validation of their collective worthiness and hard work – is wilting before their eyes, acceptance of change is difficult to say the least. When such economic changes are accompanied by population shifts that bring residents of different ethnic, racial, and/or religious identities, seldom is an effort made to embrace the more recent arrivals and acknowledge the role they play in shaping a landscape in a manner that speaks as well to *their* cultural values and needs (to say nothing of the negative associations that some of those *restored* historical social environments might conjure up).

In such instances of contested social settings, preservation – as an institutional formation – runs the risk of inscribing inflexible political motivations into their heritage practices. These are not easy issues; yet, they are being faced increasingly in the USA and around the world as urban areas infringe upon traditionally rural settings, and new in-migrations alter the character of local communities and patterns of human behavior. Expanding the historical narrative of a locale to illuminate both the old and evolving identities of Place increases community stakeholders and increases not only economic but human investment in the future success of the shared enterprise. Such a position also returns the commercial district to meeting the specific economic needs of its local residents, not just the anticipated needs of the tourist viewing a reconstituted presentation of Place.[6] (For a demonstration

Architecture as cultural production **31**

FIGURE 2.12
Regionally adjusted southwestern North Carolina mobile home embedded in its cultural landscape. (Drawing by the author and Gregor Weiss.)

of an economic revitalization planning strategy in a non-historic commercial district that draws from current local needs and social practices see the case study on Darren Petrucci later in this text.)

Urban historian Alison Isenberg offers an interesting juxtaposition of two extreme forces that shaped urban form in her book *Downtown America:* *A History of the Place and the People Who Made It.*[7] Chapter Six, 'The hollow prize? Black buyers, racial violence, and the riot renaissance,' assigns social relevance to the racial riots that called out for change and reshaped commercial urban practice during the 1960s. Chapter Seven, 'Animated by nostalgia: preservation and vacancy since the

FIGURE 2.13
Woodlawn Plantation, Assumption Parish, Louisiana, an example of the efforts of Historic American Building Survey (HABS) photographers during the 1930s to document endangered heritage resources. (Photograph by Richard Koch, HABS, 1937, public domain.)

FIGURE 2.14
Members of the Vernacular Architecture Forum (VAF) photodocumenting the ruins of an eighteenth-century plantation in the Tidewater region of Virginia in 2002. (Photograph by the author.)

1960s,' addresses the variety of heritage development schemes that attempted to convince people to repopulate and shop in older urban centers by offering up reassuring expressions of a sanitized past. Often, these reconstituted historic sites functioned, Isenberg notes, on a commercial level as settings for consumed tradition, where one *acted* the native, versus *being* the native.

This dichotomy offers a challenge to the architecture and planning professions addressing older commercial districts. One may either follow the past as a reference point (the extinct vernacular) in an effort to affirm notions of cultural continuity, or, as Nezar Al Sayyad suggests, address the immediate present: one of multiple identities, current realities, and transformative states of social and environmental change (the evolving vernacular).[8] For example, one effort to confront the tension that exists between gentrification and revitalization goals is the 'Restorative Listening Project' of Portland, Oregon's, Office of Neighborhood Involvement. The goal is to provide a forum for local city dwellers to speak, listen, and eventually heal. The case in point: African–Americans who for decades have lived in North and North-east Portland (the heart of Portland's African–American community) are invited to tell whites how it has felt to see them move into and remake their neighborhoods. In the face of escalating housing prices that have begun to force out many long-time residents, the storytelling project has become an exercise in 'shared humanity,' whereby 'the fundamental acts of telling and listening can heal ... Similar projects have grappled with much weightier issues – the horrors of apartheid, the Holocaust and World War II ... Seeing what you have in common opens the door to becoming allies. It allows [a person] to be connected to everyone else, and in that connection is the medicinal value.'[9]

Hence, Historic Preservation or Heritage Conservation, as the field is referred to outside the USA, often embraces broader concerns today than it did when the 1964 Venice Charter and the 1966 Historic Preservation Act in America were adopted. This is especially true of Historic Preservation programs that are affiliated with architecture and planning departments. Inventories, surveys, site designation – as well as the documentation, stabilization, restoration, and rehabilitation of those resources – are still staples of the field. Yet, many professionals are acknowledging that the spectrum of issues addressed must focus more directly on improving the livability of various communities through sustainable heritage development. Sustainable stewardship is accomplished, in part, by rescuing buildings and places important to our collective heritage, and by incorporating preservation principles into responsible land use policies.

The challenge put before architects, as Richard Moe, president of the National Trust, puts it, 'is to lighten the environmental footprint while preserving a building's historical integrity.' Moe's National Trust initiative is to protect and enhance buildings and landscapes in a manner that has a 'tangible impact on who we are – and can be.' By enhancing the viability and livability of our habitats as part of a smart growth environmental development ethic, preservation becomes an essential tool for the environmental viability of the planet.[10]

Often sustainable stewardship means active partnerships among university programs, non-governmental organizations enlightened developers, local communities, business and political

Architecture as cultural production **33**

FIGURES 2.15 AND 2.16
The 1916 Goodhue Company Cooperative Department Store in Red Wing, Minnesota, was converted to a shopping center during the 1960s with a modern metal 'slipcover.' It has since been restored to its 1916 likeness, though it is presently used as a storefront church rather than for its original retail purposes. (Photographs prior to restoration are courtesy of Brian Peterson, Planning Director, City of Red Wing, Minnesota.)

leaders, and local professionals. The level of involvement, of course, varies. Such collaborations take the form of adaptive use and sustainable renovation projects dealing with an abandoned warehouse, school or factory, sensitive design infill, sustainable retrofitting for affordable housing, community development, disaster planning and relief, and preservation planning (Figures 2.17 and 2.18). Such meaningful collaborations will make it possible for humanistic concerns to be addressed among wider groups of participants and, hopefully, improve the way we shape our environments from multiple perspectives of what constitutes *value* in today's society.

The following section of this text offers a series of case studies that, while they are conceived from different vantage points from each other, illustrate a common concern for designing socially responsive and environmentally responsible buildings.

FIGURE 2.17
An exterior view of the 1892 Armory in Portland, Oregon. It is listed on the National Register of Historic Places and received the nation's first Leadership in Energy and Environmental Design (LEED) Platinum Rating for its renovation into a performing arts facility. (Photograph courtesy of Ralph DiNola.)

FIGURE 2.18
Interior view of the Portland Armory adaptively reused as a performing arts facility, the Gerding Theater, by Green Building Services, Portland, Oregon. (Photograph courtesy of Ralph DiNola.)

Notes

1. Dolores Hayden (2004), *A Field Guide to Sprawl*, Norton, 70.
2. An 'I-house' is a two or two-and-a-half-story, one-room-deep residential structure. It is generally two rooms wide with a central hallway on each floor. Chimneys in the gable walls are common on nineteenth-century houses, though in North Carolina they tend to be placed behind the ridge and closer to the hallway. Such houses are often enlarged with the addition of rear extensions forming an overall L- or T-shape configuration.
3. For more on this issue see R. Melnick (1999), Strangers in a strange land: dilemmas of landscape integrity, a paper presented at *Multiple Views, Multiple Meanings: A Critical Look at Integrity, the First National Forum on Historic Preservation Practice*, Goucher College, Baltimore, Maryland, March 11–13, 1999.
4. For distinctions between vernacular and ethnographic landscapes see A. R. Alanen, Considering the ordinary: vernacular landscapes in small towns and rural areas, in *Preserving Cultural Landscapes in America*, A. R. Alanen and R. Z. Melnick, editors (2000), The Johns Hopkins University Press, 112–142.

    Efforts to expand National Register criteria to be more responsive to issues of diversity have been made most recently by Ned Kaufman and Antoinette Lee. Among the earliest voices to challenge the National Register criteria for 'significance,' 'integrity,' and, most recently, the notions of 'authenticity' and 'change' were those heard at a series of conferences at Goucher College. People like Barbara Wyatt and Caroline Torma, who work in state agencies and Historic Preservation programs, have also raised concerns regarding National Register criteria. See also the article regarding the importance of including vernacular structures among potential National Historic Landmark designees by C. Lavoie (of the Historic American Building Survey) and B. Savage (of the National Register of Historic Places) in the *Vernacular Architecture Newsletter*, 106 (Winter 2005), 6–8. For a method that addresses the 'architectural evaluation' phase of historic urban sites and traditional houses in Turkey, see B. Ipekoglu (2006), An architectural evaluation method for conservation of traditional dwellings, *Building and Environment*, 41 (March), 386–394.
5. Richard Moe, the President of America's National Trust for Historic Preservation, discusses how Main Street programs 'tell America's stories,' illustrate the power of preservation to strengthen communities, and make Main Streets livable in his text, *Changing Places: Rebuilding Community in the Age of Sprawl*, Henry Holt, 1997.
6. Twenty years ago, the Main Street program focused almost exclusively on economic and commercial development. Today, the program functions at different scales from cities to small towns, and seeks measurable standards for defining *success* that are more broadly defined than economic stimulus alone. Diversity issues that will enrich traditional commercial districts balance revitalization, building restoration, and entrepreneurship. Note the phrasing for the National Main Street Conference (March 30 to April 2, 2008) in Philadelphia, Pennsylvania: 'These unique qualities [entrepreneurship and diversity] add to local flavor, create a true reflection of community, contribute to an authentic identity, and attract an exciting business mix ... Embracing diversity brings multiple perspectives and a wider range of talent to your organization and your community.' Of particular interest to this discussion is the tour entitled: 'The Challenges and Benefits of a High Immigrant Population on Commercial Redevelopment.' The tour description reads, 'This tour focuses on efforts [that] Upper Darby's municipal government and nonprofit organizations have taken to involve new immigrant communities and businesses in the first-generation suburb. The Township of Upper Darby, Pennsylvania, has opened a welcome center to give new immigrants information they need to get involved in the community. The Township has also significantly invested in streetscape and redevelopment efforts in the area through the Upper Darby Gateway project.'
7. University of Chicago Press, 2004.
8. I have reached the conclusion that the awkward synthesis of old and new patterns of effect within a landscape provides evidence of an evolving vernacular. These patterns of contradiction call out for critical examination on the part of vernacular scholars and offer opportunities of accommodation on the part of architects and urban planners willing to address the emerging situational context. Of interest, in this regard, is the work of San Diego, California, urban designer Teddy Cruz; Phoenix, Arizona, architect and urban planner Darren Petrucci; and Detroit architect Dan Pitera. Rather than embracing vestiges of the past for their reassuring associative value, current, complex urban realities define their work.
9. E. H. Barnett, Voices of change and pain: a project gives North Portlanders a chance to talk about gentrification, *The Oregonian*, April 17, 2008, A1 and A7.

    It is clear that with the intervention of new people and new ideas about what constitutes cultural identity of a neighborhood in transition something will be lost and gained. The key seems to be to make genuine efforts at understanding and collaboration, and address many points of view without losing focus. It is really community building in the end.

    Other studies worth noting are the *Social Impact of the Arts* (findings from a number of related studies conducted by the University of Pennsylvania on the presence of cultural activity in neighborhoods, social cohesion, and revitalization; available at www.ssw.upenn.edu/SIAP). Special thanks to Bill Bulick, Creative Planning, Portland, Oregon, for pointing me to this study.
10. 'Global crisis and preservation,' a lecture delivered by Richard Moe on February 28, 2008 in Portland, Oregon, at the Gerding Theater (located in the Old Portland Armory, a Platinum LEED Certified renovation). The critical point made was that while America's population is only five percent of the world's population, it produces twenty-two percent of greenhouse emissions. The culprit is not our auto-dependent culture alone (that contributes twenty-seven percent of the total amount), but the energy consumption of our buildings and how we use them

(forty-seven percent of the total). Not only do we need to be wiser about how we build, Moe contends, but reusing existing buildings is a productive way of conserving energy over demolition, landfill, and new construction. The critical issue is capturing the embedded energy that already exists in buildings – particularly those constructed prior to 1920. The Armory building was used as a case in point. Constructed of stone, brick, iron, and wood, it covers 55,000 square feet. This is 700,000 gallons of equivalent embodied energy, he states, and capable of driving a car that averages twenty miles to a gallon fifteen million miles. His point: 'We can't build our way out of the energy crisis, we have to conserve our way out. Preservation plays an integral part in sustainable development.'

Section Two

From regional theory to a situated regional response

3

Introduction

> The true basis for any study of the art of architecture still lies in those indigenous, more humble buildings everywhere.
>
> Frank Lloyd Wright

In the previous section of this text, the focus was on the collective forces that determine our regional settings: how human habitats are socially constructed, how environmental and cultural forces shape distinctive landscapes, and how patterns of contradiction are as relevant indicators of Place as patterns of continuity. In attempting to understand a particular landscape, it was suggested that documenting its environmental determinants, analyzing its material culture, and exploring the ways in which spaces are used and transformed allow for a more nuanced perspective of our environments. In addition, it was recommended that investigations seek out multiple narratives of both users and makers to understand a locale's *lived experience*.

In this section of the text, attention shifts from a proposed theoretical model for interpreting regional distinctiveness and Place-based research methods practiced in the field of vernacular architecture to various case studies on architects and urban designers who address a broad range of human concerns and environmental determinants within distinctive global settings. These case studies feature work that is characterized as *situated regional design*. Drawing from the lessons of regional formulation discussed earlier in this text, the goal of situated regionalism is to design from the point of view of the people within a locale – how they address their physical environment, derive meaning, and express their rituals and beliefs by ordering human activity spatially and formally amidst changing regional circumstances.

James Ackerman in his article 'The history of design and the design of history' makes three observations concerning the levels of experience involved in designing in accordance with the dynamics of Place: (1) experience of the culture, (2) personal experience with the locale, and (3) experience of the environment. This experiential approach to design does not suggest that such knowledge is obtainable only by being born to the place. In fact, native participants may often be overly familiar with the characteristics of a locale and fail to see its full complexities, multiple perspectives, or evolving patterns that demand alternative regional responses than what has been the customary practice. There is value in the freshness of outlook that comes from experiencing a place for the first time, and judging its uniqueness against one's own cultural biases. One cannot stop there, however. As Ackerman suggests, gaining experiential knowledge of a human setting is contingent upon acquiring the ability to understand how a society organizes itself by collaborative interaction, internal support, and the basic human understanding of its developing needs. Perhaps Ackerman's three experiential factors might be summarized as *People*, *Locale*, and *Environment*. These components of a landscape are, in fact, interrelated and, in the hands of a sensitive practitioner, are approached collectively when considering design intervention. At its best, design goals will link social equity with ecological performance. Parts One, Two, and Three divide the case studies among the three components of People, Locale, and Environment in an effort to focus on the recognized strengths of each professional under discussion. Though not arranged in the sequence listed above, three case studies address housing issues; three case studies investigate various scales of urban intervention; and two studies explore

Copyright © 2009 Elsevier Ltd. All rights reserved.

FIGURE 3.1
San Francisco De Assisi adobe mission, built 1813–1815, Rancho De Taos, New Mexico. (Photograph by the author, 2006.)

museum design and interpretation from different sets of design inquiry. All address the particularized regional philosophy of the practitioners.

Vernacular architecture and the architect

The vernacular landscape is different from an architect-shaped or planned landscape, but how is it different, and why is this important? And, what can the architect learn by exploring vernacular settings, and by employing methods of regional analysis drawn from vernacular studies during the pre-design stage? Can, or should, an architect design in a vernacular way? Can there be such a thing as a *New Vernacular*?

Amos Rapoport draws a critical distinction between architectural design and vernacular building processes in his meaningful chapter, 'Learning from vernacular' in his seminal book *House, Form and Culture* (considered to be the first book to tackle the human motivations behind diversity in house forms). He states that the important point in attempting to create regionally recognizable cultural landscapes is not that vernacular design is created without architects, but rather that vernacular design is achieved through a system of shared rules. By being culture specific and place specific, these rules are shared and widely accepted within a discrete locale; the resulting environments communicate clearly to their inhabitants and are then capable of being adjusted and varied to suit local specific conditions.

In contrast, the *regionalist* renditions of Robert Venturi, Denise Scott-Brown, and Steven Izenour, or the so-called New Vernacular interpretations of Frank Gehry, Eric Moss, or Morphosis during the 1980s relied upon hyperbolized cultural symbols, recontextualized design features, and reformulated modern materials as *commentary* on Place to an outside audience (Figures 3.2 and 3.3). These works represent highly personal design statements of what the locale meant to the architect, speaking to other architects.

Hence, what precludes high-style representations of vernacular architecture from becoming a true vernacular expression is that vernacular works often focus on broader goals of utility, social accommodation, and/or environmental appropriateness that is *locally* based. In contrast, high-style interpretations of vernacular processes or design features tend to be directed toward aesthetic communication, or present a built manifesto of design theory to a *global* professional audience. This is not to suggest that vernacular architecture is without an aesthetic intent, or that it does not harbor pretensions; this was clearly demonstrated in the gentry houses of Annapolis discussed earlier in this study. But as a rule in vernacular architecture, the regional dynamics are addressed first. Such distinctions are not made simply to glorify the vernacular. Instead, it is a matter of shifting the lens through which we view our landscapes and the priorities that govern our work.

Sue Clifford, in the Introduction to *England in Particular: A Celebration of the Commonplace, the Local, the Vernacular and the Distinctive*, describes her goal as developing a way of 'seeing,' so that one can explore, at the local level, a particular circumstance. During a phone interview with the author, she noted: 'Regions are so varied in England, some "invent" regions, some share, but assemble the components differently.' Clifford feels, 'It is more useful to apply the term "local distinctiveness" rather than the term "regional."' 'Heritage conservation,' she adds, 'is similar to natural conservation in that if we lose local distinctiveness, we lose regional diversity.'

This discussion points to several conditions for contributing to the *truth to locality*. First, there is recognition – a way of seeing, fostered by heritage stewards and design professionals in concert with the inhabitants of a locale – of what holds meaning and embodies cultural relevance within the community. Further, the cultural (not just economic) revitalization or continuance of Place is contingent upon the involvement of the people who reside in a particular setting. Then, there is acknowledgement that the use of building features and materials is not arbitrary but, instead, is tied to their appropriate task, time, and place. And, it is not enough to preserve buildings and spaces alone but, whenever viable, to preserve the local life ways, natural resources, and local economies that created the distinctive setting.[1] Therefore, members of Common Ground, the group founded in 1982–1983 and publisher of *England in Particular*, look to more indices of Place than architecture. This organization encourages people interested in holding on to what they recognize as the *best* of what defines their local culture. This grass roots organization embraces the special meanings that these distinctive practices hold within the locality today, from working to reopen the local stone quarry or preserving an orchard of antique varieties of apples. The various activities collectively demonstrate what

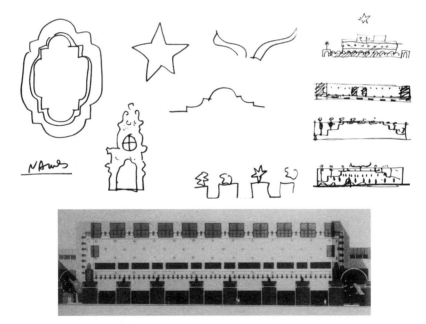

FIGURE 3.2
Robert Venturi, Denise Scott-Brown, and Steven Izenour – from symbolic essence to concept development. Staunchly critical of dominant functional modernism, the firm's early schemes for the Austin Museum of Art (formerly Laguna Gloria Art Museum for Austin, Texas) drew upon vibrant images and recognizable historical features of Texas' cultural identity as a starting points for regional design. These schemes appeared in *Center Magazine*'s 'New Regionalism Issue,' volume 3, 1987. Originally designed as a museum specializing in twentieth-century American art and as a centerpiece for its neighborhood context, the museum's board halted the project 'to accommodate art from the community's ethnic cultures, address other changes in the museum's function and focus, and reconsider the location and size of the museum's site.' (Images and commentary courtesy of Venturi, Scott-Brown, and Izenour.)

FIGURE 3.3
Eric Moss's Petal House for Brad and Maritza Culbertson, Los Angeles, California (1981–1983) as published in *Progressive Architecture*. (Photograph courtesy of Tim Street-Porter.)

people can achieve together, whether it is initiating or continuing time-honored festivals or developing orchards. Such shared activities lend *ownership* to the locale by its inhabitants.

This said, a situated regional approach is achievable; it requires immersion in a specific local condition in order to understand its environmental and cultural lessons. The work of Michael Pyatok (see his Tower Apartments, Rohnert Park, California, 1993) provides examples of sensitively designed, low-rise, subsidized housing that addresses population density issues at the same time as providing internal landscaped courts that engender personal identity and community. Rob Wellington Quigley's work during the early 1990s in San Diego offered a dignified solution to the gap between homelessness and permanent dwellings in the form of Single Resident Occupancy housing (SROs). And, Samuel Mockbee, through his Rural Studio in one of America's poorest rural settings (Hale County, Alabama), merged social service with unsentimental, imaginative, and place-responsive modern design.[2]

In this text, the work of Nina Maritz in Namibia, Carol A. Wilson in northern Maine, and Glenn Murcutt in New South Wales, Australia, stresses respect for local building processes that are in harmony with their environment, and the necessity of utilizing appropriate technologies to optimize energy conservation while touching the earth lightly. These practitioners offer insights into environmental regionalism by demonstrating, respectively, how a paucity of materials and building infrastructure do not have to translate into a poverty of expression; how spatial economy can provide richness in daily living; how sensitive attention to the siting of a building respects the intrinsic characteristics of Place that brought the clients to the locale in the first place; and how an informed understanding of regional environmental factors can provide varying levels of mediation between the dwelling and its surroundings, introduce sustainable living practices, and foster an appreciation for the transcendent power of nature.

A situated regional approach also requires addressing existing humanistic needs, sensibilities, and values. Ideally, such a design response enlists the active collaboration of the people for whom a work is being designed – not just as labor support, but also in a manner that respects the human dignity of those whom the design project is intended to serve. Of note are the case studies on Howard Davis, who works collaboratively with other design professionals, social workers, and future occupants to provide affordable housing for the rickshaw taxi drivers formerly relegated to the slums in Vellore, India; and urban designer Teddy Cruz, whose community-based planning efforts within the border town of San Ysidro, California (less than a mile from the US–Mexico border), seek to understand how essential human needs and living practices can be identified and implemented in new design. These case studies provide insights into diversity issues of regional design: how issues of race, ethnicity, gender, social class, and world view require the professional to adopt effective tactics when working with communities radically different from himself/herself in order to ensure a voice critical to the success of the design process and to the community being served.

In contrast, Michael Graves' 1981 San Juan Capistrano Public Library (an icon in its day of 'regional' expression) possesses design elements derived from the once regionally manifest Spanish missions (e.g. stucco finish, visually prominent bell towers, terracotta roof tiles as well as many other design overlays, Figure 3.4). Yet, the cultural relevance of these features—once vital to the traditional meaning of place is elusive in any tangible sense to the local population. Responding to strict design guidelines for the area, the features are culled from the past, reinterpreted, and recontextualized to summon up references of a public library instead of their original function as a mission. Even the materials, while superficially appearing like adobe, function differently in terms of their structural and thermal properties from the wood, adobe, and lime plaster coating originally used and, ultimately, project a different sense of palpability and mass (Figures 3.5 and 3.6). It is more a caricature of a past heritage than a genuine engagement with it.

The San Juan Capistrano Library might best be characterized as a product of *personal or symbolic regionalism*; regional reference is achieved by an omniscient observer/designer who synthesizes critical design features from an assortment of California missions that he feels constitute the visual representation of Place. Graves' approach to the Reginal library responds to the physical context but at the same time ardently resists *becoming* context. Instead of performing a supportive role to the existing building stock, Graves strives to declare the building's elite status as an internationally recognizable work of art. To do so, it must set itself apart (in various ways) from the local context and become a visual landmark.

The very concept of *context* may differ from area to area. San Diego, California, architect Rob Wellington Quigley, for example, suggested during an interview in 1991 that context, as a discernible physical environment, served in his work 'as a genesis to creativity' (Figures 3.7 and 3.8). Conversely, in the eastern USA a random assortment of historical associations often are viewed as the context. Hence, the collective memory of images that form a landscape of the mind – unbound by time and place – can constitute the context of a building program in some schools of thought. As a result, urban planners, developers, and design professionals today frequently respond to context (in its many guises), and recreate – or create anew – a manufactured and promoted sense of Place.

If the gap between image making and social and environmental relevance is to be bridged, the mere imitation of local features or the recalling of the distant – often mythical – past is not enough. Note,

FIGURE 3.4
Michael Graves' Regional Library, San Juan Capistrano, California, 1983. (Photograph by the author, 1991.)

44 Vernacular Architecture and Regional Design

FIGURES 3.5 AND 3.6
Detail of Michael Graves' Regional Library, San Juan Capistrano, California. (Photograph by the author, 1991.) Detail of San Francisco De Assisi adobe mission built 1813–1815, Rancho De Taos, New Mexico. (Photograph by the author, 2006.)

for example, the steep angular volumes used by Hardy, Holzman, Pfieffer Associates of New York in the Hult Center for the Performing Arts in Eugene, Oregon, of 1979–1982 designed to *complement* the silhouettes of surrounding mountains and its use of nearly 100 foot Douglas fir posts in the lobby as design gestures to anchor a modernist building into its local fabric through visual association (Figure 3.9).

Similarly, one might consider the fanciful creation of Seaside, Florida, that attempted to recreate

FIGURE 3.7
Villa Maria, located in the Little Italy district of San Diego next to the Mexican Embassy, was developed by Barone Galasso and Associates and completed in 1999. This mixed-use, redevelopment, affordable housing project brought in various area architects to ensure diversity of design, materials, and spatial complexity that responded to specific local concerns. (Photograph by the author, 2006.)

the *vernacular past* by appropriating older building types from Alabama and Virginia and codifying other spatial conditions like sidewalk, fence line, and house set back relationships in hopes of capturing the image of a small, pre-1940, Southern town (Figure 3.10). The many layers of images and allusions at Seaside are purposefully derived from 'self-effacing, anonymous buildings' and small town streetscapes as typical manifestations of social coherence. The evocative forms and features are interspersed with works by internationally known architects and are, in turn, bound together and

FIGURE 3.8
This Villa Maria Apartment unit designed by Rob Wellington Quigley addresses local social concerns. The varied grouping of buildings provides flexibility of use – ranging from ground floor eating establishments and stores, to a glazed-in laundry room immediately adjacent to a children's play area that allows parents the ability to monitor their children while doing laundry. The project earned an AIA Award for Excellence. (Photograph by the author, 2006.)

FIGURE 3.9
Hult Center for the Performing Arts in Eugene, Oregon, of 1979–1982 designed by Hardy, Holzman, Pfieffer Associates of New York. (Photograph courtesy of Dennis Galloway.)

encouraged by the Urban Code established by the husband and wife architectural team of Andres Duany and Elizabeth Plater-Zyberk along with developer Robert Davis. This highly successful development strategy has spawned many imitations that offer a form of *nostalgic regionalism.*

Some planning schemes under the heading of New Urbanism/Traditional Neighborhood Development in the USA provide enlightened responses to pedestrian paths over a dependence on the automobile and promote the notion of community and sustainable life ways over suburban sprawl. However, far too many of these community prototypes function as momentary solutions to crime by offering gated living, the longing for community (by bringing brand name 'anchor stores' to the suburbs as simulated neighborhood shops), and the desire for reassurance that comes with a sanitized past devoid of social strife, diverse populations, and visual disharmony.[3] Critics have also pointed to the reliance on private development without public ownership of public spaces and streets, and the targeted market of high-income buyers leaving Main Street, as anything but a bastion of diversity. As one scholar put it, 'After all, real cities have rough edges, poor people, industry, a diverse building stock, real competition in land transactions, and continuous change.'[4]

Simply stated, a regionally situated design response involves effective communication with the user(s), and an informed awareness of the built, social, and natural environments as collective determining factors. Design tactics are synthesized within the framework of these various levels of experience, and the solutions are carried out in such a manner that the resultant work not only addresses the complex realities of the locale, but also is capable of communicating back to its constituent' positive human values. One of the unacknowledged design constraints the planners of Seaside had to face, for example, in what was once a largely undeveloped

FIGURE 3.10
Seaside, Florida, planned and designed by Andres Duany and Elizabeth Plater-Zyberk along with developer Robert Davis. (Photograph courtesy of Jenny Young.)

section of the Florida panhandle (Seagrove Beach near the Seaside development had a population of eight in 1981, according to resort architect Scott Merrill) lies not only in the 'lack of indigenous housing stock' for site references and historic precedent, but the lack of observable patterns of human behavior from which to generate, accommodate, or articulate a cultural and environmental response.

Hence, a situationist ideology recognizes that the *context of place* is not comprised of alienated, anonymous users living amidst undifferentiated environmental settings. Instead, design investigations seek solutions that are critically engaged in the worldly situation. A true postmodernist expression, therefore, will not be one that simply divorces itself from the images of the Modernist past, but from the thinking and methods of the Modernist past as well. It involves a new set of responsibilities and priorities from the architect of utilizing environmental and sociocultural knowledge of the locale, and developing that knowledge in a manner that accommodates change within the context of local sensibilities.

In this regard, the role of history as a subject area within architectural education needs to shift from merely functioning as a source for precedent studies from which plan-types, form-types, and features can be lifted, to a genuine understanding of the past and the collective, interrelated forces that shaped its expression in built form. Conversely, vernacular architecture studies need to stress the roles that architects, planners, and urban designers play as agents of change in shaping the form and character of our landscapes. Vernacular landscape scholarship is no longer limited to the exploration of resources and settings shaped by the non-professional. All aspects of culture shape the contours and meanings of our living/working/spiritual environments. In support of this sentiment, effort is made in this section of the text to employ methods of analysis gleaned from contemporary vernacular architecture studies, and apply them to significant demonstrations of the manner in which the profession responds to changing (and sustained) patterns of use, cultural identity, technological innovation, and environmental phenomena in addressing environments both familiar and distant to them.

Achieving situated regionalism

All the case studies that follow are considered by the author to be exemplars of regionally situated design; yet, it is recognized that there is not one way to design in a regionally integral manner. Architects will continue to reach beyond the application of learned messages of the locale and the mere practicalities of place to inspire, interpret, or inform by means of architectural expression, because that is what architects generally do. But, whether the design response is conceived principally to address the social concerns, local physical context, or environmental determinants of Place, such premises are likely to become a more integral part of the locale and its people, and begin to replace image with substance.

In the case studies on Jo Noero (a native of South Africa) and Glenn Murcutt (who works exclusively in Australia), a profound understanding of culture, environment, and climate has been internalized. Instead of a heavy reliance on user participation or community control that others like Teddy Cruz, Darren Petrucci, and Nihal Perera advocate, the engagement with a wide spectrum of regional factors in their work allows for situated regionalism to be achieved by other means. In Murcutt's example, the dissemination of the deep structure of regionally appropriate environmental strategies is passed on through built examples and his various teaching and lecturing venues.

In Howard Davis's case study, there is a combination of the rules of thumb offered by Clifford (a way of seeing the various critical components within a locally distinctive setting), and Rapoport (a way of understanding what the rules or patterns are and applying them in a regionally appropriate way). Davis has stressed to the author, 'apart from the political/power importance of user participation, the primary importance is to get at accuracy in the process and therefore in the result.' In this manner, the end product resonates with the user by demonstrating an understanding of her/his cultural values and essential needs. He further notes, 'My own view is that ultimately, it is a question of process – and that the best the architect can do is to be a catalyst for a shared cultural process in which everyone is responsible. This is not to say that the architect is not involved, but that in the end, control devolves to people – who are [ultimately] the most accurate about their own needs and wants. Otherwise, even if [an architect] can do a better job at capturing the rules of a culture or place, the rules remain as expert knowledge' – a singular rather than a collective awareness of regional design tactics. He adds, 'Communities and educational institutions may come to see the advantages of both inside and outside knowledge and experience. Indeed, vibrant cultures have often maintained their life by assimilating knowledge from outside themselves. The critical thing is that they should not be overwhelmed in the process [for example, the scale of development and/or the manner in which the project is undertaken].'

Nina Maritz, on the other hand, regards her role as a socially and environmentally responsive architect to reach local design consensus, utilize local resources – both natural and human – and create civic structures in Namibia that are fully sustainable. The end product, she feels, must speak to the economic realities, needs, and environmental factors of the area's inhabitants as well as inform cultural outsiders. Her work is completely deferential to its locale. In Maritz's Visitors' Interpretation Centre for Prehistoric Rock Cut Art, for example, every effort is made to have her building disappear into the natural environment, giving primacy to the rock art that the building is designed to serve, and do as little harm to the environment in the process by being fully reversible. Similarly, in Jo Noero's museum, the building form is meant to be permeable and be experientially part of the local context, while also being expressive (not by visual reference alone but by community involvement) of the collective historical/sociopolitical experiences under apartheid.

The following case studies are grouped under the regional components of *People* (Improving the Human Condition through Design), *Locale* (Interpreting and Accommodating Characteristics of an Evolving Landscape), and *Environment* (Appropriate Technologies and Design Tied to the Dynamics of Place). The works under investigation demonstrate various strategies – or opportunities – for addressing these priorities effectively. Some approaches addressed in this book are admittedly experimental in nature (and not always successful as conceived), while others are time proven and have been celebrated by professional accolades. In all the case studies, *design process* is stressed, and the architects, planners, and urban designers under discussion are asked to reflect upon the choices they made in responding to a particular human, physical, and/or environmental situation. All case studies are keyed into global context maps, and there is a brief description of each case study at the start of each chapter that summarizes its perceived contributions to situated regional inquiry.

If there is one overarching aspect that unites all the case studies, it is that Situated Regionalism is a *principled* way of addressing the habitats in which we intervene. In his recent chapter in the text *Vernacular Architecture in the Twenty-First Century*, entitled 'Architectural education and vernacular building,' Davis calls for a 'new kind of professional education,' where 'professionals are humbler, draw their knowledge from the situations in which they find themselves, and have a deep respect for other professionals, builders, clients and members of communities.'[5] The case studies that follow fit this description. In many cases, the design teams are facilitators; they choose to design collaboratively and listen to a full range of stakeholders. In other instances, the architect or urban designer functions as a sole practitioner, but fully understands the cultural and environmental dynamics at play. New ideas, evolving technologies, and innovative design solutions are introduced that are often different from what has come before, but the resulting works are true to the present human and environmental situation. As such, the work is at one with the people, place, and time. This, I feel, is designing in a vernacular way: a situated regional response.

References

Ackerman, J. (1980). The history of design and the design of history. *VIA: Culture and Social Vision IV*, 12–18.
Rapoport, A. (1969). *House, Form and Culture*. Prentice Hall.

Notes

1. Phone interview from Oxford, England, between the author and Sue Clifford of Common Ground on July 25, 2006. See S. Clifford and A. King (2006). *England in Particular*. Hodder and Stoughton.
2. See A. O. Dean and T. Hursley (2002). *Rural Studio, Samuel Mockbee and an Architecture of Decency*. Princeton Architectural Press.
3. For a critique from the proponents of Seaside, see T. W. Bressi, editor (2002). *The Seaside Debates: A Critique of New Urbanism*. Rizzoli International Publications.
4. H. Davis (2006). *The Culture of Building*. Oxford University Press, 279.
5. H. Davis (2006). Architectural education and vernacular building, in *Vernacular Architecture in the Twenty-First Century*. Taylor and Francis, 231–232.

Part One

People – improving the human condition through design

4

Finding patterns within the local building culture, and preserving the continuity of tradition through participatory housing and community development

> Discussions between clients and professionals remain abstract and general. They are not about the product, but instead about the 'values,' or 'needs,' or 'functions.' The professional goes away and designs the product with these abstractions 'in mind' – but essentially by his own lights and according to his own habits. Within such a situation, the whole corpus of existing tradition is ignored – it is after all only a 'product' – and then buildings are built that neither client nor professional love or admire.
>
> Howard Davis, David Week, and Paul Moses in *Architecture & Design* (March–April 2003), 53–54.

Project: Housing Initiative for Rickshaw Drivers and their Families, Vellore, Tamil Nadu, India
Location: Vellore, Tamil Nadu, India
Design team: Informal organization called The Center for People's Housing/Tamil Nadu (ILLAM)
Official participants:
   Howard Davis, Professor of Architecture, Center for Housing Innovation, University of Oregon
   David Week, Director of Pacific Architecture, Sydney, Australia
   M. Nelson, Founder and Director, Center for Development (CEDMA), Tamil Nadu, India
   Thomas Kerr, Architect, Field Recorder
   Paul Moses, Director of Architecture South in Madras and Site Manager
Time frame: 1990–1995

Introduction

By exploring the specific living patterns of a particular user group, Howard Davis demonstrates how such information can contribute to our cultural perceptions of a landscape – particularly life ways beyond the architect's realm of personal experience. Willing to listen, observe, and question, he and the design team acknowledge the useful role of a cultural outsider to provide valuable insights without controlling every aspect of the design process.

This case study offers an alternative to a singular reliance on formal analysis or stylistic reference in addressing place-based design concerns. Instead, Davis and the design team explore buildings and their settings from interrelated sets of human behavior. Design seen in this manner supports the notion of social regeneration. New ideas fold into familiar ways of doing things, allowing for the continuance of social practice amidst improved living conditions.

Project description

A team of architects, social workers, and members of the community set out to collaborate on designing a participatory housing initiative for 130 rickshaw drivers and their families living in Vellore, India. Howard Davis and David Week employed the principles of a *pattern language* (the site layout

Copyright © 2009 Elsevier Ltd. All rights reserved.

FIGURE 4.1
Detail of a bicycle rickshaw and driver in Vellore, India. (Photograph courtesy of Howard Davis.)

FIGURE 4.2
Location of the site. (Map courtesy of US Central Intelligence Agency, *World Fact Book*, 1996.)

procedure builds on work developed by Christopher Alexander[1]). By undertaking extensive fieldwork on existing settlement patterns in Vellore and surrounding villages, team members Thomas Kerr and Paul Moses developed about thirty-five specific observations that had implications for the site layout. Davis points out, 'These observations constitute, in effect, a translation describing significant differences between the language of the local building culture, and a language more familiar to us as modern professionals.' These characteristic living patterns and street layouts were incorporated into the final site plan. Recording relationships with camera, sketchpad, and computer (that is, 'always a temple' as in Figures 4.3 and 4.4, or 'women usually fetch water at least twice a day ... The well or pump is usually located at a road widening or intersection' as in Figure 4.5), critical design elements began to emerge and were discussed with the intended users for verification.

The narrative of the settlement plan, as articulated by Davis, reads like the *social mapping* of a site by a vernacular scholar dedicated to revealing culture through careful site analysis of the smallest informal sector activities. Here, vernacular studies and contemporary design process find a fruitful balance.

The government-donated tract was laid out by the design team who worked alongside the future residents (Figure 4.6); room configurations were decided upon; enough latitude existed for the addition of elements that reflected personal identity and local custom. In the end, current conditions, a collaborative spirit, and a collective will enabled permanent homes and businesses to take root. Beyond the specific project definition of providing improved housing and developing a mechanism for self-sufficiency for a politically marginalized group through collaborative strategies, the broader issue was 'to understand how development may be possible while preserving the continuity of tradition.' In other words, how can positive social and economic *change* be balanced with cultural *continuity*?

Before the project began, team members visited other housing projects laid out by local firms and based on Western planning ideas and building standards. This exercise set the tone for a design strategy that reacted against imported design ideas. The design team asked the questions, 'What can we learn from the local condition? How can we come up with actual patterns from the *local* building culture?'

Design intent

In clarifying the role of professionals in helping to provide housing in the developing world, Davis and Week wanted people to take responsibility for the layout and design of the houses they were going to inhabit. This attitude corresponded with CEDMA's philosophy toward self-help, preferring to encourage the city's urban poor to take charge of their own lives. Accordingly, emphasis was placed

FIGURE 4.3
'Always a temple' – this pattern element is a small temple located in its traditional position within the community. The layout is recorded by camera. (Photograph courtesy of Howard Davis.)

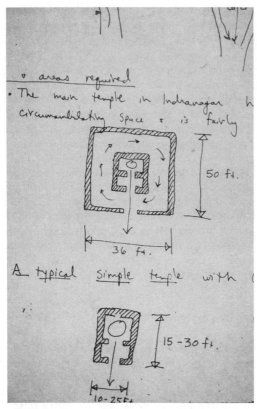

FIGURE 4.4
Observations of the various temple's spatial relationships and physical features were recorded in field notes by Kerr and Moses. (Photograph by Howard Davis.)

FIGURE 4.5
Site locations (top), street sections, and field notations (below) by Kerr and Moses. These social and spatial patterns are related to collecting water in the village. (Photograph of drawing courtesy of Howard Davis.)

on the social *process* of the building initiative, rather than on the *product* as an end in itself. The effort to improve the housing conditions of the rickshaw drivers, it was understood, must also be linked to changing the drivers' own perception of their power relations within the community as it related to their economic development. The architects were not there as 'foreign experts transferring expertise,' Davis notes. 'We were there simply to offer another point of view' in the effort to empower individuals through improving their living situation.

Design process

In the five years that the project took to complete (1990–1995), Howard Davis traveled to India six times. Over the years, his regional knowledge increased, and he gained the trust of the client. Gradually, social worker Nelson (the client) revealed more of himself and his organization's work with disenfranchised groups in India over the past twenty-five years that included education, employment generation, job training, human rights advocacy, rural sanitation, housing, and small-scale manufacture. Together, the architects and client collaborated with the formal association of the Rickshaw Drivers' Association in Vellore. Nelson organized mostly Hindus (many of them untouchables), who had migrated relatively recently from rural villages and were, therefore, new to city life. While they were mostly lower caste, they were not among the poorest. They had started their own rickshaw business and paid loans, but were relegated to living in slums with their rickshaws (Figure 4.7).

CEDMA went about helping the rickshaw drivers to carry out several stages of development: to free themselves from the financial exploitation of the rickshaw owners for whom they worked, CEDMA helped the drivers to obtain loans to own their own rickshaws. The rickshaw drivers were then encouraged to assert claims for land. On behalf of the rickshaw association, CEDMA next went about initiating house financing and self-construction in order to build houses on their land.

In 1991, the government purchased land from local farmers and made it available for the CEDMA self-help building project. At this point, architect Howard Davis became involved in this international collaboration project. By the spring of 1992, investigations of local settlement patterns were completed; 136 house sites had been laid out on the ground (Figure 4.8); the site plan had been

Finding patterns within the local building culture 55

FIGURE 4.6
A site-marking ceremony at the start of the house construction. Each lot was exactly 13.5 square meters. (Photograph courtesy of Howard Davis.)

FIGURE 4.7
Existing housing in Tamil Nadu, where bicycle-rickshaw drivers and their families lived prior to the completion of the new project in Vellore. (Photograph courtesy of Howard Davis.)

FIGURE 4.8
Vellore community members walking the perimeter of the site. (Photograph courtesy of Howard Davis.)

approved by the district surveyor; and an experimental building was under construction. This collaborative spirit among all participants, according to Davis, 'forced [Davis and Week] to put aside normal attempts to control the process. Yet all the participants, despite their differing perspectives and experiences, were able to work with remarkable synergy and fluidity to get quite a bit done.'

As discussions with the community continued (Figure 4.9), a commonly understood and accepted product that embodied people's values and ways of life began to emerge. The image of things to come served as a touchstone, Davis recalls, that drove the process. As members of the design team put it, 'Our experience has been that unless the product is thus made central, the process is impoverished.'

Drawing from the extensive field observations undertaken by Thomas Kerr and Paul Moses, about thirty-five simple rules of thumb guided the site layout. Believing that professionals and clients should cooperate as equals in the design process – each learning from the other – the layout of the settlement proceeded on site with members of the community. Major physical features of the settlement were fixed before going on to details. Boundaries were walked; community leaders were asked where they thought the entrance to the settlement should be; the main square was defined in relation to the main entrance; and the temple was sited.

'Decisions about the extensions of the street beyond the square, the shape and size of the square, and the shape and size of the streets followed.' Kerr and Moses coordinated these social and pragmatic decisions related to the patterns recorded in the survey data. 'A main street leads into the settlement from the public road, passing through a main square

FIGURE 4.9
Community members in Vellore being asked to contribute their ideas about what they wanted in a home. (Photograph courtesy of Howard Davis.)

with a temple facing down another lane; the street winds its way along the length of the settlement, including another public place for a meeting hall. There are tiny squares where the streets join wherein are located places to serve as water sources.'

Assessing the regional filter

Southern India relies on a rice-growing and coconut economy. The climate is very hot, which determines work patterns that begin early, halt between the hours of two and five in the afternoon, and resume near sundown. Davis recounts that between midday hours he often attempted to sleep. Sometimes the electricity would go off; there would be no fan and he would remain in bed, motionless from the heat.

Social dynamics

'When working with individuals who have never owned a home, they often grasp onto a vision of domesticity shaped by what they see being built around them. In Vellore, these were flat-roofed, concrete buildings; however, brick is better than concrete thermally, and a pitched roof is cooler [due to vertical stacking] than a flat roof,' Davis notes. In this instance, the architects made design decisions that disagreed with the first impressions of the potential residents regarding issues of human comfort and lifecycle energy requirements in the project.

In contrast, the client (Nelson), following Western principles of modern housing standards, thought that the bathrooms should be connected to the individual houses. Hindu social customs, however, separate toilets from the house and often place them on the opposite end of the courtyard. One factor in reaching successful resolutions of such differing perspectives, Davis notes, is time and immersion in the culture. Davis' intent was to reach that balance of what geographer Edward Relph refers to as *empathetic outsidedness* where, generally speaking, one maintains the objectivity of an outsider, while attempting to understand the local situation from the vantage point of the local participant. Or, as Davis put it himself, 'The architect has to maintain a sense of respect for the realities of the situation and not imagine that what he has to offer is better than what local knowledge offers. Learn to withhold judgment; be observant about every detail. See everything anew; notice more. It is easy to miss details that make a difference.' His solution for the dilemma of the bathroom placement was *phased construction*, where current users gauged their attitudes over time, and the architect adjusted his response accordingly in the later phases of the project.

Developing the housing program

In blocking out the simple plan-types for the tiny housing units, discussions with the potential inhabitants revealed that simply maximizing interior space was less important to them than defining the *social accommodations* of selected spaces. For example, in a typical two-room longitudinal plan (Figure 4.10), the architect might assume that by aligning doorways from the outside to the interior rooms along the exterior wall, it would allow for

FIGURE 4.10
The first two experimental houses in Vellore. (Photograph by Thomas Kerr.)

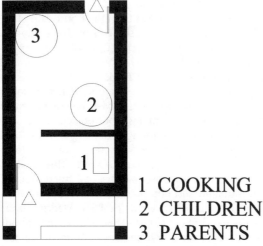

FIGURE 4.11
Annamalais house plan. (Drawing by Orrin Goldsby for the author after plan by David Week.)

1 COOKING
2 CHILDREN
3 PARENTS

greater space opposite the circulation path. However, the future occupants, the Annamalais, wanted the entries placed diagonally across from the room plan to allow for two pockets of space in the back room, creating private corners for the parents and children when they slept facing the wall (Figure 4.11).

Additionally, women knew where they wanted to place the vent hole next to the stove, so that smoke would escape properly. By placing the stove diagonally across from the door separating the front and rear rooms, the kitchen maintained its social function as a private space and provided both a dining and sleeping space. The wife in the family, Davis observed, often stood in the doorway between both rooms during meals when guests were present and contributed to the conversation while replenishing dishes as needed.

Architect's reflection

The trips to the building project by Davis and Week were not frequent, but they involved intense design activities. Together the team blurred the traditional professional roles, where 'architects make the buildings' and 'the social worker cares about the people.' 'Social change takes time,' Nelson notes. These socially based projects need to 'flow like the river.' They have to yield to the 'natural process of human change … If you are serious [about addressing the current critical realities of Place], you need to do the same.' Ultimately, the phased, owner-built and occupied, housing project was successful because it arose from – and was shaped by – members of the community themselves. 'Projects like this are catalytic – a product that depends on understanding, and being responsive to the process of cultural and economic change' (Figures 4.12–4.14).

FIGURE 4.12
View of an experimental house during construction. Fired brick was transported by truck from another site that the NGO ran in an attempt to keep resources within the regional community. Though similar to the Mexicali Project under Christopher Alexander, where families designed their own houses, the Vellore settlement, in contrast, used local, well-understood, methods of construction.
(Photograph courtesy of Howard Davis.)

Finding patterns within the local building culture

FIGURE 4.13
A Vellore family and rickshaw shortly after their home was completed. (Photograph courtesy of Howard Davis.)

Author's comment

This case study addresses the challenge that both an architect and regional scholar face when attempting to understand a culture unfamiliar to them. William Somerset Maugham, for example, confronted this problem in his travel books such as *The Gentleman in the Parlor (A Record of a Journey from Rangoon to Haiphong)* written in 1930. He states: 'He puts himself into the shoes of his characters; but there are shoes he cannot get into … When he describes them he will describe them from the outside, and the observation divorced from sympathy can seldom create a living being.' This reference is similar to reducing a culture's architectural expression to basic physical attributes divorced from their function and social meaning. Maugham continues: 'Here time is the prime agent. The writer is fortunate who can wait till this has effected such a change in him that he can see what is before him with fresh and different eyes.' (Ackerman's point of the value of personal experience with the locale as a condition of designing in accordance with the dynamics of Place is made clear here.) But time in a place and a change of scene alone are not enough. Maugham adds: 'I have known writers who made adventurous journeys, but took along with them their house in London, their circle of friends, their English interests and

FIGURE 4.14
A Vellore home culturally weathered with ceremonial rice flour threshold art, pottery, and a raffia shading device added in the months following occupation. (Photograph courtesy of Howard Davis.)

their reputations; and were surprised on getting home to find that they were exactly as when they went. Not thus can a writer profit by a journey. When he sets out on his travels the one person he must leave behind is himself.'[2]

In this self-help housing project, methods of analysis that had been valuable elsewhere were adapted to a new locale, but *a priori* decisions of what this village would look like based on past experience were left behind. By immersing themselves in the situational context of daily life, and recording and verifying related spatial uses with the future inhabitants, the design team began to see the emerging village plans and housing designs through the priorities and values of the people who would soon inhabit the village. In essence, the design team 'left themselves behind' when they traveled to Vellore.

Recommended reading

Alexander, C., *et al.* (1985). *The Production of Houses.* Oxford University Press.
Davis, H. (2000). *The Culture of Building.* Oxford University Press.
—— (1993). Learning from Vellore: low income housing project in India, *Arcade*, XIII (2), 8–10.
—— Week, D., and Moses, P. (1993). The village meets the city. *Architecture & Design*, X (2), 51–57.
Verhelst, T. G. (1990). *No Life without Roots.* Zed Books.

Notes

1. As Daves describes it, his is a bottom up approach to planning that provides order through local means, and creates locally empowered communities.
2. William Somerset Maugham (1957). *The Gentleman in the Parlor.* New York: Marlowe & Company, Preface.

5

Facing the challenge of a framework approach

Unlike the restructuring of the village and Buddhism in the nineteenth century, this [design tactic of *critical vernacular*] architecture has no direct connection with the past. Instead, it uses indigenous and historic spatial concepts, elements, architectural details, and construction methods to construct a built environment for contemporary institutions and functions. This is, however, not a 'vernacular architecture' nor an 'architectural style constructed by borrowing elements of an historic architectural vocabulary to provide mere visual signs.' Nor am I referring to Western architects' attempts to create stylistically defined place-specific architecture, or to modern hotel complexes designed for the visual consumption of tourists, simulating built forms of the indigenous environments. What I am concerned with here is the conscious or unconscious construction of a historic continuity through a particular cultural response from within the society concerned where the trajectory of history has been ruptured by colonialism, or other aspects of European expansion.[1]

Nihal Perera

Project: The Mahaweli Development Project
Location: Towns built as part of the Mahaweli River, Democratic Socialist Republic of Sri Lanka
Design team: The Mahaweli Architectural and Planning Unit of the Government [Twenty architects and planners – Nihal Perera (Chief Architect-Planner beginning 1983) and Urlik Plesner, Principal Consultant]
Time frame: 1981–1989

Introduction

Unlike Howard Davis' preceding study, where socially specific evidence was drawn upon to inform a cultural outsider about community and residential design, Nihal Perera's design team faced the challenge of planning and constructing town centers that were being newly created for residents as part of a national dam relocation project. Though a native of Sri Lanka, not knowing the agricultural habits of the future inhabitants, their everyday patterns of behavior and belief, Perera called upon other tactics for socially relevant design intervention.

In providing schemes for positive urban intervention, a phased redevelopment plan (that allowed time for inhabitants to adapt, personalize, and transform spaces to fit their needs and means) had proven to be the most successful approach in this region. Perera and his team, therefore, provided sufficient flexibility – beyond the provisions of structure, form, space, and systems – for the vernacular matrix to take hold. As part of a *loose-fit planning strategy*, human activity would shape the character of a locale.

The planned town centers (and their collective readjustment through use) were intended to allow the builders and occupants alike to recast dramatic change into the familiar. Given this project's inception on the heels of national political independence, the design intentions were emblematic of a search for identity that encompassed scales of reference ranging from the local to the international.

Project description

The reference to the *familiar* in the form of vernacular design constructs was intended to serve not only the pragmatic requirements for housing solutions in the Mahaweli relocation project, but as a salve for emotional yearnings on the part of the future residents as well. Thousands of residents were

Copyright © 2009 Elsevier Ltd. All rights reserved.

FIGURE 5.1
Pre-existing site condition of a Mahaweli Dam site. (Photograph courtesy of Nihal Perera.)

forced from their habitats and community ties as land was cleared for one of the world's largest irrigation projects. Seven irrigation dams, new designs for relocated hamlets and town centers, their incumbent infrastructure, and public and commercial services all had to be conceived in an accelerated planning cycle that shifted from its initial planning projection of thirty years to a ten-year development process. Perera's design team took on as their directive to rebuild not only the lost physical structures for the displaced population, but to create a means by which these communities could reconstruct their sense of belonging. This study focuses on one of these newly designed towns for displaced persons, Dehiattakandiya.

Design intent

This case study illustrates a sincere effort on the part of the design team to draw upon familiar spatial elements and design features that were critical to the region's environmental response and to its shared cultural identity; these forms and features were used as starting points for modern urban design inquiry that sought to provide cultural continuity in the face of the sweeping physical transformation of the inhabitants' living environments brought about by political change and, subsequently, a massive dam and irrigation relocation project.

Nihal Perera led the Mahaweli Architectural and Planning Unit of the Sri Lankan government beginning in 1983. As a native of Sri Lanka, Perera called upon his regional awareness, as a 'cultural insider,' to decipher regionally appropriate design elements that could be adapted for use in this enormous government relocation housing project. Tile roofs with broad overhangs, long verandas, and wall openings (connecting interior and exterior spaces in response to the region's hot, humid climate) became critical design elements integrated into the new design. Perera now refers to such essential design tactics as the *critical vernacular*. Perera is quick to note that 'with over ten years of experience developing critical vernacular design responses in Sri Lanka, Urlik Plesner's [the design team's Principal Consultant] input was critical' to this design approach.

This notion of an architecture rooted in the present circumstance, yet simultaneously connecting Sri Lankans to their inherent cultural ties, underscores the dialectical tension that existed in the country following independence from colonial rule. Recognizing that architecture can be a powerful communicative vehicle for projecting political ideologies, the challenge for design professionals was how to balance the desire to be recognized in a global political sphere through the physical expression of architecture, and yet respond to the country's emotional need for a regional identity that speaks to their underlying cultural roots. Design and planning projects during this post-colonial era, therefore, are conceived within the framework of this global–local duality. The Mahaweli project, by combining local architects and foreign consultants in the design team, directed local, regional, and international expertise toward creating a 'hybrid architecture and urban form.'

Regional filter

In order to understand the motivations that prompted and shaped the development of this irrigation relocation project some historical context is necessary.

Sri Lanka's long history began with its settlement in the sixth century BCE, but in more recent times its regional identity was determined by external influences of hegemony. In the fourteenth century, an Indian dynasty established a Tamil kingdom in the northern part of the island. In the sixteenth century, the coastal regions of the island were controlled by the Portuguese and, in the seventeenth century, by the Dutch. Ceded to the British in 1796, it remained under some form of British control until 1948.[2] Thus, reassertion of Sri Lankan national identity has been an important aspect of governmental efforts since independence in 1948, and it has colored many of its national policies and physical expression even as it has made efforts to join in the processes of globalization and the world marketplace.

In the late 1970s, the government initiated more market-oriented policies, encouraged exports and foreign investment, and looked more and more to the outside world, while attempting to maintain its national identity as being uniquely Sri Lankan.[3] Its attempts to balance these dual roles might be best exemplified by the separation of the global–economic functions (centered in Colombo) from the national–political functions (relocated to the outskirts of the capital in a new government seat). After assuming control of the government in 1977, the United National Party quickly established the Urban Development Authority (1978) to promote integrated planning and the development of important urban locations.[4] International banks and financial agencies were invited to invest in the central business district of the capital city of Colombo. This new central business district was rebuilt in the International Style (at the government's encouragement), situating it visibly within the world marketplace and within widely recognized progressive design principles. At the same time, a new government center was developed on the outskirts of Colombo, showcasing a new national Parliament House, which, 'in its subtle blend of modernity and tradition,' was a visible expression of this national effort to represent and express a sense of the new nation's Sri Lankan national character apart from any previous colonial references. This impulse to address the cultural and environmental determinants of Sri Lanka in a manner that represented its post-colonial political identity was best illustrated by its most influential architect, Geoffrey Bawa.[5]

Rather than seeing Bawa's influence as a *neo-vernacular* subcategory within postmodernism – thus reducing it to a stylistic classification – his work represents a significant shift in attitude toward regionally reflexive design that focuses on the continuation of cultural traditions within the exigencies of the immediate present. Bawa's work during the 1970s set the stage for a postcolonial Sri Lankan architecture that spoke of a revised political and ethnic identity for his country. It drew upon local vernacular traditions to forge a new architecture that addressed its independent status as well as its critical environmental factors (heavy rainfall, high humidity, and heat). In addition, he drew together (and worked closely with) talented young designers and artists who shared his interest in Sri Lanka's architectural heritage, thereby exerting a significant influence on the emerging architecture of the newly independent nation and on successive generations of younger architects. In addition, many believe that Geoffrey Bawa's ideas directly affected the lives of ordinary people as they spread across the island, providing a bridge between the past and the future, a mirror in which ordinary people can obtain a clearer image of their own evolving culture.'[6] In addition to Bawa's influence, Perera is quick to underscore the importance of Ulik Plesner (with whom Perera later developed what became known as critical vernacular design) to the design approaches brought to bear on the planning and design of the Mahaweli housing project.

Project definition (phase one)

As mentioned above, the government of the United National Party launched an ambitious public

64 Vernacular Architecture and Regional Design

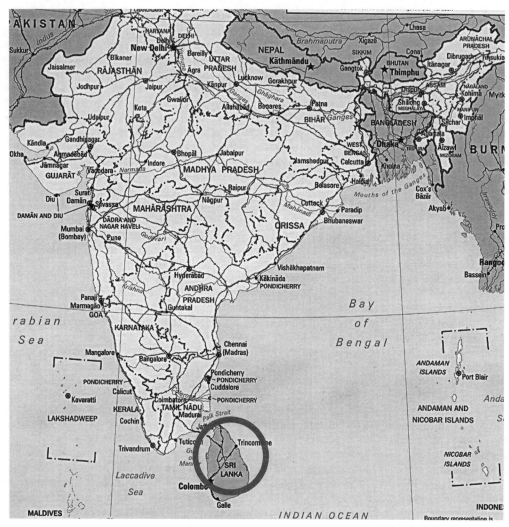

FIGURE 5.2 a & b
Regional reference map with Sri Lanka designated. (Map courtesy of US Central Intelligence Agency, *World Fact Book*, 1996.) Reference map with the town sites located. Dehiattakandiya, the subject village, is denoted by the red circle. (Illustration courtesy of Nihal Perera.)

investment program after taking control. Between 1977 and 1980, these government projects expanded the construction industry at an annual rate of some twenty percent. The Urban Development Authority was established in 1978 to promote integrated planning and development of important urban locations. Its responsibilities included the new parliamentary buildings and the reconstruction of St John's fish market in Colombo.

Under the direction of the Urban Development Authority, a policy based on such support systems was implemented in 1984 (known by the name The Million Houses Program) to coordinate both public and private housing construction.[7] The Mahaweli relocation planning project under the direction of Nihal Perera (between 1983 and 1989) was conceived within these governmental parameters.

Project definition (phase two)

The largest construction project of this post-1977 period was the Mahaweli Irrigation Project. Originally developed in the 1960s as the Mahaweli Ganga

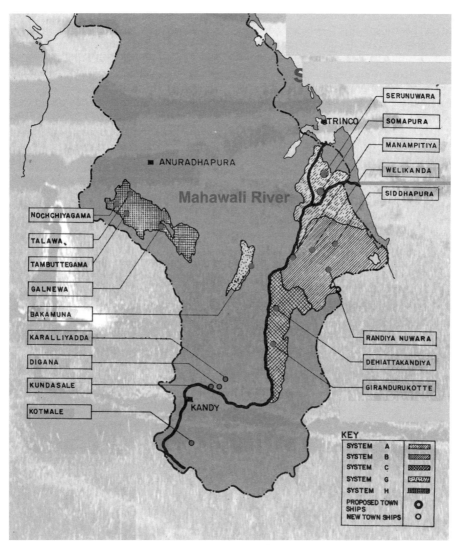

FIGURE 5.2 cont'd.

Program, the project had been expected to provide some 364,000 additional hectares of land in the *dry zone* under irrigation to significantly increase agricultural output, and to provide an additional 540 megawatts of hydroelectric power. Completion of the overall project was expected to take thirty years.

The first two dams were completed in 1977 and opened about 53,000 hectares of new land to irrigation in a general area south of the old capital of Anuradhapura in the central arid or dry zone of the country. In 1977, however, the government renamed the project the Accelerated Mahaweli Program (AMP) with a completion time of ten years. Construction began at five new sites between 1979 and 1982, with the intent of increasing the hectares under irrigation and generating an additional 450 megawatts of hydroelectric power for the national grid. The seven reservoirs that were constructed, however, also flooded agricultural land and displaced pre-existing communities, requiring a master plan to address the relocation and reconstruction of hamlets and towns along with their necessary infrastructure.[8]

By the early 1980s, even after years of planning, the new towns in north-central Sri Lanka still had very few buildings. What existed were partially developed rural areas, rather than real communities replacing the critical social, economic, and religious services that had been lost. In the 1980s, the decision was made by Perera and the design team to provide the displaced communities with town centers from the beginning, along with the appropriate infrastructure necessary for the inhabitants to resume familiar life patterns in the newly irrigated areas.

Design process

When Perera became the lead architect-planner in 1983, he and his team designed these new town centers around a dense urban core created by the clustering of the institutional and commercial buildings built in the first few years. The plan would be updated annually based on progress, funding, and other factors. The design intent behind the creation of various town centers was to connect critical social and practical functions with socially meaningful spatial accommodations. Thus the town would be anchored by its center, but there would be sufficient flexibility for the families to adapt their habitats in accordance with their personal needs and values through a *loose-fit* or *framework approach*. The term 'loose fit' was coined by Wes Janz, a colleague of Perera's at Ball State University (Indiana), to describe this design approach.

Akin to John Turner's premises regarding government subsidized housing, wherein people determine the type of housing they need and then the government provides it, these towns were conceived to begin their lives as urban centers but develop within the framework of a planning process that could be adjusted over time by the occupants themselves. Relinquishing much of the planner's role to prescribe a building's program, basic form-types were provided and spaces were blocked out. Decorative features and the resultant social relevance of the spaces were left up to the occupants to shape over time (Figure 5.3).[9] In this loose-fit planning approach, Perera expected that the physical and spatial adjustments to the building framework would be part of the design process carried out by the

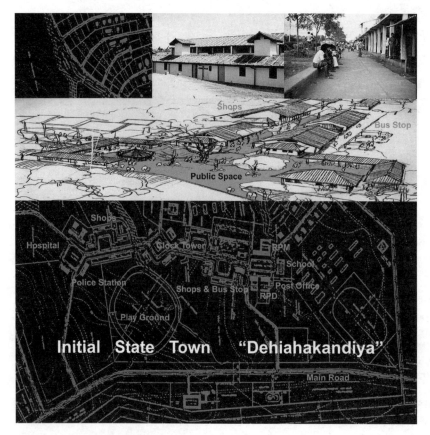

FIGURE 5.3
Figure of various design schemes of the initial state towns of Dehiattakandiya and Girandurukotte (top two rows). Both are located in the downstream area. The design of Girandurukotte was led by Vodek Wynman, consultant and member of the design team. (Illustration courtesy of Nihal Perera.)

FIGURE 5.4
An affected site in the planned reservoir bed at Randenigale. (Photograph courtesy of Nihal Perera.)

inhabitants. Hence, in accordance with performance theory, *use* would define meaning and determine, collectively, local distinctiveness and identity.

Design development

The Mahaweli project was comprised of two kinds of townships. Downstream: townships were constructed in the newly irrigated areas where towns had not existed previously to accommodate the expected increase in population. Upstream: new towns replaced the commercial, institutional, and residential infrastructure lost in the construction of the seven reservoirs built for the irrigation project (refer back to Figure 5.2, and to Figures 5.4 and 5.5).

The Architectural and Planning unit of the Mahaweli development project recognized, early on, the need to quickly rebuild housing and to provide basic urban necessities for those communities and adjacent settlements whose city services would be destroyed. Central to the planning of

FIGURE 5.5
Opening of the completed Victoria Dam, flooding down river village sites. (Photograph courtesy of Nihal Perera.)

these new settlements was the desire to offer familiar reference points to the residents to ease the adjustment period, and to counter, as much as possible, their dislocated sense of well-being.

In the newly developed downstream areas, farmers were settled in hamlets and villages and a hierarchy of urban centers was provided. Each town center was equipped with institutional facilities critical to the maintenance of public life, such as high schools and courthouses. These township services accommodated from 8,000 to 10,000 farming families. The Mahaweli Architectural and Planning Unit was involved in planning twelve town centers between 1983 and 1989 for newly developed and redeveloped areas (Figure 5.6 and 5.7). Dehiattakandiya was one of the newly developed downstream towns.

Mahaweli town: structure and relationships

1. Towns to serve the newly irrigated agricultural areas downstream, for example Dehiattakandiya, Welikanda, Girandurukotte.
2. Towns to replace those facilities inundated by the reservoirs in upstream areas, for example Rajawella (Digana), Teldeniya (Karalliyadda).
3. Reinforcement of the existing towns to cater to the increased catchment population due to the development of those areas under the Mahaweli Project, for example Bakamuna.

Mahaweli town: composition and systems

1. Hamlets: the smallest composition of the system comprised
   (a) 250–300 families, farmers.
   (b) Acreage for irrigated lands, acreage for homesteads.
   (c) A hamlet center comprised of a primary school, a post box, and a few shops.
2. Towns: served by
   (a) 3–4 hamlets, 800–1,200 families.
   (b) A village center, provided with a higher level of infrastructure, for example Dehiattakandiya.

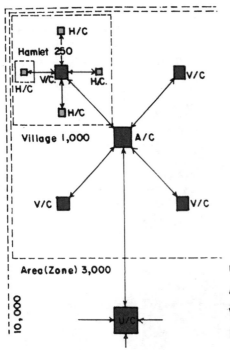

FIGURE 5.6
Mahaweli town: structure and relationship chart to serve the new irrigation settlements in downstream and upstream areas. (Content and illustration courtesy of Nihal Perera.)

Facing the challenge of a framework approach **69**

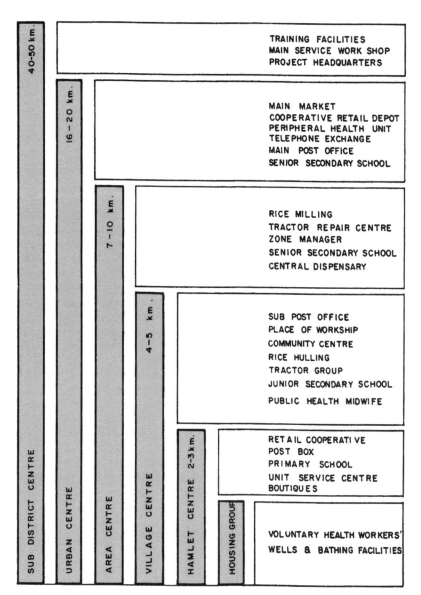

FIGURE 5.7
Hierarchy of service centers.
(Illustration courtesy of Nihal Perera.)

3. Initial stage towns: comprised of
   (a) Approximately 500 families
   (b) A bus station
   (c) A senior secondary school with hostel facilities
   (d) A post office
   (e) A police station
   (f) A hospital
   (g) Shops
   (h) Bank
   (i) *Pola* (a weekly market)

Design implementation

When interviewed, Perera stated that '… there were economic forces and challenges that occurred from not knowing who the clients were, not knowing their life ways, and not fully understanding their place as farmers who were recently displaced.' (Since these were newly designed town centers, rather than replacement villages, there was no opportunity to observe and accommodate existing patterns of behavior.) Rather than making assumptions about the residents' cultural values and social priorities, enough latitude was built into the design project for the residents to define what was essential to their sense of self. Perera noted that '… in the core of the new towns, we provided store designs with spaces above for living or for storage. We built only the structural shell and the roof; these were not finished, some plastered, some with windows' (Figure 5.8).

Perera continued, 'the interior spaces were generic and designed for the occupants to use as they wished. As a result, the residents were able to customize their buildings and houses using the structures we provided as a beginning point and within the government's rules and guidelines' (Figure 5.9).

'In some respects, the design process was a reaction to [contemporary building practices],' Perera added. 'The basic designs were inspired by vernacular and historical form-types in the region that provided an alternative to the culturally insensitive Western type boxes which were becoming more and more popular.' It was a conscious decision, therefore, that 'the designs did not follow the messy post-colonial built forms without roof overhangs and verandas. [Instead] the resulting forms were hybrids composed of compatible spatial elements that worked in vernacular, historical, as well as post-colonial environments. They were both modern (in their ability to provide contemporary amenities) and culturally friendly.'[10]

With regard to the commercial infrastructure, the team provided three plan-types for stores lining the main streets: a double-story plan, one-story hip roof form, and a salt-box form with overhang (Figures 5.9 and 5.10).

The project planning team also imagined creating town squares out of the institutional buildings earmarked for the initial period of development. The buildings skirted an open area with the verandas forming an arcade around the square – framing views of open space and providing a sense of enclosure to this public space area. Simple structures with fixed windows at a higher level were designed for the buildings facing the square. The windows were equipped with trellises for ventilation and privacy (Figure 5.12). The rear courtyards of the buildings addressed the parking and loading functions, while making the buildings culturally more familiar through their spatial associations (Figure 5.13).

Consistent with the intent for defining the character of individual businesses and dwellings, occupants were encouraged to recreate their own vision of the townscape in relation to the new regional context of Mahaweli settlements. In an effort to retaliate against their recent sense of dislocation, a new critical-vernacular expression (comprised of an amalgam of old and new building elements) began to emerge. Additionally, the units were

FIGURE 5.8
Structural shells under construction in the center of the town of Teldiniya. (Photograph courtesy of Nihal Perera.)

Facing the challenge of a framework approach **71**

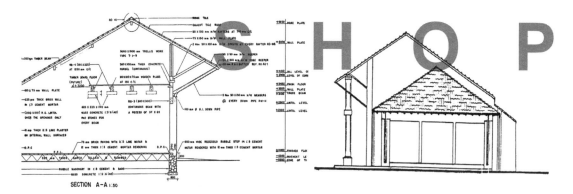

FIGURE 5.9
Drawing of one of the three plan-types for stores with living spaces above that lined the main streets of the town center of Dehiattakandiya: this scheme illustrates the salt-box form with overhang. (Illustration courtesy of Nihal Perera.)

grouped in such a manner as to afford creative collaboration among the newly constituted town dwellers and to foster creative use of open public space, thereby establishing community ownership. The first phase of state-sponsored buildings served as a framework upon which to build the next phase.

Architect's reflection

Perera concedes, 'the project both failed and succeeded as intended. People incrementally changed what we built, and our initial input was a significant springboard for the development of the town.'[11] Architecture and urban design, however, never exist in a sociopolitical vacuum. The uneasy peace between Tamil separatists and the Sinhalese-dominated government soon erupted into civil war in 1983; tens of thousands died in the ethnic conflict in the decades that followed.

With the civil war between the government and the separatists, security became a primary requirement. For example, the spatial conditions of the government offices in Dehiattakandiya were altered and then fences were put around them. 'The loose fit notion did not actualize in the manner that we had imagined. Some of the public spaces were gone, and the government and political conditions determined the quality of the spaces – not the local people.'[12] With the abandonment of the idea of public squares anchoring the foreground spaces of the buildings, it was now left to the privately owned commercial establishments to enhance the public town. Perera notes, however, 'this is just one square in

FIGURE 5.10
Three-quarter view of the salt-box form's structural shell shortly after construction.
(Photograph courtesy of Nihal Perera.)

72 Vernacular Architecture and Regional Design

FIGURE 5.11
Three-quarter view of the double-story post office in the new town center of Teldeniya after storeowners and clients responded to Perera's loose-fit design, and reclaimed the building and foreground spaces in a manner meaningful to them. (Photograph courtesy of Nihal Perera.)

one town (Dehiattakandiya). The others are working as public squares. Another change that the people did was to encroach [onto] some of the sidewalks. This is pretty common in south Asia – we discouraged it a bit, but it is up to the stakeholders to negotiate this space.'

The choice for the designer, Perera feels, is either to assume the role of *architect as author*, or the role of *architect as instigator* (facilitator). He concedes, 'The latter role (which we opted for) becomes difficult when dealing with governmental power relations.'

FIGURE 5.12
Simple structures with fixed windows at the higher level were designed with the façades facing the square to maximize the view of the foreground space. This view is of the hospital in Dehiattakandiya. (Photograph courtesy of Nihal Perera.)

FIGURE 5.13
View of the rear courtyard of the Mahaweli office in Dehiattakandiya designed as a multipurpose space for parking and outdoor activities.
(Photograph courtesy of Nihal Perera.)

Author's summary

In the end, Perera's collaborative decision-making process and decentralized design control approach, where the design team merely provided the technical infrastructure and formal and spatial framework, opened itself to conflicting ideologies. One ideology (Perera's) was to serve the needs of the displaced persons both emotionally and pragmatically. The other ideology (the government's) addressed the prevailing political climate and stressed security measures for both the local inhabitants and the country at large. Both concerns were relevant. Ultimately, the nature of the project changed as the regional dynamics changed.

Perera's regional design philosophy was put to the challenge on this project. Recognizing that regional determinants do not remain constant, Perera now embraces more fully the design premises of hybridity, post-colonial identity, and post-structural theory to guide his planning concepts. However, by establishing a framework (or loose-fit design approach), the Mahaweli project did overcome the authentic single-use premise and the 'designer as author and designer as provider approaches.'[13] More importantly, the relocated inhabitants' dignity was honored by trusting them to define their homes, commercial activities, and community settings in a way that was meaningful to them.

Suggested reading

Davis, H. (1999). *The Culture of Buildings*. Oxford University Press. Introduction and Chapters 1, 6, 12.
Turner, J. F. C. and Fichter, R. (1972). *Freedom to Build: Dweller Control of the Housing Process*. Macmillan.
Perera, N. (2004). Contesting visions: hybridity, liminality, and authorship of the Chandigarh plan. *Planning Perspectives*, 19 (April), 175–199.
——(1998). *Society and Space: Colonialism, Nationalism, and Post-colonial Identity in Sri Lanka*. Westview Press.

Notes

1. Nihal Perera, *Society and Space: Colonialism, Nationalism, and Post-colonial Identity in Sri Lanka*, 144. Though the focus of this case study is on town planning, Perera's argument about 'critical vernacular architecture' addresses the approach carried out by the Mahaweli project design team that qualifies for this characterization. Perera cites Geoffrey Bawa and Ulik Plesner as the leading architects of this tendency.
2. Sri Lanka, in *The World Factbook* (2008). United States Central Intelligence Agency. Available at https://www.cia.gov/library/publications/the-world-factbook/geos/ce.html

3. Ibid., Economic overview section. Available at https://www.cia.gov/library/publications/the-world-factbook/geos/ce.html#Govt
4. Sri Lanka: A Country Study. Washington. JPO for Library of Congress, 1988. Available at http://www.countrystudies.us/sri-lanka/52.htm
5. The Aga Khan Award for Architecture Chairman's Award, The Eight Award Cycle, 1999–2001. Available at http://www.akdn.org/agency/akaa/eighthcycle/bawa.htm
6. Khan, H. U. (1995). *Contemporary Asian Architects*. Taschen Books.
7. Sri Lanka, in *The Library of Congress Country Studies*; *CIA World Factbook* (1989), Economy section. Accessed at http://www.photius.com/countries/sri_lanka/economy/index.html. See also Perera, *Society and Space*.
8. *Sri Lanka Construction* (republished from *The Library of Congress Country Studies* and the *CIA World Factbook*, 1988). Available at www.geographic.org
9. Unless otherwise indicated, all quoted remarks by Perera are from an interview conducted with this author at Ball State University, Muncie, Indiana, April 12, 2006.
10. Perera perceives this approach (what he terms *critical vernacular*) as an important architectural design trend that emerged since the 1970s following Sri Lankan independence – with Bawa being its most acclaimed proponent. It is an approach that moves beyond so-called 'Modern architecture and its relation to historic Lankan architecture.' He notes that he is 'not referring to a mere *style*, the main trait of which is that it is distinguishable from others, but to a cluster of broadly defined design practices that draw upon historic Sri Lankan concepts of space in creating culturally, climatically, and technologically more appropriate buildings in independent Sri Lanka.' The rise of critical-vernacular architecture, Perera stresses, 'has been a particular indigenous cultural response to post-colonial economic, technological, ideological, and historic conditions.' Such architectural premises consciously break with the political past and the contested colonial system that shaped Sri Lankan living environments for centuries.
11. Interview at the ICOMOS: Thailand Conference, November 2006 and subsequent written correspondence, January 24, 2007.
12. Correspondence with the author January 24, 2007.
13. For an expanded discussion of this argument see Nihal Perera (2004), Contesting visions: hybridity, liminality, and authorship of the Chandigarh plan, *Planning Perspectives*, 19 (April), 175–199. In this article, Perera contends that the 'Corbusier plan' is generally celebrated 'largely [as an] architect-centric, descriptive and positivist' creation. Instead, Perera offers another narrative whereby he sees the plan as negotiated among 'multiple agencies and is not the creation of a single author … No single imagination emerged victorious; no one author created the plan … the plan is much more chaotic, hybrid, liminal and diverse than its architect-centered discourse suggests. Missing in the discourse is the idea that people – including administrators, politicians and planners – are not passive recipients of external ideas; ideas do not get transmitted across cultural boundaries without mediation' (p. 175).

6

Rewriting history through architecture

Architecture is not just form making. Architecture can influence lives; contribute to the local economy; and add to the cultural life of the local people. It is exciting for an architect to be part of the process: to listen to the local community, add something meaningful that was not there before, and in the process enrich people's lives.

Jo Noero, 2007

Location: New Brighton, Port Elizabeth, South Africa
Design team: Jo Noero, Principal, Noero Wolff Architects, Cape Town, South Africa
Time frame: 1998 – Project is awarded through an international competition
2002 – Project begins
2005 – Phase I, the museum is completed. Six additional bulidings in the cultural precinct are planned

Introduction

Jo Noero's design for the Museum at Red Location speaks to the collective struggles of a people, the invisible structures of power that defined the social experience of apartheid, and the promise of a reimagined cultural identity that the very premise of a post-apartheid heritage museum represents. National and international in importance with regard to its inspired design concept and execution, the museum succeeds most brilliantly in its ability to connect to the local human experience, local residents, local building features, local spatial relationships, and the realities of the local economy. It is community-centered design – a true *civic* building.

The Museum at Red Location presents a built forum, where through the medium of a memorial, the local, regional, and national South African population can transmit their narratives of struggle and hope to present and future generations. The museum project and its planned cultural precinct offer an optimistic view of the future while acknowledging South Africa's troubled past. The project demonstrates how architecture can help shape a vision of positive change, while enriching people's lives in the process.

The regional filter – addressing the political, social, and physical context of the museum

'The challenge at the outset,' Noero notes, 'was to overcome centuries of constructed cultural perceptions of Place: South Africa as a place of darkness, nascent violence, primitive superstition, huge inequality and, most recently, a center of a progressive economy among emerging nations.' How, then, does one begin to forge a built statement of cultural identity amidst the vestiges of the many layers of transplanted colonial masks? Noero asks, 'What constitutes our heritage?' He describes a consciously constructed view of the past, offered up as history, that the Dutch colonists discovered and cultivated an *uninhabited* land. By 1652, the Dutch began imprinting on the South African landscape expressions of an identity foreign to the indigenous people. By the 1870s, Chicago's urban grid was overlaid, at 1/4 scale, onto Johannesburg's topography. During the 1920s and 1930s successive waves of Eastern European and Jewish immigrants made the city their home, once again adding to a diversity of cultural expression that included some of the best examples of *European* modernism internationally. However, the progressive urbanism of the mid- to late 1900s must be juxtaposed against

Copyright © 2009 Elsevier Ltd. All rights reserved.

FIGURE 6.1
Entrance view of the Red Location Museum, Port Elizabeth, South Africa (Photograph courtesy of Jo Noero.)

the retrogressive national political ideology that mandated the oppression of an ethnic minority.

In addressing all the contradictions that are South Africa, Noero wonders, 'What is the fitting memorial that will trigger the past for the largely poor, uneducated populace that has never stepped inside a museum before?' This question was the generative concept that Noero and his firm embraced as they joined other cultural institutions in South Africa subscribing to a post-apartheid national heritage agenda.

The inception of the Museum at Red Location is set against the backdrop of a transformation process initiated after the advent of democracy in 1994 with the expressed goal of addressing issues of heritage, culture, and identity. As one spokesperson put it,

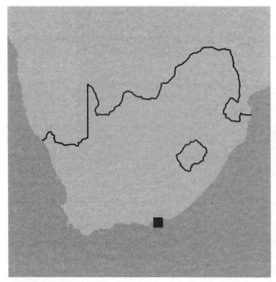

FIGURES 6.2 AND 6.3
Map of South Africa with the location of the site in Port Elizabeth marked. (Maps courtesy of US Central Intelligence Agency, 2002.)

Rewriting history through architecture

such issues are 'deeply emotional – after all these are issues that are at the very core of the transformation agenda in South Africa.' Seminal in these policy debates was the official White Paper, tabled by the Minister of the Arts, Culture, Science and Technology (DACST) in 1996 which preceded the passing of a series of heritage-related Acts of Parliament towards the end of the 1990s.

Despite these progressive political initiatives, the daunting reality for Noero and his firm was the realization that sixty-five percent of South Africa's population still lived in informal shanty settlements built by the urban dwellers themselves out of their own experiences and limited resources (Figure 6.4).

During the period of time when the museum was being designed, the government was initiating efforts to eradicate some of these impoverished and densely populated resettlement communities that had segregated the black South African population under apartheid rule. A dilemma presented itself; dismantling human habitats that had grown out of the very forces of apartheid's political and economic marginalization policies over generations of settlement also eradicated the built testimony of the struggle, perseverance, and enduring hope of the majority of black South African people.

Concept development: reading the cultural landscape

Noero recognized early on that the challenges of the museum project could not be met by 'turning to magazines' for conventional design strategies. In order to produce a situated regional response, Noero admits he 'had to learn to see, and learn to listen' instead. Some observations translated directly into form-givers and spatial strategies (such as addressing local determinants of use, climate, materials, and structure), while others did not but led to a better understanding about how objects expressed the values and frustrations of the people for whom the museum was being built.

Noero continues: 'what, then, is the *authentic* history and where does it reside in South Africa?' He notes that the government expunged many of the official records attesting to apartheid's political abuses – especially from the 1950s on when apartheid, as social engineering, was concretized. In this documentary vacuum, the posters of protest artists of the 1980s and 1990s, whom Noero knew during his own efforts to end apartheid, became the historical record: 'the tale of an unrecorded past that includes relocation and the apartheid struggle.'

FIGURE 6.4
Unplanned urban habitats built during apartheid. (Photograph courtesy of Jo Noero.)

In one linocut by John Morangyo, the rage and frustration of an oppressed people is given agency in art. As Noero explains, 'the notion of a *recolonization* by tourists is unfolding in the depicted scene.[1] The *innocent savage* is being attacked by the capitalist class, counting money, and accompanied by an indifferent government.' This poster reference by Noero speaks, on the one hand, to the loss of an authentic regional identity through the commodification of culture. Often tourist art reduces a region's essence to stereotypical images. Such purveyors of place manufacture a more palatable and, hence, saleable expression of a locale. On the other hand, it speaks to the poignant reality of a three-tiered economic structure in South Africa of a poor, middle income, and tourist economy. His design for the post-apartheid museum had to avoid such stereotypical expressions of collective identity.

Recovering history

Some historical accounts were preserved through Africa's tribal oral tradition. Noero mentions an employee of the South African Council of Churches, who listened to and recorded stories of the apartheid struggle. One narrative recounts the early roots of twentieth-century apartheid in the Second Boer War. This war was fought by the British against the Boers (also called Afrikaners), descendants of the early Dutch settlers of South Africa. The Second Boer War is a matter of historical record, but accurate records of the effects of the war on the native population are nearly non-existent. The various names used to refer to the conflicts themselves reflect the differing perspectives on the nature of the wars and the reasons for which they were fought. Outside of South Africa (particularly by the British), it is called the South African War or simply the Boer War; among some South Africans, it is referred to as the Anglo-Boer War; and among the Boers, it is known as the Anglo-Boereoorlog or Tweede Vryheidsoorlog – the Second War of Independence.

A frame of reference for some of the events that took place during the Anglo-Boer War needs to be addressed if we are to understand the design premises of the museum. The conflict between the British Empire and the two independent Boer republics of the Orange Free State and the South African Republic began on October 11, 1899 and lasted in a protracted manner until May 31, 1902. Following the war, the two independent republics were absorbed into the British Empire. However, the final stage of the war (September 1900 to May 1902) was extended considerably by a shift to guerrilla warfare on the part of the Boer and native forces who outnumbered and outmaneuvered British troops. This prolongation of the conflict led directly to the establishment of concentration camps (the contemporaneous term used by the British) for both

FIGURE 6.5
A British concentration camp built during the Anglo-Boer war. (Photograph circa 1900 in the public domain.)

FIGURE 6.6
Former concentration camps today.
(Photograph courtesy of Jo Noero.)

white Boers and black Africans who might aid and resupply the guerrilla insurgents (Figure 6.5).

The British settled on a slash and burn approach to deal with the Boer commandos who refused to surrender. As the native and Boer farmsteads were destroyed, Boer women and children and Africans were forcibly removed from the farms by the British and imprisoned in camps. There were more than forty camps built for Boers and sixty-four for Africans. By July 1900, Africans started to leave their tribal areas, seeking protection with the British. As the British cleared more and more areas, the number of camps for the native population increased. By the end of the war there were between 107,000 and 115,000 black African prisoners controlled by a separate Native Refugee Department.

Overcrowding, poor diet, and unsanitary conditions within the camps led to epidemics of measles, pneumonia, typhoid, and dysentery, resulting in tremendous loss of life in both the Boer and African camps. Official estimates for total deaths among Boer prisoners range from 18,000 to 28,000. Deaths in the African camps were even more seriously underreported at the time than those in the Boer camps and few records were kept. Various estimates suggest that at least 12,000 to 20,000 black South Africans died in the concentration camps.

Following the war, as the camps were deconcentrated, some were initially used as schools for children. However, many camps continued to house the impoverished and dislocated native South Africans who did not have the resources to return to their traditional homes.

The Port Elizabeth camp was disassembled and moved to a new site. Between 1902 and 1903, these reassembled buildings served as the first relocation camps created for the African population (Figure 6.6). The former native internees in the camps had few alternatives but to continue to work for the poor wages offered by the British. Those who had hoped to recover some of their former lands from the defeated Boers were to be seriously disappointed as the British assisted the defeated Boers in the recovery of their prewar land holdings and paid compensation to help in their economic recovery. While the British paid some compensation to black South Africans as well, it was far exceeded by that paid to the Boers. Those who had hoped that wages in the gold mines would improve under British control also were to be disappointed; in fact, labor conditions worsened and wages were cut after the war.

By the 1940s, these relocation camps had become the most densely settled black African communities in South Africa, and the source of intense passive resistance. Hence, these buildings encapsulated several layers of South African history. Pregnant with meaning, this was the site chosen for the museum (Figure 6.7).

Design intent

During the design concept phase of the project, Noero asked himself 'How do you go about making a museum that deals with a struggle that takes place on the site of the struggle, and the people whose story is being told live in the area? What can be done to make the museum experience resonate with them?'[2]

One consideration was to analyze the spatial dynamics that the site and its existing buildings imparted. 'I saw the street as discourse,' Noero adds. 'This was the public zone. Because of harassment by the government, the shacks literally turned their backs to the street. There were, in effect, two faces: a public face of dilapidated rows of buildings

FIGURE 6.7
View from the former barracks toward the museum. (Photograph courtesy of Jo Noero.)

closed against a world of terror, and a private face, clean and socially inviting interior rooms that constituted a world apart from governmental control and fear' (Figures 6.8 and 6.9).

These shacks, imparting multiple meanings and histories for their former inhabitants, have been reinscribed yet again. They have been designated national landmarks and the people (on their own accord) are moving out, many just a few steps away, to new government-built housing that they requested as part of the museum negotiations (Figure 6.10).

These new homes built by the government are within sight of the shack settlement that represents the struggle of the relocation period. The shacks will, in fact, be part of the interpretation of the museum complex. The challenge for preservationists will be how to maintain these substandard houses in a manner that neither sanitizes nor romanticizes the past in its interpretation of the relocation period from a black South African perspective. 'There is a palpable desire,' Noero recounts, 'to keep a physical record of what the living conditions were like under apartheid.' Similar to the filmmaker Steven Spielberg's efforts (housed at the University of Southern California) to archive the stories of the Holocaust survivors, 'if the memory of that community is wiped out, then the memory of what it meant to live in – or around – that place is wiped out. I think of memory as the only way any person knows who he or she is, and it's also the only way any community knows what it is.'[3]

Building program

'Museums do not become museums on their own,' Noero reflects. 'They are not isolated objects. They are part of a wider community of buildings stitched into the local area: archives for the history of struggle, library, museum school, cinema for African artists, art school, council chambers for the city mayor.' The apartheid museum, the first structure to be constructed, then, is part of a massive program that includes other facilities, such as a cinema to display films by African filmmakers and an art school (one of 30 arts centers in rural South Africa planned by Noero and commissioned by the country's Ministry of Arts and Culture). All will be conceived in such a manner as to foster community empowerment and 'to attempt to rewrite the history of black South Africa.' Noero stresses, 'We wanted to adjust the "official" history – by creating a regional and national museum complex that tells the history of

Rewriting history through architecture 81

FIGURES 6.8 AND 6.9
Two faces: (public face) houses closed to the street and (private face) a socially inviting interior room.
(Photographs courtesy of Jo Noero.)

82 Vernacular Architecture and Regional Design

FIGURE 6.10
View of the new government-built housing with the former barracks in the foreground. (Photograph courtesy of Jo Noero.)

South Africa through the representative experiences of relocation, apartheid, oppression, and struggle' (Figure 6.11).

Design process

In an effort to design a museum that 'constructs a public idea of how architecture can initiate positive social change,' Noero relied on 'intense community consultations.' 'Such buildings are tangible symbols that reassure people that the State is committed to a better way. It transmits to optimism.' Having worked earlier in his career with Anglican leader Desmond Tutu and black community activists in the anti-apartheid movement, Noero discovered how architecture, initially used by the South African government as a tool of oppression and racial

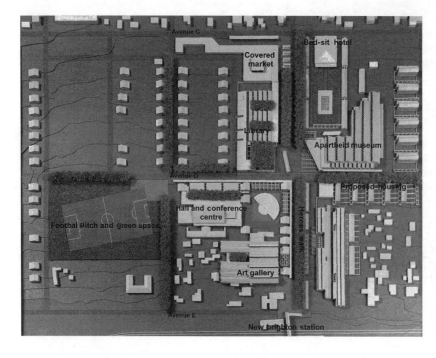

FIGURE 6.11
Plan view of the entire museum complex as presently envisioned. (Illustration courtesy of Jo Noero.)

segregation, could be transformed under the resistance movement to create a sense of hope and belonging.

Recalling the passion of the resistance movement, Noero turned again to some of the posters he had collected by the protest artists of the 1980s and 1990s for inspiration. Iconic images emerged. Temple form government buildings of the colonial past were represented as instruments of oppression. On the other hand, the school, the house, the saw-tooth factory (often a staging ground for protests) were symbols of civic virtue that were embraced widely by the local population (Figure 6.12).

The trade union struggle against white capital on the shop floor was won in 1994 with the end of apartheid. The saw-tooth factory roof, as symbolic essence, was incorporated by Noero into the design vocabulary of the museum as a reference point for those who participated in the union struggle (Figure 6.13).

Following Walter Benjamin's injunction that history distorts truth and omits too much, cultural memory becomes the touchstone for the past in the

FIGURE 6.12
Council of the South African Trade Union poster (1980). Note the saw-tooth factory to the upper right. (Illustration courtesy of Jo Noero.)

museum spaces. The vehicle used by Noero to recognize the important role that each visitor brings to the museum (in the form of his or her own

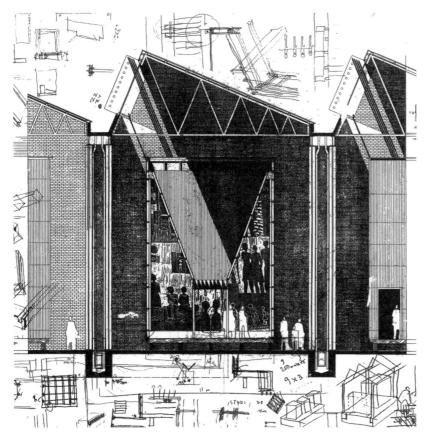

FIGURE 6.13
The saw-tooth factory becomes a symbolically loaded feature in this museum section. (Illustration courtesy of Jo Noero.)

FIGURE 6.14
Memory boxes as repositories for objects of cultural value in the home. They serve as a metaphor for preserving cultural memory related to the struggle against apartheid. (Photograph courtesy of Jo Noero.)

connection to the past) is the *memory box*. The memory box is an actual artifact known to all South Africans and is used as a repository in the home for people's personal history. Objects of cultural value reside in the memory box (Figure 6.14).

Twelve gigantic memory boxes were constructed of ungalvanized, corrugated sheets of steel designed to rust quickly, suggesting the passage of time. Noero states that the goal was to demonstrate 'how to make architecture a scaffold, upon which people can place both predictable and unpredictable elements from their own experience without narrative.' These somewhat brooding monoliths serve as places for contemplation and commemoration (Figure 6.15). The form of the memory box, as metaphor, sprang from a shared regional experience and, therefore, needed no interpretation. As a result, the new was instantly familiar.

Noero describes the spatial conditions of the memory boxes and their interstitial settings as the 'relocated space of reflection – past and present – where the present slips into the past.' Invoking Andreas Huyssen, Noero sought out what he refers to as *twilight spaces*. Noero stresses that the interstitial spaces intended for contemplation between the memory boxes 'should be mysterious, quiet, solemn spaces, where one is compelled not to talk, where they can hear the ghost of their ancestors rustling around. It is not a prescriptive setting but should have an anonymous quality charged with creativity.'

In this completely uninterpreted museum, the visitor chooses to write, read, or reflect. The architect merely provides the *opportunity* for a social experience by placing the demand on the visitor to engage with the environment and to relate his or her own stories. The museum, in this manner, is very inclusive. Everyone has a voice and a story to impart if he or she chooses to.

To stress the notion of inclusivity and to attempt to link the museum grounds to its social and

FIGURE 6.15
A single figure sits in contemplation at the foot of the memory box. (Photograph courtesy of Jo Noero.)

FIGURE 6.16
The pedestrian traffic flow through the museum grounds stresses the notion of permeability built into the museum design. (Photograph courtesy of Jo Noero.)

physical setting, the street and the base of the building share the same material and texture. A good deal of the building is permeable, opening itself to a variety of experiences with little distinction between public and private realms. Noero points out that the notion of spatial freedom is important in light of the apartheid experience.[4]

Prior to 1994, the marginalized and dispossessed township populations living in the former internment shacks that wanted lives of greater dignity and freedom became nurses or teachers. There was little other choice. After forty-three years of enforced segregation, moving freely through public space is an affirmation of post-apartheid freedom and social mobility. Traffic flow within and around the museum, therefore, is treated as social space placed within a museum setting. 'These are reconstituted private spaces,' Noero notes, 'filled with public intentions. People pass through spaces like the portico on their way to work. The museum is not a place apart but part of the everyday experience' (Figure 6.16).

Design resolution – addressing the region's intangible heritage

Upon arrival, visitors view three wattle posts that serve as part of the structural system for the entrance portico. The posts read like saplings joined together by rope or wire and recall the support system used in traditional dwellings. This reference to the vernacular as visual association may seem like yet another superficial gesture to link modern architecture to a regional past – a trope aimed at outside visitors so common today among post-modern architects. However, this visual device is aimed at the *local* population explicitly to make the museum, as a civic structure, socially friendly to those unaccustomed to visiting a museum, and who are experiencing the feelings of dislocation tied to dramatic political and social change (Figure 6.17). Similar to some Pacific region museums that encompass 'living and transforming cultures' and include both tangible and intangible components, museum interpretation has gone from the 'elitist and authoritative voice of the institution to a more inclusive and culturally sensitive approach.'[5]

The effort to engage the local participant extends beyond the use of materials, symbols, visual associations, and building techniques ubiquitous in the area. Using an exterior wall of the museum as a canvas for a photo-transferred image, a billboard size picture documents a relocation scene taken by a local photographer. Because these are local events – albeit with national import – that have been experienced by the local inhabitants, identification is immediate. The very participants captured in the photograph often become storytellers to the visitors, relating their historical ties to the events depicted. This is first-person narrative interpretation at its most authentic, and at its most meaningful level for those cultures that draw from a strong narrative base (Figure 6.18).

One hopes that the museum administrators will make the effort to have such exchanges between an impromptu interpreter and onlookers recorded or videotaped as a means of making the intangible

FIGURE 6.17
Wattle posts are visible in the pavilion to the rear of the image. (Photograph courtesy of Jo Noero.)

(experiences, skills, practices) tangible (documents, objects, museum installations). Though the memories of the events recounted are part of the recent past and, therefore, are very palpable to those who revisit them, they are temporal and will soon take on different historical dimensions. The Museum at Red Location, as an interactive medium for the exchange of memories, emotions, and events, will itself be the product of a continual act of creation and reassessment.

The participatory education approach in this post-apartheid museum reinforces Thomas J. Schlereth's definition of a museum as 'a site where people learn about people (including themselves) primarily through objects that people have made, used, or found meaningful.' In this case, the 'museum becomes the object,' the communicative vessel, or even the 'performance.' People learn about their collective heritage by communicating their shared human experience of apartheid. As

FIGURE 6.18
Storyteller mural, center left. (Photograph courtesy of Jo Noero.)

historians Barbara and Cary Carson suggest: developing relationships from things to people, to activities, to ideas must be of primary importance in the interpretation process.[6]

On the other hand, if the vernacular, by definition, is regionally relevant, one might ask: 'How meaningful are these self-referential artifacts and narratives to cultural outsiders visiting the museum for the first time?' Frank Delaney, in discussing his book, *Ireland, A Novel*, states, 'The vernacular tradition captures as much as modern literature the condition of what man is. In terms of a vernacular culture, almost any form of communication will do; it comes from the people. Every diverse culture is that of our blood. It is the rock of origin: buildings, language, art, music. What the vernacular tradition offers is a universal culture.'[7]

With regard to the relevance of embracing a region's oral tradition as history, Delaney continues:

> *Beneath all the histories of Ireland, from the present day, through her long troubled relationship with England and back to the earliest times, there has always been another, less obvious reporter speaking – the oral tradition, Ireland's vernacular narrative, telling the country's tale to her people in stories handed down since God was a boy.*
>
> *This fireside voice took great care to say that imagination and emotion play their parts in every history and therefore, to understand the Irish, mere facts can never be enough; this is a country that reprocesses itself through the mills of its imagination.*
>
> *But we all do that, we merge our myths with our facts according to our feelings, we tell ourselves our own story. And no matter what we are told, we choose what we believe. All 'truths' are only 'our' truths, because we too bring to the 'facts' our feelings, our experiences, our wishes. Thus, storytelling – from wherever it comes – forms a layer in the foundation of the world; and glinting in it we see the trace elements of every tribe on earth.*[8]

The pervasive sense of informality sought after by the architect to encourage reflection and to foster social commentary may continue to hold true for the local population, but increasingly the museum and its cultural precinct are being conceived in much broader terms by regional and national governmental authorities. Government officials plan to move into the precinct and some leaders, like the Mayor of Port Elizabeth (a Marxist Leninist), may be interred in the Community Hall. The debate between family members and the government regarding who has primacy over commemorating the memory of a departed one – the family or the nation – holds true for the museum's interpretive mission as well. This is the question often raised: 'Is this a museum that commemorates a national struggle in local terms, or is it truly a regional and national museum in the range of narratives it embraces?' Or, put another way, '*to whom* does national heritage belong (if anyone): the host community, where important events occurred and resonate among its occupants – or the nation, whose struggle for freedom (in this instance) was widely shared?' Perhaps, as Delaney infers in the statement above, every diverse culture that has suffered under oppression will see a glint of itself here (Figures 6.19 and 6.20).

Environmental and social factors

The climate of Port Elizabeth is benign. Accordingly, there is no air conditioning and the museum uses all natural lighting. However, while the climate was not a determining factor, other forces gave Noero 'the satisfaction that comes with designing in extreme conditions.' The project was to proceed into the construction phase using skilled contractors and local workers. The agreement was that fifty percent of the unskilled workers were to be locals from the relocation settlement. To maximize the job opportunities among the local population, the community held firm to a policy of rotating the workforce every three months. The transfer of skills thus took longer (having to retrain a new crew just as the quality of work was improving), and costs (due to the retraining time) were accrued.

Architect's reflection

Noero understands the importance of grassroots building projects, having been appointed by Tutu as architect for the Anglican Church at Transvaal, South Africa, where he trained the local black population in construction methods necessary for building desperately needed housing using readily available materials.

With the museum project, Noero notes that the experience with the work crews made him redefine his priorities. 'If the project takes longer and you can

FIGURE 6.19
Portrait exhibit of those who fought against political oppression in this region of South Africa. (Photograph courtesy of Jo Noero.)

engage the local people in the process, that's great.' Similar to Nihal Perera's project, discussed earlier, government intervention influenced the outcome of the project. In this instance, it produced socially meaningful results. Also similar to Perera's *loose-fit approach*, Noero learned that by not having control over the actual materials installed in the memory boxes, the effects hoped for of commemoration, reflection, and 'retold history' stand the risk of not being achieved. 'Can such decisions be entrusted to local participants?' he wondered.

A case in point presented itself. One group designed the interior of a memory box to resemble the kitchen space of a relocation shack. Noero thought this odd, since the shacks themselves were just outside. What followed, however, was unexpected and remarkable. After the room was completed, elders came and sat at the kitchen table and recounted stories of oppression to onlookers. Instead of the kitchen artifacts remaining static and unrelated to their human context, the elders offered up the many intangible and anecdotal meanings

FIGURE 6.20
A memory box with the haunting reminder of political abuses. (Photograph courtesy of Jo Noero.)

FIGURE 6.21
The installation (within a memory box) of a kitchen space resembling one in a relocation shack. (Photograph courtesy of Jo Noero.)

behind such social settings as they existed under apartheid. Also fitting is the maintenance of the *public* versus *private* nature of the exterior and interior spaces of the relocation settlement households. By depicting a kitchen space as a museum installation (instead of utilizing an actual relocation shack), domestic privacy is respected and someone's everyday experience is not objectified under the gaze of tourists (Figure 6.21).

More importantly, the kitchen space memory box offers an opportunity for 'restorative listening' to take place. In South Africa during the 1990s, the Truth and Reconciliation Commission held meetings 'in which torturers and victims told their stories, compelled the government to pay reparations and grant amnesty.' As South African journalist Lizeka Mda notes, 'validation came from telling "heart-rending stories." At last they were heard and recorded for all time.' The process revealed the fate of relatives who had disappeared, perpetrators who had found absolution, and victims who had glimpsed their suffering.[9] If cohesion is to be found between blacks and whites over a shared history, insights of each other's pain and participation can be gained over this kitchen table.

Hence, one of the many lessons that Noero's collective work imparts is the recognition that a situated regional response does not spring solely from

FIGURE 6.22
Sectional views of the Post-Apartheid Museum at Red Location. (Illustration courtesy of Jo Noero.)

evocative images of place from which many of his initial design references began. It stems from a sincere involvement with the critical circumstances of the present human condition – the issues of political empowerment, economic realities, labor issues, domestic living patterns, existing belief systems, cultural identity – that give such elements their authenticity. When he created opportunities for individual interactions within the museum setting (which became performances in their own right), some of the most meaningful goals for the museum were achieved. Finally, socially oriented design can also exhibit a mastery of execution that speaks to a global audience without sacrificing its utility and meaning within its local context. This juncture marks the most relevant interface of the vernacular and the profession (Figure 6.22).

Recommended reading

Benjamin, W. (1969). Illuminations. Schocken Books.
Deckler, T., et al. (2006). *Contemporary South African Architecture in a Landscape of Transition.* Double Storey Books.
Huyssen, A. (1995). Twilight Memories: Marking Time in a Culture of Amnesia. Routledge.
Turner, J. F. C. and Fichter, R. (1972). Freedom to Build: Dweller Control of the Housing Process. Macmillan.

Notes

1. Similarly, M. K. Smith (2003) in *Issues in Cultural Tourism Studies* (Routledge), Chapter 3, discusses the affects of tourism on developing countries and traditional societies. She raises the issue of tourism as the new 'imperialism.'
2. Unless otherwise noted, all quotes are from an interview by the author with Jo Noero on January 31, 2007, following his lecture organized by Howard Davis and sponsored by a Savage Grant at the University of Oregon, Eugene, Oregon.
3. Quoted by D. Greenberg, in Voices of change and pain, *The Oregonian*, April 17, 2008, A7.
4. A similar effort to convey the notion of governmental transparency and public participation was made by incorporating a slit window at foot level of the recent Constitutional Court, Johannesburg – designed by architects OMM Design Workshop & Urban Solutions – as a constant reminder to the court authorities of the people that the government is entrusted to serve. A special thanks to Nina Maritz for bringing this project to my attention.
5. Kolokesa Uafa Mahina-Tuai (2006). Intangible heritage: Pacific case study at the Museum of New Zealand Te Papa Tongarewa. *International Journal of Intangible Heritage*, 1, 14–24.
6. In an effort to respond to the issue of preserving intangible heritage, the National Museum of the American Indian (completed in 2004 on the national mall in Washington, DC), for example, uses holographic images and recorded narratives to capture the memories, values, and heritage of the tribal cultures being interpreted. One might ask if it is even reasonable to expect such contemporary forms of museum installations and media technology in undeveloped nations from the vantage point of both expense and cultural appropriateness.

    Schlereth, T. J. (1992). Object knowledge: every museum visitor an interpreter. *Patterns in Practice: Elections from the Journal of Museum Education*, Museum Education Roundtable, 102. Also, Barbara and Cary Carson (1992), Interpreting history through objects, in *Patterns in Practice: Selections from the Journal of Museum Education*, Museum Education Roundtable, 129.
7. Simon, S. (2005). Stories by the fire: Frank Delaney's *Ireland*. NPR National Public Radio, broadcast March 12, 2005. Available at http://www.npr.org/templates/story/story.php?storyid=4532548
8. Frank Delaney, Author's Note, *Ireland, A Novel*. Available at http://www.frankdelaney.com/work.php?id=10&info=author_note
9. Lizeka Mda, journalist for the Johannesburg, South Africa, *Mail and Guardian*, quoted in Voices of change and pain, *The Oregonian*, April 17, 2008, A7.

Part Two

Locale – interpreting and accommodating characteristics of an evolving landscape

7

Embracing the urban contradictions of a border zone

For today, socially responsible architects must serve as a bridge across borders, to develop architecture that responsibly serves people and their communities without imposing arbitrary restrictions – an architecture that understands real human needs, such as privacy, space, and freedom.

From 'Teddy Cruz and the wall: an architectural discourse,' in *GLFEA News*, accessed at www.glfea.org/html/gn-tcatwaad.htm

Project: Casa Familiar, Mi Pueblo – San Ysidro Pilot Village
Location: San Ysidro, California
Architects/urban designers: Estudio Teddy Cruz design team (Teddy Cruz, Giacomo Castagnola, Adriana Cuellar, Mariana Leguia, Kathleen Roe, Alan Rosenblum, Jota Samper). Teddy Cruz, Estudio Teddy Cruz (established 1994), San Diego California[1]
Partnership organizations:
 Casa Familiar
 San Ysidro Business Improvement District
 LandGrant Development
Time frame: 2002–2006 – Concept development
 2006–2009 – Design development

Introduction

Teddy Cruz offers a post-colonial perspective for providing housing and community centers to the densely occupied neighborhoods that encircle San Diego, California. Born in Guatemala, but working along the Mexican border for years, his firm aims at providing an insider's vantage point for addressing a community's planning needs and aspirations. Far from embracing the notion of *architect as author*, Estudio Teddy Cruz (its designers hail from diverse backgrounds and nationalities) employs a teaming approach. Coupled with a commitment to community engagement, Cruz seeks to redefine the limits imposed by rigid zoning and planning laws in San Diego. In doing so, the team responds to the existing urban conditions, patterns of spatial occupation, and social interaction that define both the tangible and intangible aspects of Place for many of the Spanish-speaking inhabitants of California's US and Latin America border zone – an area that encompasses eighty square miles.

Among the contributions Cruz makes to our understanding of a place-based planning strategy is his clarification of how ethnicity is imprinted on the landscape. In our increasingly diverse urban neighborhoods, there is a need to rethink long-standing planning policies originally implemented to serve different users than those that presently inhabit a locale. Cruz's photographic studies of borderland habitats demonstrate the power of a subculture over physical form. By degrees, these individual acts of 'transgression' and 'appropriation' transform the character of the land within which people reside, and embody the values of the people who live there. In their totality, these disparate human responses (expressed in built form) define the distinctiveness of a region such as the California–Mexico border zone.

Design intent

Teddy Cruz has designed what he calls *Pilot Projects* that will rehabilitate and redevelop distinct communities connected to the historic core of San Ysidro. These community improvement efforts will be carried out through the lens of Latina/Latino needs, priorities, and values through phased development plans.

Copyright © 2009 Elsevier Ltd. All rights reserved.

FIGURE 7.1
View from the Mexican side of the ten-foot steel border wall separating Tijuana, Mexico, from San Diego, California, in the USA. (Photograph courtesy of Teddy Cruz.)

Working with receptive community planning offices that have provided a special demonstration classification that eases zoning restrictions, Cruz wants to reform what he calls 'Puritan urbanism' – an urbanism 'driven by a desire for homogenized architectural styles and exclusionary planning practices [that] has resulted in zoning for San Diego that opposes the forces and influences arising out of this continually changing and expanding border condition.'[2] In contrast to what he perceives as an *urbanity of sameness*, Cruz brings a radically new urban vision to bear. Conditions of 'complexity, hybridity, and improvisation' – elements that add cultural texture and festiveness to the border towns he studies – also bring creative energy and cultural relevance to his own work. This is regional distinctiveness that is rooted in a cultural experience that may be different from America's dominant culture, but that is inextricably part of our times – a situated regional response.

Cruz stresses that his approach is relevant and transferable to other urbanized locales. In fact, the Casa Familiar Organization that helped initiate the project adds, 'This tool can be replicated in San Diego's older urbanized communities [and] will allow for communities to focus on the area of development they choose and provide their own design values.'[3] *The New York Times* reporter Nicolai Ouroussoff goes a step further. He feels that Teddy Cruz 'has found a humane model for rethinking America's suburbs,' and 'his ideas could be applied to the new immigrant suburbs of the Midwest or the flood-ruined neighborhoods of New Orleans.'[4] The key, Cruz argues, is recognizing the need to look at urbanism differently – beyond objects and formulas, to *people*. Cruz calls for a 'trans-border urbanism' involving government, non-governmental organizations (NGOs), and communities. Through a meaningful and equitable

FIGURE 7.2
View from the Mexican side of the ten-foot steel border wall separating Tijuana, Mexico, from San Diego, California, in the USA. (Photograph courtesy of Teddy Cruz.)

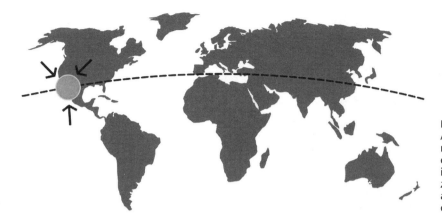

FIGURE 7.3
Architect's global reference map of converging economic influences in the border zone between the USA and Mexico. (Illustration courtesy of Teddy Cruz.)

collaboration among these stakeholders, 'cultural thresholds of imagination, community, and realism' can be crossed.

The community-based premises that grew out of brainstorming sessions with Casa Familiar reinforced Teddy Cruz's frustration with the design trends expressed in New Urbanism. Cruz feels that, in practice, New Urbanism 'only addresses aesthetics, creating a fake façade of difference without considering the lifestyle of the community.' He continues: 'the downtown redevelopment of San Diego is an example of this kind of suburban planning – dressed up urban aesthetics without proper consideration given to zoning policies for higher density, mixed use, and affordable housing options.' Cruz states, 'We should be turning our attention away from the wall [the physical border separating Mexico and the USA] and towards the landscape, the ecology, and communities' that define different aspects of contemporary life and the sociocultural and political implications of shaping space within the border zone.[5] In the post-9/11 atmosphere of heightened security that stresses the need for such border barriers, Cruz reminds us of the benefits of cultural exchange and tolerance that can enrich life on both sides of the border (and beyond) in lieu of policies of exclusion and division.

Concept development

When Cruz was interviewed in 2006, the planning scheme was less of a built project and more of a vision statement for trans-border urban strategies. Cruz looked for inspiration from the 'particularities of bicultural territories.' His attention was drawn to the adjacent cultural landscapes of Tijuana, Mexico, and San Diego, California. These two human habitats presented 'two radically different cultures, societies, and economies ... that occupy the same geography.' He photographed a series of evocative images of opportunity and struggle, of bounty and deprivation. He found optimism in the variety of resourceful ways in which other people's waste was transformed into another's opportunity (Figures 7.4 and 7.5).

A case in point is the California bungalows that were literally discarded by San Diego developers during the construction of a new housing project; they were purchased by a Tijuana developer, loaded onto trucks, and moved across the border. These discarded goods from America's affluence were placed in a row on raised steel frames and sold to local residents who then refashioned them to meet their particularized needs. Lifting the wooden-frame houses onto a metal superstructure, the ground floor space eventually accommodated, alternatively, a garage/auto repair shop, a second apartment, or a store, while there was always ample foreground space on each lot for street marketing or yard activities in keeping with local priorities and social practices. One tactic utilized the *ad hoc* space over a narrow driveway separating two pre-existing cottages on which to perch their house (Figures 7.6 and 7.7). (See the chapter on Nihal Perera where he employs a similar planning strategy in Sri Lanka of providing volumes of space for markets and living accommodations along with a basic infrastructure of systems from which

96 Vernacular Architecture and Regional Design

FIGURE 7.4
Improvisation: A dwelling made out of discarded packing crates and corrugated sheet metal erected on the eastern edge of Tijuana. (Photograph courtesy of Teddy Cruz.)

displaced inhabitants could shape their own culturally meaningful habitats.)

In another stage of his investigations, Cruz manipulated images to stress (to cultural outsiders) the oppositional dynamics that he feels exists on both sides of the border. These hyperbolized images reveal the *landscape of contradiction* that defines the border zone where San Diego meets Tijuana, just

FIGURE 7.5
A habitat in Tijuana made from found objects, such as an old garage door used as an end wall. Note the illegal tapping into an electrical power source – what Cruz refers to as an architecture of insurgency.
(Photograph courtesy of Teddy Cruz.)

FIGURE 7.6
California bungalows scheduled for demolition by San Diego builders are purchased by a Tijuana developer, moved across the border, and placed on a row of steel superstructures for appropriation by the new owners. (Photographs courtesy of Teddy Cruz.)

a twenty-five-minute drive from each other. These fictionalized photographic landscapes might be thought of as exercises for seeing the often-intangible social divisions and contested boundaries existing within the region. Cruz states that they are used as 'tools to reveal that which is hidden in the urban fabric – fields of observation and infrastructure, photographically stitched together'[6] (Figure 7.8).

FIGURE 7.7
Densification: An *ad hoc* use of space to support one of the California bungalows moved across the border. Here, the transplanted house is perched over a narrow driveway that separates two pre-existing cottages. Cruz draws attention to such moments of transgression over private property boundaries for insights into solutions for San Diego's urban density problems. (Photograph courtesy of Teddy Cruz.)

FIGURE 7.8
Cruz's manipulated images serve as visual tools for stressing the paradoxes that exist on either side of the ten-foot-high steel wall separating San Diego and Tijuana. Here, the wall serves as both boundary and threshold for citizens living within the border zone. (Image courtesy of Teddy Cruz.)

For other evidence of place-specific social behavior, he turned to *non-conforming business practices*, like appropriated commercial spaces; *moments of transgression* over boundaries, such as international borders, private property boundaries, and illegal energy use; *acts of spatial, formal, and economic intervention/opportunities*; appropriations of the least expected, least utilized places in the city that often become *unofficial centers* of community and commerce (Figures 7.9 and 7.10).

Many of these sociospatial relationships of human context were explored in the Tijuana workshop and Latin American/Los Angeles ('LA/LA') studios that Cruz conducted at the SCI-ARC architecture program in southern California from 1994 to 2000. His goal was to have his students find suburban solutions that did not apply the rigid, often sterile, stamp of spatial and stylistic regularity of American subdivisions on culturally diverse neighborhoods (Figure 7.11). His critical analysis of case studies helped his students turn their eyes away from iconic images of American prosperity cultivated by trade magazines, and draw instead from the very marrow of life represented by Tijuana's squatter culture living in the hilly terrain east of the city. Here, *earth ship* retaining walls made from used tires packed with earth, and makeshift housing constructed of discarded packing crates, corrugated sheet metal roofing, and used garage doors prevailed.

The suburban reality Cruz perceived was not that people would choose these materials and living conditions if given other options; he recognized, however, that in such humble habitats lay the essence of human accommodation. In other words, he sought to discern what was essential to one's survival, social accommodation, and individual expression. This type of urban archeology – the close examination of objects/spaces, their use, and value within a community – informed various design concepts later when working with the non-profit community center Casa Familia.

Teddy Cruz sees a 'transformed urban morphology' as the end product of transcribing the array of observed and experienced social evidence he has amassed into urban design. Eschewing stereotypes and nostalgia as devices of urban narrative, he presents an *urbanism of insurgency*. His work embraces spaces of ambiguity and indefinite programmatic clarity as familiar urban relationships among Hispanic urban dwellers in and around San Diego. In attempting to respond to the true complexity of class that shapes domestic space in this border town, programmatic layering, multiple identities (and uses) for spaces provide elasticity of living accommodations for multigenerational families. 'Living spaces need to be able to expand or reduce as family units change,' Cruz feels. These elements serve as the basis for his affordable housing planning strategies.

Beyond Cruz's design intent to provide flexibility within the living spaces of multifamily residences is a commitment to address San Diego's larger issue of population density. Whereas architect Carol A. Wilson (see the chapter on her work later in this text) strives to meet the needs of her affluent clients who 'summer' in rural coastal Maine in the least amount of single-family, detached living space, Teddy Cruz recognizes the urban realities of neighborhoods like San Ysidro and City Heights of high urban densities, low incomes, and a largely pedestrian population (around forty percent of the residents do not own cars). As architectural historian and *Architectural Design* editor Denise Bratton notes, 'Intensified global trade and population explosions on both sides of the border ensure that Tijuana and San

FIGURE 7.9
Simultaneity: An example of 'unofficial centers of community and commerce.' The addition to the right serves as a repair shop – one of several 'non-conforming business practices' found in Tijuana. (Photograph courtesy of Teddy Cruz.)

Diego will undergo massive transformation in the 21st century as a result of global forces that converge in Southern California … [Cruz has drawn these issues] to the surface, riveting international attention (positive and negative) on the question of how cities in the border zone will respond to the need to densify when the horizon of suburban sprawl is finally foreclosed, and the pristine and picturesque urbanism cultivated in affluent neighborhoods proves incapable of meeting the needs of growing number of residents.'[7]

Project description

The urban plan that emerged was developed through the support, consultation, and collaboration of the non-profit community center Casa Familiar, whose client base is predominantly Spanish speaking. Founded in 1972 to provide basic services to Spanish-speaking immigrants in the San Diego area, Casa Familiar now addresses the needs of all racial and ethnic groups, and focuses on the economic revitalization of the historic core of San Ysidro.[8] Added to this collaboration were enlightened clients and influential developers from the community. Though place-centered in inspiration, support, and implementation, these were not urban strategies that were intended to isolate the pilot communities from the outlying urban core. Cruz states, 'Every effort has been made to integrate both of the City of San Diego projects – the [recently completed] San Ysidro Library and the new San Ysidro Fire Station – [into the design scheme].'[9] Two affordable housing schemes and a community center for immigrants living in San Ysidro generated two pilot projects.

FIGURE 7.10
Illegal energy use in Tijuana. (Photograph courtesy of Teddy Cruz.)

FIGURE 7.11
A photographic juxtaposition of 'two urbanisms:' an urbanism of difference and contrast (Tijuana to the left), versus an urbanism of sameness (a San Diego subdivision on the right). (Photograph courtesy of Teddy Cruz.)

Scheme One: 'Living rooms at the border'

With the assistance of public housing funds and private grants, a three-layered, phased-construction plan will incrementally transform a 1927 church and surrounding parking site into much needed affordable housing and community services (Figures 7.12 to 7.16). As supplemental funding is provided, additional parcels will be purchased to accommodate other community programs.

Phase I began in 2001. The old church was adaptively reused as a community center with an upstairs office space provided for Casa Familiar (Figure 7.13). The familiar community icon of a church became the social focus for a 14,000-square-foot, mixed-use, high-density plan to be carried out in Phase II. Recall the strategy used on the houses moved across the border and placed on a steel superstructure with shops below and foreground market space provided. Similarly, poured-in-place concrete arcades support flexible *urban rooms* at street level and connect to the public garden and market corridor. Above the arcades, wood-frame affordable housing units are planned (twelve in all) that will provide flexible living spaces.

A two-bedroom unit, for example, can be converted into two small studios sharing a kitchen. (Formerly zoned for no more than three housing units, mixed-use was disallowed as well under the existing zoning laws. The multifamily units will be constructed during Phase III.[10]) Though partly inspired by Donald Judd's sculptural cubes, the abstract formalism of the exterior yields to an informal and flexible social organization within. A series of interlocking rooms are conceived in such a way as to allow them to be divided into two one-bedroom units or be combined for large family occupation.

By concentrating a variety of necessary services in close proximity to each other, greater accessibility will be afforded to the predominantly pedestrian population living in the area. Similar to the human context studies undertaken earlier, Cruz makes use of underutilized alleys and narrow streets as circulation paths, connecting the residential units to the market, park, and tram station serving the border (San Ysidro is less than a mile from the US–Mexican border). Interstitial building spaces are intentionally left undesignated in use as a way of promoting organic and flexible development through time.

Embracing the urban contradictions of a border zone

FIGURE 7.12
Site of 'Bedrooms at the Border' prior to construction. The 1927 church is located in the bottom right of the highlighted square. (Image courtesy of Teddy Cruz.)

Scheme Two: 'Senior gardens: housing with child care'

The second scheme continued the social commitments inspired by Casa Familiar. This neighborhood project also embraced the community benefit of combining public and domestic spaces. Here, the family structure of seniors raising their grandchildren, common in this area of the city, is given validation, and daycare facilities for children with working parents are provided as part of the interweaving layers of public and private spaces (Figures 7.17 to 7.19).

Fourteen affordable housing units of 600- to 1,000-square feet, and six studios of approximately 400-square feet are connected to a semi-public lobby, a restaurant counter, and small private living spaces. Private entrances are provided to each unit off the main entry, accessible through a private garden that connects to a communal garden space, and another is located off the alleyway. In an effort to promote permeability, the communal garden promenade also provides access to the childcare facility, the existing public park, and other Casa Familiar housing developments.

Service walls contain kitchens, bathrooms, and storage spaces. The kitchens are able to open out to the garden promenade for social activities. In keeping with the goal of flexibility and personalization of living spaces, some units have loft apartments with their own entrances so that they can either be rented out or serve as extended family living (Figure 7.19).[11]

Author's summary

Cruz characterizes his practice – admittedly as much policy oriented as design oriented – as *temporal urbanism*, an urbanism constructed out the current social realities and emergent necessities of Place. His design premises specifically tackle existing urban contradictions. It is the transformed physical nature of Place – a local context appropriated and reimagined to address different expressions of cultural identity and use than originally intended – that serves as his various design cues.

Among Cruz's many strengths is his ability to articulate clearly and effectively his beliefs and goals among the critical entities of community, government, and NGOs (Figures 7.20 and 7.21). Through

FIGURE 7.13
Perspective sketch of the remodeled 1927 church with offices for Casa Familiar located in the top floor. Opposite are the 'urban room' arcades for informal markets to be created on the ground level, with affordable housing above. A block-long public garden is situated between the arcaded housing structure and the community center. The garden space, in turn, connects West Hall Street to an alleyway that is presently used as a pedestrian corridor for locals on their way to work. The emphasis is on re-energizing inert urban pockets, the layering of activity zones, mandating spatial flexibility, and implementing high-density planning. (Sketch courtesy of Teddy Cruz.)

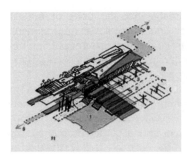 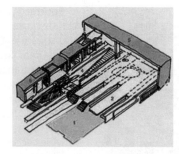 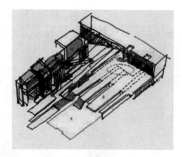

FIGURE 7.14
Living Rooms at the Border for Casa Familia, San Ysidro, San Diego: sketches of the three phases of development. As labeled: (1) existing church; (2) terrace garden above parking; (3) parking; (4) garden corridor; (5) concrete arbor; (6) church's studio units below garden terrace; (7) community center's kitchen; (8) access to the existing senior housing and garden; (9) link to existing public park; (10) alley; (11) street; (12) affordable housing; (13) market. (Sketches courtesy of Teddy Cruz.)

his efforts, an atmosphere of mutual trust, respect, and receptivity prevails in the uneasy task of engendering effective urban change.

At this point, however, Cruz's urban visions are more conceptual than literal, since they are conceived as long-term, multiphase operations. Most often, the schematics are demonstrated in expressive geometries and blocked-out spaces for social accommodation, in addition to experimental adjustments to the local building codes. Cruz

FIGURES 7.15 AND 7.16
Drawing from Cruz's earlier field observations on how recycled housing was placed on a steel superstructure, he conceives of domestic space located similarly over concrete urban rooms to allow for flexibility of social use. The computer model to the right is of Phase III, where the ground level is used for market space and the upper story is for affordable housing. (Photograph and image courtesy of Teddy Cruz.)

FIGURE 7.17
This view is one of a series of slender building blocks and linear gardens proposed by Cruz in the 'Senior Gardens' scheme. (Computer model courtesy of Teddy Cruz.)

acknowledges the problem of trying to reconcile bicultural living patterns within 'current forms of governance that cannot absorb nonconformity.' This frustration is expressed, often, in his visual couplings of bland conformity with images of social richness. He intentionally stresses 'difference and contrast, versus an urbanism of sameness' as the ultimate goal of a transformed urban planning policy (Figures 7.22 and 7.23).

Following the lead of architect-developers like Ted Smith and Rob Quigley in San Diego, as well as a new breed of non-profit local developers who work toward transforming existing zoning to better accommodate current and evolving urban circumstances, Cruz's vision may soon become reality. His concepts, it should be noted, have received accolades from the profession. The San Ysidro Affordable Housing Project won the 2001 PA *Architecture* magazine award. Teddy Cruz also won the 2004–2005 James Sterling prize for *Border Postcard: Chronicles from the Edge*, a project exploring urban strategies for the international border zone between San Diego and Tijuana. Recently, he joined some developers in securing a small parcel of land in the

FIGURE 7.18
View of the angular rhythm of rooflines alternating with large open spaces. This arrangement is designed to strengthen the spatial flow among housing units, to provide a flexible climate response of sunlight and shade, and to enhance community-oriented activities like the street market to the left. (Computer model courtesy of Teddy Cruz.)

FIGURE 7.19
View of the public garden space and living units at 'Senior Gardens' designed to accommodate positive social interaction and supervision by grandparents who are caring for their grandchildren. (Computer model courtesy of Teddy Cruz.)

northwest corner of Tijuana that butts up against the steel border wall. Cruz notes, 'It is the absolute corner of Latin America. We'd love to turn it into a cultural center, maybe with a local university.'[12]

The two award-winning, multiphase projects for Casa Familiar have set the stage for greater attention by the city, and beyond, to apply similar planning tools that are specifically situated in the present human condition and the cultural make-up of the communities they serve.

Regarding the Casa Familiar Project, Teddy Cruz stated, 'practices of encroachment, strategies of informality, patterns of use, and contamination' have defined the conceptual framework of the project over the past four years. But, these concepts, in themselves, are not enough to ensure successful, long-term commitments to neighborhood housing projects and economic revitalization policies. As Denise Bratton notes, 'The sustained engagement with specific communities has privileged Casa Familiar with insight that municipal planners and commercial developers do not necessarily possess; thus, planning in their hands is driven by cultural and site specificity rather than the proverbial bottom line ... The logical next step is to turn this accumulated knowledge into policy, [whereby non-profit developers that possess a strong civic sense can grow communities].' Bratton notes the following components as being critical to Cruz's success in providing schemes for positive urban intervention: 'small projects that acknowledge the histories and identities of culturally specific communities; collaborations involving architects, nonprofit developers, city planners and other agencies; transformations of modest idiosyncratic parcels to create space in which small economies

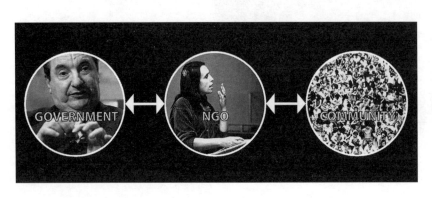

FIGURE 7.20
Teddy Cruz feels that a sustained engagement with local communities can only be accomplished through collaborations involving multiple stakeholders. (Image courtesy of Teddy Cruz.)

Embracing the urban contradictions of a border zone **105**

One may ask, 'How do you balance the need for increased density with a desire to maintain the urban character of older San Diego communities?' Ultimately, these issues have to be negotiated through citizen involvement, what some urban planners term *contributive democracy*, as to what are the desired and negative implications of such urban planning policies. Such issues are also facilitated by taking small steps – phased development of small projects that allow the collective bodies to visualize the impact of a fully realized planning scheme.

The proposals for 'Living Rooms at the Border and Senior Gardens' are in the process of being cleared to begin as a three-year experimental urban design project. Rezoning for the pilot projects was approved by the San Diego City Council in 2008. The challenge still lies ahead, however, as to whether four years of field observations, concept development, and theoretical propositions will yield enriching community-based social settings that speak to the needs and values of its inhabitants. With the memories still alive of the modernist-era public housing schemes that won national design awards when completed yet failed miserably over time as social solutions, such as Pruitt-Igoe in

FIGURE 7.21
Small projects that acknowledge the histories and identities of culturally specific communities spring from collaborative efforts involving architects, non-profit developers, city planners, and other agencies. (Image courtesy of Teddy Cruz.)

can flourish; and phased redevelopment efforts that allow communities to adapt, personalize and transform spaces to fit their needs and means.'[13]

FIGURE 7.22
Juxtaposed images of conformity and non-conformity/aesthetic blandness and ethnic texture. (Image courtesy of Teddy Cruz.)

FIGURE 7.23
Cruz's vision for overlaying planning strategies of hybridity, simultaneity, improvisation, and flexibility onto a landscape of sameness. (Image courtesy of Teddy Cruz.)

St Louis (constructed in 1954 and celebrated by Charles Jencks as the moment that the postmodern movement began with its implosion in 1972), many are hopeful that Cruz's vision will yield positive results.

Selected reading

Cruz, T. (1999). Tijuana workshop – border chronicles of a vertical studio at Sci-Arc. *Architecture of the Borderlands/Architectural Design*, 69 (July/August), 42–47.

Dilworth, D. (2006). Cruz finding new solutions for border living. *Architectural Record* (May 25), 1–2. Retrieved at http://archrecord.construction.com/news/daily/archives/060525cruz.asp

Ouroussoff, N. (2006). Border-town muse: an architect finds a model in Tijuana. *International Herald Tribune*, March 13. Retrieved at www.iht.com/articles/2006/03/12/news/shanty.php

——(2006). Shantytowns as a new suburban ideal. *The New York Times* (March 12), 1–3.

For more on border territory constructions of identity, space, and place see Dr Yael Navaro-Yashin's work in Northern Cyprus since 1998. Her work addresses the construction of a wall between Turkish and Greek Cyprus as the basis for a study of 'affective energies as they are retained in and produced by public and private sites of violence, militarized spaces, and zones of ruin and abandonment …' She uses vocabulary to connect anthropology to the field of public policy. Nostalgia and emotion, she feels, have a place in public policy, but often they are discounted because of the lack of professional language to address such human factors. As noted on her internet site, this is a multidisciplinary investigation that combines her interests in psychoanalytic and political theory with her emerging interest into 'the anthropological study of space, the built environment, material culture, law, and bureaucracy.' Her book-in-progress is entitled *The Make-believe State: Governance, Law and Affect in a Border Territory*. Special thanks to Azhar Tyabji for bringing this reference to my attention.

Notes

1. Unless otherwise indicated, quotations from Teddy Cruz are derived from his lecture at the University of Oregon on February 10, 2006, personal interviews prior to and following the lecture, and a site visit to his studio in San Diego on March 27, 2006. Teddy Cruz is an Associate Professor of Fine Arts, University of California, San Diego. Cruz received his Bachelor of Architecture degree in 1987 from California State Polytechnic University, San Luis Obispo, and a Masters in Design from the Graduate School of Design, Harvard University. He received the Rome Prize in Architecture, American Academy in Rome,

Italy, in 1991. Prior to forming Estudio Teddy Cruz, he was Project Designer for Rob Wellington Quigley in San Diego from 1989 to 1993.
2. Quoted in Denise Bratton, Estudio Teddy Cruz, *Practice Profile* (n.d.), 118 and 120.
3. Quotes from Teddy Cruz and commentary from Dilworth, D. (2006). Cruz finding new solutions for border living. *Architectural Record*, May 25, 1–2. Accessed at http://archrecord.construction.com/news/daily/archives/060525cruz.asp
4. Nicolai Ouroussoff (2006). Shantytowns as a new suburban ideal. *The New York Times*, March 12, 1.
5. Ibid., 2. Also, Teddy Cruz's design philosophy is outlined at http://california-architects.com
6. These images were published as a series of Hybrid Border Postcards as part of the issue on *Architecture of the Borderlands* in the summer 1999 issue of *Architecture Design*. Also cited in D. Bratton, Estudio Teddy Cruz, *Practice Profile* (n.d.), 118.
7. Ibid.
8. Bratton, 120.
9. Casa Familiar – San Diego non-profit organization in San Ysidro, 'Mi Pueblo' San Ysidro Pilot Village, http://www.casaFamiliar.org/mipueblo.html
10. Bratton, 119–120.
11. Dilworth, 1; Bratton, 120.
12. Quoted in Ouroussoff, 3.
13. Bratton, 122.

8

Overpainting sprawl as a sustainable landscape

Built space expresses a society's material and political priorities.

Dolores Hayden in *A Field Guide to Sprawl*.[6]

A constellation of factors, including the activities of the outdoor advertising industry, laid the groundwork for the commercial strip [in America] of the postwar period. By the 1920s, central business districts of small and large cities were overrun with automobiles, congesting streets designed to handle only a fraction of the demands put on them. Real-estate developers and merchants recognized the growing frustration of shoppers and, with and without the benefit of extensive market and traffic studies, they went to the fringes of the central city, where land was less expensive, parking ample, and congestion not yet an issue. Businesses logically migrated toward the arterial highways.

Catherine Gudis in *Buyways: Billboards, Automobiles, and the American Landscape*, 151.

Project: Stripscape – 7th Avenue Urban Revitalization Project
Location: Phoenix, Arizona
Design team: Tactical Design Matrix x, Darren Petrucci, Design Director, in collaboration with the City of Phoenix (Department of Streets and Transportation, Neighborhood Services, Public Art, Planning, Economic Development, and Signage), the 7th Avenue Merchants Association, and the Melrose Neighborhood
Time frame: 2000–2003

Introduction

Stripscape is the result of a three-year research and design project that was undertaken from 2000 to 2003. Its charge was to transform the barren strip development along Phoenix's 7th Avenue into a sustainable, vibrant, and community-responsive commercial district. What once had been governed by the uncontrolled commercial exploitation of undervalued land at the edge of city's urban core during the 1960s was now shaped by a different set of urban design priorities. Green infill, pedestrian pathways, climatically and socially responsive *outdoor rooms* were layered onto the streetscape. Through a collaborative initiative among a wide spectrum of stakeholders from the city, the merchants, the arts, and the community, Darren Petrucci sought 'to develop an urban revitalization strategy that form[ed] a new multi-use pedestrian network linking together the disparate fragments of the commercial strip with the surrounding neighborhoods, parks, retail, restaurants and schools.'[1]

Similar to the work of Teddy Cruz, Darren Petrucci delved into the cultural and site-specific particularities of the locale as transformed by its urban inhabitants. Small projects were undertaken (sections of streetscape commercial neighborhoods, in fact) to acknowledge distinctive community behavior patterns and priorities. In doing so, he chose to reconsider current urban conditions of sprawl – most specifically underutilized or degraded urban spaces that others tend to ignore as an inevitable byproduct of unchecked development. Beyond cultivating a positive working relationship among neighborhood groups that, in turn, became active participants in the new development planning strategies, Petrucci's community effectiveness was strengthened by his belief that enlightened city

Copyright © 2009 Elsevier Ltd. All rights reserved.

FIGURE 8.1
New graphics speak to the neighborhood's revitalized image. (Photograph courtesy of Daniel Greene, 2008.)

planning offices can become willing partners, working in the best interest of often underrepresented neighborhoods, instead of being inflexible guardians of long-standing urban policies.

In lieu of a 'regional' response to place, Petrucci stresses 'local distinctiveness.' By gauging the environmental transformations of the commercial strip to the particular needs, character, and goals of various communities on the outskirts of Phoenix, Arizona, the partnerships that are forged among city planning offices, local professionals, and neighborhood groups provide a basis for change in other sectors of the city. Though the 7th Avenue study stresses analysis and classification of patterns of use, it is not formulaic. Rather, it is understood that each community relates to its urban context differently, and these distinctive patterns of behavior should be acknowledged in any neighborhood planning proposal.

Project description

Phoenix, Arizona, is a classic example of a western US city that, other than the Native American reservation that defines the city's eastern edge, has no urban growth boundary. Commercial interests continually spill out to the urban periphery, decentralizing the urban core, and creating greater demands on the

FIGURES 8.2 AND 8.3
On the left is a before view of a section of 7th Avenue as a consequence of car-dominant, barren strip development. On the right, the same view after green infill, pedestrian pathways, and climatically and socially responsive outdoor rooms are layered onto the streetscape. (Photograph and computer image courtesy of Darren Petrucci.)

city's infrastructure for highway maintenance, schools, water, and sanitation. Typically, the urban streetscapes supporting such development are comprised of paved expanses catering to vehicular traffic, while the 'big box store' developments that are a corollary of sprawl too often are aesthetically impoverished and socially isolating.

Urban designer Darren Petrucci aims at reversing this cycle. With the local merchant and neighborhood interests in mind, the goal is to transform the standard pedestrian and automobile infrastructures that exist in generic strip development (such as sidewalks, street lighting, and parking spaces) into such upgraded amenities as shaded parking, display areas, outdoor seating, and recreation areas through creative place-based design.

Petrucci points out that these prototype interventions, or *demonstrations*, are installed by the city in public rights-of-way; then they are made available for purchase by the merchants for their own commercial use and maintenance – 'creating a seamless transition between the public and private realm.' The *Amenity Infrastructure* 'caters to both work and leisure activities allowing both merchant appropriation (displaying wares) and neighborhood occupation (recreation and leisure activities).' The design interventions contribute to the site as both pedestrian destinations and connections.

Concept development

Petrucci draws upon the Situationist artist Asger Jorn for the notion of *overpainting*. This approach involves the process of appropriation, modification, and creative reinvestment in an artistic work. Specifically, kitsch paintings produced solely for commercial consumption and lacking in aesthetic and intellectual import, according to Jorn, are painted over in an attempt to restore creative value and new meaning to the work. The artistic intent is a conversion of value '… the transformation of paintings as commodities (objects bought in the market) into sites of spontaneous, natural creativity.'[2] Similarly, Petrucci (facilitated by the city municipality) aims at transforming the kitsch landscape of the strip through strategic urban overpainting. It is an effort to reverse the modernist planning practices that proliferated across American cities particularly during the post-World War II era of isolated, compartmentalized, lower density growth. Within the general characterization of *sprawl*, Petrucci points to its incumbent manifestations of the shopping mall, the planned unit development (PUD), and the commercial strip. His target in this case study is the generic zone – a place neither here nor there – of Phoenix's one-mile long commercial corridor known as 7th Avenue.

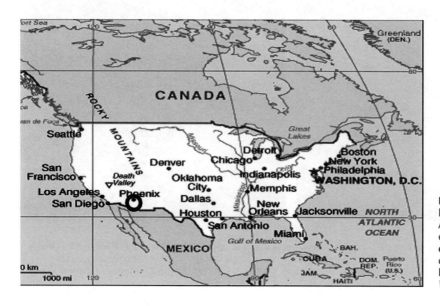

FIGURE 8.4
Location of Phoenix, Arizona, in the context of the contiguous forty-eight US states. (Map courtesy of US Central Intelligence Agency, *World Fact Book*, 2008.)

Project site: why 7th Avenue?

Petrucci relates the physical and economic reasons behind the site selection as follows: 'In 1968, 7th Avenue was widened by the Arizona Department of Transportation to create a high volume north/south transportation corridor in excess of 60,000 cars per day. Landscape improvements typically located between the street and sidewalk were absorbed by the increased width of the street. The City of Phoenix was unable to make conventional infrastructure "beautification" improvements. This condition combined with the strip's decay caused by competition with regional malls, power centers, and strip malls called for urban action. In 1997 over sixty merchants along this one-mile commercial corridor formed the 7th Avenue Merchants Association to develop a strategy for revaluing their properties and businesses. Their objectives were three fold: first, to establish a character for the strip that would be identifiable in the greater metropolitan area; second, to increase business by promoting renovations of existing businesses and new development; and third, to reduce discursive and undesirable conditions by forming a stronger pedestrian connection with the surrounding neighborhoods.'

A demonstration site was selected that was capable of establishing a strong connection between 7th Avenue's commercial strip in Phoenix and the surrounding neighborhood. A new infrastructure was created within the generic landscape, and a landscape feature functioned as a visible gateway at the quarter mile cross streets to engender a recognizable community identity. The first demonstration project was located at the intersection of 7th Avenue and Glenrosa (refer to Figure 8.5).

The focus of the planning project was to energize and promote commercial strip amenities in the target area: namely, public spaces that provide shade, display, recreation, and leisure activities. This collaborative planning scheme rethought and modified the programmatic priorities and car-dominated access that historically shaped this section of Phoenix. In its place, the existing rights-of-way, alleyways, utility easements, required setbacks along property lines, and retention areas that are perpendicular to the street operated as a 'connective tissue of experiences' linking sidewalks to the service alley, parking lots, and adjacent neighborhoods. Drawing, in part, from the conceptualization of 'infrastructure' as offered by Stan Allen in his book *Points & Lines: Diagrams and Projects for the City*,[3] constructed surfaces and landscapes became integrated urban spaces and were divided into four zones: circulation, commercial, recreational, and art.

Methods of analysis

Petrucci concedes that in order to have the strip modified into 'a dynamic urban typology, it needed to be examined with unconventional methods.' A master plan with flexibility was needed. For example, smaller tactical interventions (such as merchant improvements to their buildings) typically

FIGURE 8.5
Detail map of Phoenix's 7th Avenue stripscape demonstration project located at the intersection of 7th Avenue and Glenrosa. (Map courtesy of Darren Petrucci.)

create delays because of the paperwork related to variances and permits. His urban 'Modifications Strategic Overpainting' method employed a *kit of ideas* for a synthetic and coordinated series of individual improvements that complemented the whole by following previously agreed upon planning concepts. He cites three methods of intervention: *tactical evaluation, strategic overpainting,* and *emergent typologies.*

Tactical evaluation involves site evaluations that are documented photographically. Here, Petrucci lends importance to the realization that landscapes are shaped by more than municipal governments and professional designers. On a daily basis, a full spectrum of urban dwellers informally commits acts of social insurgency that reshape public space in a manner that accommodates their particularized human needs. This 'making do,' as Petrucci puts it, is a form of public intervention that intrudes, as well, into the 'privatized commercial landscape of the strip through productive acts of leisure.' Some scholars refer to this documentation process as *social mapping.*

To document these acts of *appropriation* and *subversion* by the public (and opportunism by the merchants), Petrucci focuses on typical use patterns within the 7th Avenue commercial corridor. The photographs are tightly cropped to define specific site conditions, like the use of *horizontal advertising* on street surfaces, or the use of foreground commercial space to display goods – characterized by Petrucci as 'Retail Garage Sale.'

The *emergent typologies* that are revealed through photographs (essentially, field data of urban performance) illustrate that users – not just makers – shape the landscape and that such evidence can set the stage for countless urban design tactics that are rooted in a particular urban circumstance (Figures 8.6 and 8.7).

The photographic evidence is distilled into various classifications that form a glossary of terms to be used in the project. The images and reductive terms provide Petrucci with an *emergent typology* that is then diagrammed as computer models to illustrate their application potential to the clients.

Existing conditions, therefore, are accepted and exploited for their distinctive localized character. For example, conditions categorized as appropriated were photographed and labeled: *found.* They were then embellished upon, or *staged,* to illustrate their applicability in the new planning model. These constructs Petrucci termed *staged public interventions* or SPIs.

FIGURES 8.6 AND 8.7
Comparative images of urban commercial use patterns along 7th Avenue are recorded and translated into emergent typologies. (Left) an *ad hoc* sidewalk space for additional customer seating is photographed and labeled as found. (Right) A rummage sale street condition on vacated space is also recorded as found. These urban situations of appropriated, underutilized, spaces later informed Darren Petrucci's concept for outdoor rooms. (Photographs courtesy of Darren Petrucci.)

Overpainting sprawl as a sustainable landscape   113

A *found* situation might be people sitting in a row of chairs in a store parking lot facing a visually compelling billboard overscaled for traffic-flow viewing. This human situation is translated into *Billboard Theater*, and generates the concept of the vertical street element used, instead, to display art (Figures 8.8 and 8.9). For Petrucci, such 'urban narratives' are capable of yielding new urban constructs drawn directly from community behavior.

Design process

Urban aggregates: Each emergent typology, such as a *retail garage sale* (namely, foreground shop space) or a *private threshold* condition, is then linked to an Amenity Infrastructure of streets, sidewalks, and service alleys located within its block to produce a *localized-urban environment* (Figures 8.10 and 8.11). Petrucci adds, 'The combination of Amenity Infrastructures, merchant improvements, existing structures, and new development within each block creates an urban aggregate that is not dependent upon the development of the strip as a whole.' These are independent entrepreneurial ventures collectively grouped – not unlike designated sales booths for public flea markets – upgraded with public amenities, uniform aesthetic appeal, and local distinctiveness. Such a scheme, Petrucci feels, 'promotes incremental growth, rather than a totalizing master plan, and is perpetuated by forces of competition [each block trying to outdo the other].'

Indeterminate programs

Architecturally specific infrastructures, like bathrooms, circulation, kitchens, and storage, prompt – rather than prescribe – the programmed spaces within each typology. Multiplicity of public/private interchange is encouraged. For example, 'interior circulation and utility cores connect different, programmatically indeterminate, housing volumes over a pedestrian path' (Figure 8.12).

Utilizing the connective tissue of the pedestrian path, other typologies can be grouped on either side, 'such as housing–commercial, commercial–commercial, housing–housing, commercial–cultural, etc., allowing uses to shift, combine, and change in reaction to the changing conditions of the strip.'

Such hybrid relationships facilitate spatial density, formal variety, and social interaction in what was formerly an uninspiring and wasteful land use policy. Petrucci proposed three combinations along 7th Avenue that complied with existing zoning regulations: 'commercial–dwelling (home–office), cultural–retail (art gallery and coffee shop), and civic–social (police substation and daycare). This low-scale, but complex, urban condition is

FIGURES 8.8 AND 8.9
Billboard Theater as found (left) and (right) public art display staged. (Photographs courtesy of Darren Petrucci.)

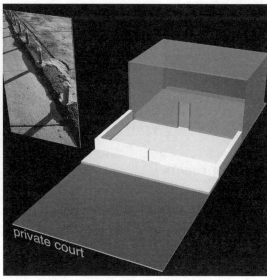

FIGURES 8.10 AND 8.11
Here, photographic documentation is translated by Petrucci into spatial constructs. The 'retail garage sale' condition (left), and the 'private court' condition (right) are cited as emergent typologies and translated into localized urban environments. (Photographs courtesy of Darren Petrucci.)

designed to transition into the residential context of 7th Avenue and Glenrosa, while functioning as a community core.

Responsive envelopes

The form and material choice of the proposed building envelopes, Petrucci clarifies, 'are determined not by their internal programs, but by their zoning, climatic orientation, and relationship to their surrounding context. Passive environmental controls such as thermal chimneys, evaporative pools, and natural day lighting are specifically detailed as environmental infrastructures that service the programmatically indeterminate volumes.' Again, flexibility and multiplicity are determining concepts as the building envelope is developed for each typology. Petrucci uses the example of the

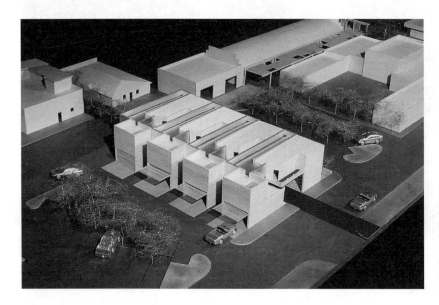

FIGURE 8.12
An axonometric blowup of the programmatically indeterminate housing volume constructed over the pedestrian path. (Computer-generated drawing courtesy of Darren Petrucci.)

Garage Sale Retail condition to demonstrate how a *folded façade* allows for exterior advertising, while functioning as a solar chimney and a vertical circulation core (Figure 8.13).

Design development

'The project required a combined process of tactical analysis based on individual merchant's improvements, with a strategic plan that the city could deploy at the end of the research.' The planning process is comprised of four layers.

Layer one: *Bands* are 'composed of concrete slabs seeded with iron filings that rust and naturally stain the concrete. Control joints are saw-cut into the concrete.' The bands define regularized intervals between pedestrian amenities of man-made shading devices and tree cover (added in layers three and four), and the paved circulation paths. These features are related to predictable urban needs, such as mass transit waiting areas (Figure 8.14).

Layer two: *Vertical elements*, such as commercial markers for local businesses, begin to be defined. 'The vertical panels [elements] act as signs with printed copy adhered to a translucent lexan panel. The interior is illuminated by twelve-volt, wired tube lights'. These vertical elements provide the opportunity to use such a medium to celebrate public art. 'A new program has been established,' Petrucci continues, 'with the Phoenix Public Art Department for the project. Vertical wall elements that function as shading devices for the lower afternoon sun are designed as light-boxes for graphic art [and one would think, digital art, through a grant program that – if connected to a computer base – could change art installations more frequently if desired.] Reproductions of the artists' work are printed on translucent panels and are illuminated at night. Every 6–12 months the panels are replaced with a new artist's work. Therefore, in keeping with the dynamism of the site, public art is conceived of as an urban gallery.'[4] Such efforts as the public art program give a community face to the neighborhood, in lieu of generic services and corporate signage, and foster ownership and pride in one's living/working environment (Figures 8.15 and 8.16).

Layer three: *Canopies* are constructed that define a variety of outdoor rooms for various merchant spaces, neighborhood art displays, and children's play areas. These so-called *Lampshades* are in essence 'a translucent lantern illuminated by the sun during the day, and by internal lights during the night' (Figure 8.17). (One wonders if these could function just as well off solar collectors.)

This amenity infrastructure combines shade, security lighting, and signage (or graphic art) into one flexible unit, thereby cleaning up the visual and physical litter along the commercial corridor (Figures 8.18 and 8.19). These elements have been

FIGURE 8.13
A computer model illustrating the hybrid construction principle as applied to the Garage Sale Retail typology. Its interior volume is 'accessible, environmentally functional, and programmatically indeterminate.' (Computer-generated drawing courtesy of Darren Petrucci.)

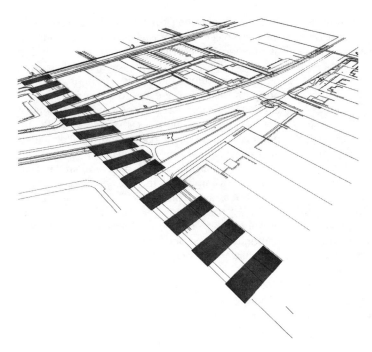

FIGURE 8.14
Drawing of the scheme for layer one: bands for the streetscape development. (Drawing courtesy of Darren Petrucci.)

optimized for cost and maintenance. They are durable and affordable for the private business owner to purchase. The Lampshade has been approved by the City of Phoenix for private installation and as a new signage opportunity for merchants.[5]

The upright steel posts are designed to resist wind loading and to optimize spatial flexibility. They consist of a few basic elements. The upright support consists of a fourteen-foot tall 8.075-inch weathering steel (also known as corten or by the trademark Cor-Ten) pole from which an eight-foot-by-eighteen-foot steel Vierendeel truss frame is supported. The pole is bolted to a two-foot-by-nine-foot concrete footing. Hence, the dimension of a typical parking space serves as the module for the canopy footprint. 'The top and bottom of the canopy are clad in 10 mm polycarbonate material. Since these panels are inexpensive, they are easily replaceable if spray-painted or damaged. The canopy is manufactured in the shop, brought to the site, and installed onto the pole.' The canopies are then arranged in various programmatic configurations (Figures 8.20 and 8.21).

The final layer is *trees* that are planted in the interstitial spaces between the bands. The bands, in turn, function as transition zones and circulation links for crosswalks, streets, and outdoor rooms (Figure 8.22).

A plan view of layer four indicates, at the detail level, the addition of concrete walkways, benches, art panels, shrubs, and trellises at the intersection of 7th Avenue and Glenrosa. Existing small businesses, such as Chester's Auto and Rapid Credit, are integrated into the low-scaled neighborhood redevelopment model as a way of investing in local enterprises in lieu of linking development with anchor stores from outside the community.

FIGURE 8.15
Illustration of the composite Lampshade function: vertical shade screen + monument sign + public art program = art/sign-shadescreen. (Illustration courtesy of Darren Petrucci.)

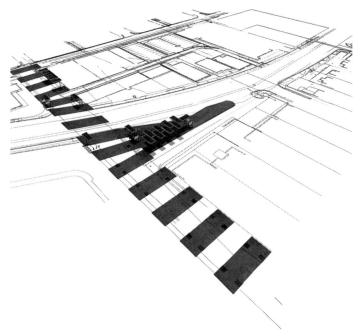

FIGURE 8.16
Drawing of the scheme for layer two of streetscape development: bands + vertical elements + canopies (Lampshades). (Drawing courtesy of Darren Petrucci.)

Typically, sprawl produces landscapes more conducive to cars and trucks than humans – with streetscapes designed with wide thoroughfares to serve heavy traffic loads not pedestrian use. Petrucci rethinks the design intensions that account for the consequences of sprawl as a process of large-scale, car-dependent real estate development; instead, he seeks to *overpaint* sprawl as a sustainable landscape. In this manner, careless and wasteful use of space yields to thoughtful planning that promotes pedestrian life accessible to all, and stresses human priorities such as social connections and personal ownership fundamental to community cohesiveness[6] (Figure 8.23).

A series of computer-generated *before* and *after* images of the various activity nodes offer locals, who are unfamiliar with urban planning maps, a glimpse of improved pedestrian amenities in both a daytime

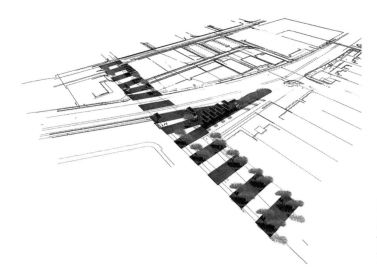

FIGURE 8.17
Drawing of the scheme for layer three of streetscape development: bands + vertical elements + canopies (Lampshades). (Drawing courtesy of Darren Petrucci.)

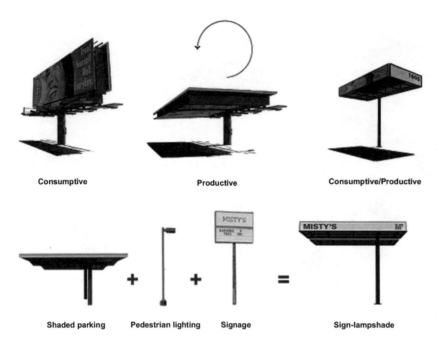

FIGURES 8.18 AND 8.19
Illustrations of the various Lampshade functions: consumptive/productive, sign-lampshade. (Illustrations courtesy of Darren Petrucci.)

and nighttime condition. Note, the emphasis on street plantings for shading and human delight; the use of vertical elements to advertise (at the pedestrian level) local services like Misty's Bar and Integrity Automotive, while utilizing light-boxes for graphic art to showcase rotating exhibits of community artwork; and the illuminated *canopies* that serve multiple functions of illuminated street markers for bus stops, shaded seating areas, security lighting, and *Greenscreen* climate control areas (Figures 8.24 and 8.25).

Petrucci offers various strategies that address a concern for preserving district identity. The first of these he labels *private merchant improvements*. In this approach, the street infrastructure is designed to be affordable for local merchants, who pay for the cost of a canopy, its installation, and maintenance. The canopies are placed either in a single or double module on their privately owned land parcels where they may serve as signage or to illuminate covered and lighted parking, outdoor eating areas, or urban markets.

By utilizing standardized graphics and uniform language on the canopies throughout the designated area of the streetscape infrastructure, a cohesive and identifiable urban landscape (requested by the Merchants Association) results which has enough flexibility built into it for individual expression.

An important part of this coordinated approach is the *contextual color palette*. A family of colors that work well in the bright desert sun is selected by the business owners from the contextual palette, and the combinations of colors are organized by a professional urban colorist. The intent is to link individual colors to various businesses without detracting from the greater whole (Figure 8.26).

The coordinated graphics include a letterform found on many of the 7th Avenue businesses. This particular font, known as *Akzidenz-Grotesk,* was selected as the identity graphic. More than just a branding issue, Petrucci argues, 'It is a sign that refers back to the colored [paving] bands that mark the entry into the district' (Figures 8.1 and 8.27).

The use of this distinctive graphic extends into what Petrucci labels *emergent corporate identity*. The M7 logo (signifying Melrose at 7th Avenue) is applied to business cards, letterheads, and envelopes to give the formal association of sixty merchants a business identity, and to denote economic empowerment for these small business owners.

The branding logo of M7 is extended in other ways. *Membership association plaques* of die-cut aluminum are made available for all merchants who are members of the 7th Avenue Merchants Association to be displayed at the entry of their establishments. Graphic designer Andrew Weed designed *T-shirts displaying the M7 logo*. Bearing the name of

Overpainting sprawl as a sustainable landscape **119**

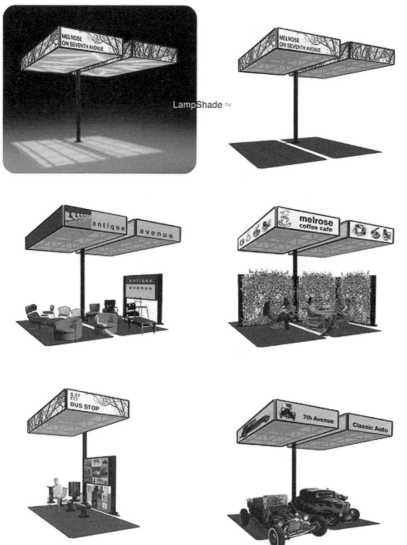

FIGURE 8.20
Illustration of the various Lampshade strategies in use. (Illustration courtesy of Darren Petrucci.)

the establishment and using the same colors designated for their business establishments, merchants wear and sell the T-shirts as promotional items.

Finally, the City of Phoenix's Streets and Transportation Department deploys *public right-of-way improvements*, at quarter mile intersections along 7th Avenue. These *iMenity Infrastructures* make improvements that will catalyze the public and private development for the emerging district.

The city's endorsement of iMenity Infrastructures allows a more flexible definition of public/private urban boundaries with the hope that neighborhood ownership of the spaces will assist in the maintenance and public safety issues of this revitalized commercial district. The intent, as well, is to 'encourage appropriation and activation of public space' that was previously underutilized or in a derelict condition. As a flexible urban revitalization tactic, Petrucci feels that it is transferable and capable of being adapted to the diverse socioeconomic conditions of the city.

Since the city provides only the infrastructure, people shape the spaces according to their own needs and values; site- and client-specific interventions engender difference, but also operate within the planning structure of the revitalized strip. The

FIGURE 8.21
Post-construction evening view of the Lampshade urban strategy implemented as a bus stop. (Photograph courtesy of Darren Petrucci.)

planning structure is designed, therefore, to balance individuality with visual and programmatic order. For example, visual cohesiveness is sought over the uncontrolled dissonance of the strip by adjusting programmatically different elements by scale. Yet, as one local resident informed the author, 'There seems to be great encouragement of artistic expression as evidenced by the number of creative shops (Bend A Light Neon, Exposed Studio and Gallery, Clay Face Tile Studio), and the amount of

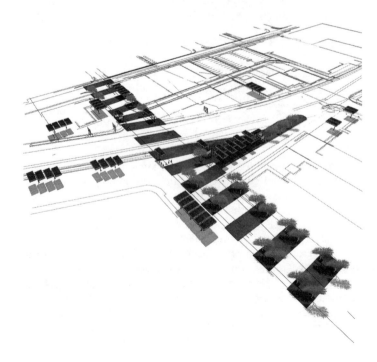

FIGURE 8.22
Drawing of the scheme for layer four of the streetscape development. (Drawing courtesy of Darren Petrucci.)

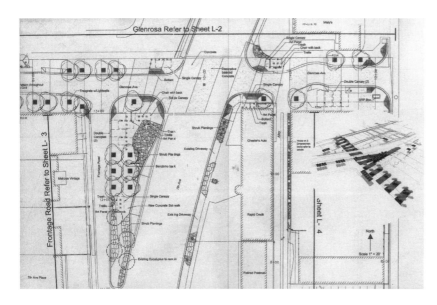

FIGURE 8.23
Plan view of the layer four redevelopment scheme for 7th Avenue and Glenrosa. (Plan courtesy of Darren Petrucci.)

unique creativity in the décor and production of goods and services. There is a business association that meets once a week, and there certainly is a good crowd at First Fridays.'[7]

In an effort to stress the *particularity of place* over generic accommodation, use–time relationships are mapped to 'identify overlaps, holes, and discrepancies in time' in such conditions as bus and automobile peak traffic flow, school-pedestrian cross-circulation, pedestrian circulation intervals, antique shopping, and entertaining and dining activity patterns. This evaluation, Petrucci feels, is 'helpful in determining new programs (such as leisure activities) that can fill gaps in time between scheduled events in the practice of the site.' This temporal map is useful in managing parking by calculating offset business hours, like Chester's Garage that operates between 7:00 am and 3:00 pm, and the adjacent Misty's Bar that operates between 4:00 pm and 2:00 am (Figure 8.28).

FIGURES 8.24 AND 8.25
Before and proposed neighborhood redevelopment schemes for Melrose Street at 7th Avenue. (Photographs courtesy of Darren Petrucci.)

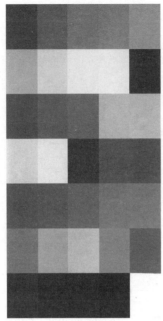

FIGURE 8.26
Image of the contextual color palette. (Colour image in online version and Black and white in printed book. Photograph courtesy of Darren Petrucci.)

FIGURE 8.28
Night scene of Misty's Bar urban context as completed. (Photograph courtesy of Darren Petrucci, 2008.)

Author's summary

To be an effective place-based planning program, collaboration among a number of stakeholders (in this instance, the city municipality, the Merchants Association, the neighborhood associations, the planner and the developer) is critical. Through documented field studies and interviews with the local inhabitants, Petrucci developed a relevant *Kit of Ideas* to frame his particularized planning strategies. Working situationally, the proposed *demonstrations* sprang from the specific social and economic practices of a subsector of Phoenix's urban core, as opposed to employing large urban redevelopment strategies that serve a statistical norm.

FIGURE 8.27
Graphic design logo for M7 'Melrose on Seventh Avenue' by Andrew Weed. (Photograph courtesy of Darren Petrucci.)

The quest was to achieve a spirited localized urban environment out of the barren soil of America's stripscapes. Inspired community-planning practices, coupled with creative individual expression on the part of the various merchant groups, illustrate the power of people to instill life into our underutilized urban pockets (Figures 8.29 and 8.30). To be sure, people have created vibrant markets throughout time and throughout the world. This planning project reinvests trust in the public and municipal government to create humane and sustainable environments. To further that endeavor, the project was used as the basis for a federal grant for the City of Phoenix's Department of Transportation to undertake further modifications along 7th Avenue and elsewhere.

Interestingly, however, there is little mention of ethnic diversity in this 'collaborative planning strategy,' particularly as it might relate to personalized color selection that stresses ethnic identity in this largely Hispanic urban area. Ultimately, this is a commercially driven planning model that utilizes current marketing strategies such as uniform graphic representation, an 'urban colorist,' branding, etc. to *economically* revitalize a bland, moribund stripscape.

FIGURE 8.29
Daytime site condition as built. Note the shaded sitting areas below the canopies and installed art/sign-shadescreen panels. (Photograph courtesy of Darren Petrucci, 2008.)

FIGURE 8.30
Bus stop, canopy, and art/sign-shadescreen as built. (Photography courtesy of Darren Petrucci, 2008.)

Such a scheme presents a different premise for local distinctiveness than that of Teddy Cruz, for example, which utilizes a socially driven model that relishes diversity of expression, juxtaposition, improvisation, density, and insurgency over spatial and visual uniformity, marketing logos, and lateral growth. Both seek local distinctiveness and neighborhood renewal by analyzing current use patterns, and modifying boundaries (whether political or physical) into connectors. Both work with cooperative planning offices and local communities in large urban cores of the American southwest. Yet, Petrucci works within current mainstream corporate strategies for commercial success. Cruz, on the other hand, seeks to work apart from traditional development formulas, adopts a community-centric model that aims at *social* revitalization, and entrepreneurial ventures for economic success that are afforded through the spatial and governmental flexibility of his urban vision.

The 7th Avenue project was part of an exhibition in Barcelona in fall 2008.

Notes

1. Quotations are taken from D. Petrucci's office publication loaned to the author, entitled *Research & Design: Selected Projects* (2003).
2. P. Wollen (1989). Bitter victory: the art and politics of the Situationists International. In *The Passage of a Few People through a Rather Brief Moment in Time: The Situationist International.* MIT Press, 48. Quoted in Petrucci (2003), *Research & Design: Selected Projects,* unnumbered.
3. S. Allen (1999). Infrastructural urbanism. In *Points & Lines: Diagrams and Projects for the City.* Princeton Architectural Press, 54.
4. Ibid.
5. D. Petrucci (2003). *Research & Design: Selected Projects,* unnumbered.
6. For an 'illustrated vocabulary of sprawl,' see D. Hayden (2004). *A Field Guide to Sprawl.* W.W. Norton.
7. Written communication, March 27, 2008, between the author and Daniel Greene.

Part Three

Environment – appropriate technologies and design tied to the dynamics of place

9

A poverty of resources/a richness of expression

There are four great motives for writing (or any other creative endeavor):
Sheer egoism
Aesthetic enthusiasm
Historical Impulse (to record)
Political Purpose in its broadest sense – a desire to push the world in a certain direction, to alter other people's ideas of the kind of society they should strive for.

George Orwell in *The Decline of the English Murder and Other Essays.*

Project: Visitors' Interpretive Centre for Prehistoric Art (also known as the Northwest Rock Art Visitors' Centre, National Monuments Council of Namibia)
Location: Twyfelfontein, Namibia
Design team: Nina Maritz, Architects with Dennis McDonald
   Community stakeholders and local community tour guides
   European Union representatives and funding authorities
   Resident archeologist – Dr John Kinahan
   Namibian Tourism Development Programme
   Structural/Civil – Uhrich
   Mechanical/Electrical – EMCON Consulting Engineers
   Quantity surveyor – C. P. De Leeuw Namibia
   Contractor – Hartmut Maletski
   Construction crew
Time frame: Opened in June 2005

Introduction

The Visitors' Interpretive Centre for Prehistoric Rock Art at Twyfelfontein is sited in an arid and remote section of northwest Namibia. Located in this dry Tropics of Capricorn in southwest Africa, the design had to address extreme climate demands of severe radiation, heat, and glare (Figures 9.3 and 9.4). In addition, the goal of the project was to provide protection and non-intrusive interpretation that would address the environmental pressures of an increasing number of visitors (over 1,000 a week), while providing a viewing experience of the twenty-thousand-year-old cultural site that would screen out the modern world.

Maritz's concept and design resolution provide an application model for a culturally sensitive and sustainable design philosophy applied to what is now a World Heritage Site.[1] The project, awarded through a competitive bidding process, was initiated by the National Monuments Council of Namibia (NMC) and funded by a 50,000-euro grant by the European Union. The Visitors' Centre is constructed of natural and recycled materials, and (as outlined in the Burra Charter of Conservation) is entirely reversible.

Nina Maritz's design philosophy sets a high standard for its recognition of the fragility of such prehistoric sites and for its acknowledgement of an architect's responsibility to consider the impact of his/her designs on the natural environment – both when the design is placed within the site and after its usable life has been reached. What follows might best be described as an integrated design approach that stretches the limits of a conventional European Union building contract. In addressing the full spectrum of the site's environmental context, Maritz's holistic approach ensures the cultural and

Copyright © 2009 Elsevier Ltd. All rights reserved.

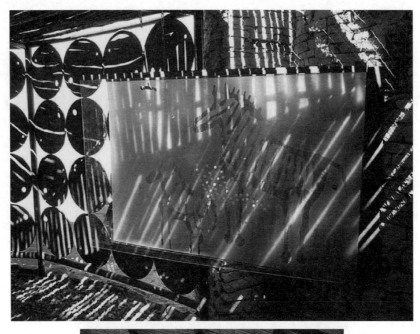

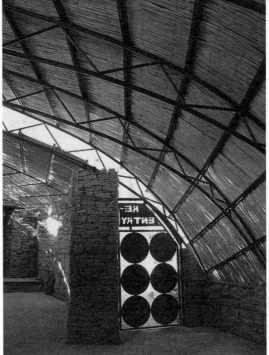

FIGURES 9.1 AND 9.2
The layering of meanings in art, the play of natural light, and an emphasis on sensory perception are all considerations of this display space made from recycled materials for the Visitors' Interpretive Rock Art Centre, northwest Namibia, 2005. (Photographs by Nina Maritz.)

environmental sustainability of a heritage site, while allowing for inevitable change.

Maritz's contribution to a situated regionalism stems from multiple strands of commitment: her desire to understand the various cultural and environmental differences within Namibia's subregions; her willingness to reach consensus on design decisions among a wide spectrum of stakeholders; and a desire to have her projects serve as teaching tools for environmentally responsible design across broad socioeconomic groups.

The regional filter

Namibia is located well below the equator along the southwest coast of Africa. Maritz describes it as 'a developing country [with] a rigorous climate and complex multicultural relations.'[2] Encompassing two deserts, the Namib and the Kalihari, the region has a hot dry climate with sandy soil. The socio-economic realities include: a low population density (1.8 million people spread over 800,000 square kilometers), restricted natural resources, virtually no manufacturing base, few skilled trades people, low levels of formal education, rapid urbanization, a subsistence economy, and a decreasing life expectancy due, in large part, to the spread of AIDS through the population. Though, at present, this population is mainly rural (seventy-one percent), it is estimated that by 2020 eighty percent of the population will be living in towns. The limited economic base that historically relied on mining (mostly uranium and diamonds), fishing, and agricultural exports (beef and lamb) is declining. In their place, tourism is expected to become the dominant economic activity. However, tourist destinations, like the one featured in this case study, must address and control the potential adverse effects of high visitation and site degradation through affordable strategies for preventive maintenance and the conservation of the heritage resource itself.[3]

Design intent: the architect's elemental design philosophy

In spite of the multitude of challenging regional forces cited above, Namibian architect Nina Maritz provides a practical and inspirational pathway of sustainable principles and practices to follow. She seeks 'a deeper level of understanding [and] different levels of "good fit" in an environment.' Maritz approaches these design intents with what architect Michael Cockram refers to as the 'aesthetics of simplicity' – aesthetic principles that sacrifice neither the pragmatics of place nor its poetic expression.

The problem of 'sustainability as a reductionist term,' Maritz asserts, 'is that it focuses discussion on only *one* issue. When we design, we need to think of *all* issues; strike a balance and not leave out the rest. We can't just say that these are *cultural* concerns, for example; climate is cultural. The seasons affect and determine behavior. Weather shapes how communities get together, and weather influences aesthetics.'

Instead, Maritz prefers an integrative approach shaped by an awareness of the environmental forces that she has come to understand. It is a design philosophy anchored in basic functionality. Buildings must work well and be comfortable to use. Tiny particulars of day-to-day use need to be taken into consideration. *Functionality*, however, is not viewed by the architect in a restrictive sense. It includes 'appropriate form and beauty, space on a sculptural level, light and serenity conducive to mental quietness.' Her sustainable design philosophy was recently put to the test in the winning competition for the Habitat Research and Development Centre in Windhoek, Namibia (HRDC Competition, Namibia, 2002–2006) (Figure 9.5).

Maritz continues, 'We should address the landscape by taking into consideration site placement, footprint, silhouette, and appearance.' By *appearance*, the architect means using design elements that are appropriate to a site's multilayered context that includes such factors as material selection, passive solar opportunities, low-maintenance (but sturdy) construction, and flexibility in use that anticipates both expansion and removal.

The project concept (as it relates to Namibia's regional realities), Maritz notes, needs to recognize its financial constraints and opportunities, such as employing low-tech, labor-intensive techniques like the *Earthship* strategy that utilizes recycled tires filled with compacted soil to serve as a retaining wall; or the imaginative use of recycled oil drum lids purchased from the air charter tourist industry and appropriated as light screens, space separators, and signage (Figures 9.6 and 9.7); or quartered oil drums used as interlocking metal roofing at the Northwest Rock Art Visitors' Centre (Figures 9.8 and 9.9).[4]

In addition, there is the issue of *ornament*. In Namibia one cannot speak only of an aesthetic function. 'We are not at a point where we have the luxury of art for its own sake.' Instead, Maritz

130 Vernacular Architecture and Regional Design

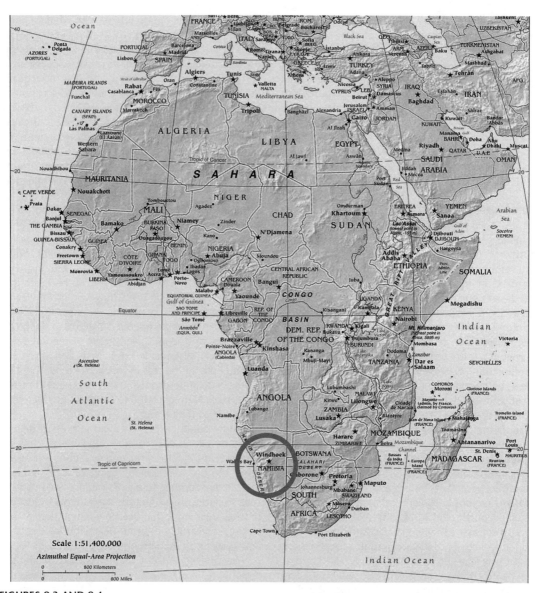

FIGURES 9.3 AND 9.4
Global representation of Namibia's place in the universe. Maritz underscores the reality that all northern hemisphere rules regarding climate orientation are reversed in the southern hemisphere. On the right is a detail image of Twyfelfontein's location in Namibia. (Map courtesy of CIA: The World Fact Book.)

recognizes that people are often creative and inventive when they have nothing, whether it is using flattened kerosene cans as roof cladding (Figures 9.10 and 9.11), or recycling sections of corporate metal signage to be hung on a steel pole frame and enclosing domestic space (Figure 9.12).

'In Namibia and other desert countries, perhaps one can say that "less is more",' says Maritz. 'For myself, this is starting to result in a kind of frugal design – one can maybe call it scavenger architecture. The "less" in this case is not the less of Miesian minimalism, but the less of means, in which poverty of resources can lead to richness of expression.'

Hence, Maritz operates from the premise that simple, recycled objects – essentially thrown-away goods – do not have to be soul-less elements. Through Maritz's thoughtful approach to design, discarded elements are either given new life and

A poverty of resources/a richness of expression 131

FIGURES 9.3 AND 9.4 cont'd. (Available at www.cia.gov/library/publications/the-world-factbook/)

FIGURE 9.5
In this view of the HRDC Building, clerestory light is softened by the roof infill matting that is made from invasive prosopis (mesquite) branches. The mesquite reeds form a pin-jointed space frame that supports a layer of low-grade wool sewn into recycled feedbags for insulation. Lavender leaves are added to each bag to prevent moths. This design feature provides lighting, ventilation, and 'mental quietness,' while reducing heat gain from the roof. Similarly, in the Visitors' Interpretive Rock Art Centre hand-made reed mats woven in Omaruru are made from invasive Spaansriet and used as insulating mats for the ceiling. The mats are placed below mesh-reinforced foil insulation and serve as a radiation barrier and drip sheet. (Photograph courtesy of Nina Maritz.)

utility in the manner in which they are reinterpreted, or conceived in such a way as to allow nature to redefine their character and meaning over time. For example, Maritz points out: 'The little bit of rain (generally once a year) adds a patina of rust to the oil can roofing tiles used on the Visitors' Centre giving the roof a uniform aesthetic.' Maritz describes the construction process as follows: 'The roof structure consists of tubular steel sections welded together in curved roof trusses, and the roof cladding "tiles" [are] made by quartering recycled 200-litre oil drums and installing them in a Roman tile fashion with a row of concave "tiles" fixed to the

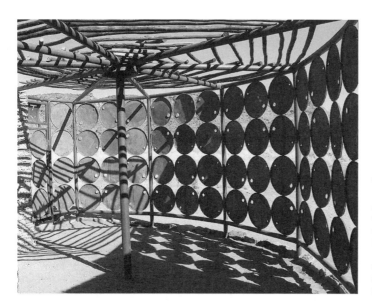

FIGURE 9.6
View of 150 liter oil drum lids refashioned into light screens and space separators. In this image they are spot-welded together into four-unit compositional groupings with the lid bung holes forming a visual pattern. Elsewhere in the site, where privacy is desired, the lids overlap like fish scales to block the holes in the lids. (Photograph courtesy of Nina Maritz.)

132 Vernacular Architecture and Regional Design

FIGURE 9.7
A restroom sign made from a forty-gallon (150 litre) oil drum lid at the Visitors' Interpretive Rock Art Centre rests against a gabion basket wall. (Photograph courtesy of Nina Maritz.)

purlins and closed with a row of convex "tiles." The metal was sandblasted before installation to remove paint remnants and to start the rusting process, which has an anodizing effect in a dry climate and will simulate the surrounding red oxide rocks.'[5] The slow oxidation of iron throughout the structure is intended to blend in gradually with the natural setting where the iron content in the sandstone provides a reddish hue.

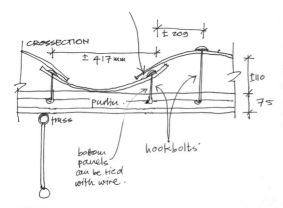

FIGURE 9.8
Original roof detail indicating pop riveted 200 liter convex drum sections sealed to prevent leakage during rain. The design also relied on sisalation to capture some of the dripping water. (Drawing courtesy of Dennis McDonald and Nina Maritz.)

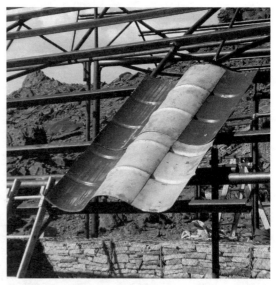

FIGURE 9.9
Construction photograph showing roofing tiles made from quartering recycled 200 liter oil drums. The tiles were sandblasted prior to assembly to remove paint and to enhance rusting for aesthetic effect. The metal cladding (applied in a manner similar to Roman tiles) was then attached to a roof structure made of tubular steel sections welded into curved roof trusses. A layer of sisalation was placed between the steel roof tiles as a waterproof barrier. Hand-made reed mats form a ceiling underneath of mesh-reinforced foil insulation. (Photograph courtesy of Nina Maritz.)

A poverty of resources/a richness of expression **133**

FIGURES 9.10 AND 9.11
Flattened kerosene cans (see detail), embellished with sponge painting, are used as cladding material on a traditional dwelling in Namibia. (Photograph courtesy of Nina Maritz.)

It should be noted that essentialism is not minimalism. 'Minimalism is not well suited to traditional Namibian habitats,' Maritz clarifies. 'Inside the wattle and daub (mud and straw) huts with straw roofs [Figure 9.13], shelves are often decorated with intricate patterns. Some call this aesthetic exuberance rendered in cardboard, corrugated iron, advertising newspaper offprints (varnished and used as wallpaper), or African printed cloth used for ruffled curtains – *shack chic*. The traditional huts may have few things in them but they are colorful and elaborate,' Maritz observes. Such aesthetic sensibilities also underscore the use of ornamentation rendered from found objects. 'Ornament has to be inherent in the function, or we can't use it at all.' Like most design decisions in her elemental approach, design features have to serve multiple functions and reflect multiple layers of meaning – they cannot simply be evocative as in the so-called neo-vernacular movement of the 1980s and 1990s.

FIGURE 9.12
Corporate metal signage is hung on a steel pole frame to enclose domestic space in a Namibian town context. (Photograph courtesy of Nina Maritz.)

Design process

The notion of doing more with less applies, as well, to the operation of Maritz's professional studio. At present, she is the sole practitioner (she would like to add another, particularly to strengthen her working drawings), and there are three technicians. Nonetheless, her design process is largely collaborative. In the Visitors' Centre it meant dealing with design concerns that ranged from local community

FIGURE 9.13
Both indigenous traditional dwellings and those utilizing hybridized features gleaned from recycled materials serve as design generators for the architect. Additionally, as in the HRDC project, rammed earth and brick construction materials are used to form massive walls for heat absorption. It is the pragmatics borne of a vernacular building culture – not the visual associations such works evoke – that inform the architect. (Photograph courtesy of Nina Maritz.)

involvement and supervising craftsmen, to oversight compliance issues from the multiple administrative and funding stakeholders. This inclusive attitude is intended to lead to an architectural solution that will be more culturally relevant when completed. Often the process begins in the community workshops that take place during the pre-design stage. Maritz notes, 'you can't approach sustainability with arrogance. You always have to be willing to change.'

In this regard, *context* involves understanding the complexities of where a building is to be placed (or situated); we can't see buildings in isolation. Some of the complexities of a site's context are revealed in the process of reaching design consensus. 'Given the legacy of apartheid,' Maritz adds, native people 'do not raise big voices.' She recognizes that in reaching design decisions 'individuals should not infringe on another's individual or community rights.' All stakeholders need to know that they have a say. 'What is important is the process of involvement. It is a critical component of African democracy that everyone has an opportunity to comment.'

In a similar manner to Howard Davis and Nihal Perera, a great deal of the creative richness that occurred during the construction phase of the Visitors' Centre was achieved by being willing to go beyond controlling *whose* project it was, and feeling that you had to detail everything. 'It is liberating,' Maritz feels, 'having people add their identity, creativity, and labor to a project.' If the local population is involved from the beginning, in the end it belongs to them. 'They take ownership of the space, and you seldom have problems such as vandalism.'

Prior to these community workshops, Maritz often camps at the prescribed site; begins to diagram relationships of circulation; and drafts out charts with lists of relationships among various components to discuss shortly afterwards with the various stakeholders (Figures 9.14 and 9.15).

'You have to look at the *whole* community life,' she notes: 'grazing, conservancy (such as wildlife management), heritage conservation practices (such as those outlined in the Australia ICOMOS Charter for Places of Cultural Significance – the so-called Burra Charter).' These issues are then balanced in light of the priorities and needs of the local culture. It is often not enough, for example, 'to fix up a community building like a school, clinic, or church. You also have to consider how communities might earn money from them.' Maritz points out, 'Demolition is the worst sustainable crime,' particularly if the embodied energy inherent in the materials is not recaptured and reused.

Working on remote building sites (sometimes 800–1,000 miles from her design studio), Maritz admits, influences her design process. She has to reduce conceptualizing to the most important issues, and produce detail drawings in such a way that unskilled workers can carry them out. She points out, 'There is a limited resource base of professionally trained individuals; with such variations in levels of training, it is important to reach an amicable agreement among all participants'[6] (Figures 9.16 and 9.17). Her communication medium is both verbal and graphic. Because of restrictive budgets, she cannot fly often enough to the site during (or toward the end of) the project. Yet, it is important to her that she reaches common agreement among the clients on the 'visual idea,' even if it is communicated via email. On this project, there were extensive meetings with the full spectrum of the Namibian community – both on the site and in the capital of Windhoek.

Project description

The National Monuments Council of Namibia initiated the project as a conservation measure in light of the increased visitation numbers (about 5,000 people a month), the subsequent damage to the site, and the need for better provisions for visitors. Foremost in the program statement was a concern that the design and construction be carried out in such a way as to contribute to the pending application of the Northwest Rock Art site being designated a World Heritage Site (World Heritage status was awarded in June 2007). The site 'is one of the richest in the world in prehistoric rock engravings, attributed to San [or Bushman] peoples of Southern Africa of about twenty thousand years ago.' The Visitors' Centre, then, could not compete with the prehistoric rock art in any way. Though the rock art is attributed to the San peoples (remnants of the San group still reside in northwest Namibia, approximately 800 kilometers away), the artwork is considered national patrimony. Entrusted with its stewardship, the project statement from the National Monuments Council addressed not only site protection of the rock art walking routes (contracted separately) and visitors' needs, but long-term management issues not usually the responsibility of project architects. These accommodations also had to be undertaken within the framework of severe cost constraints. A review committee comprised of a representative from the Namibian Tourism Development Program, the National Monuments Council, and the consulting

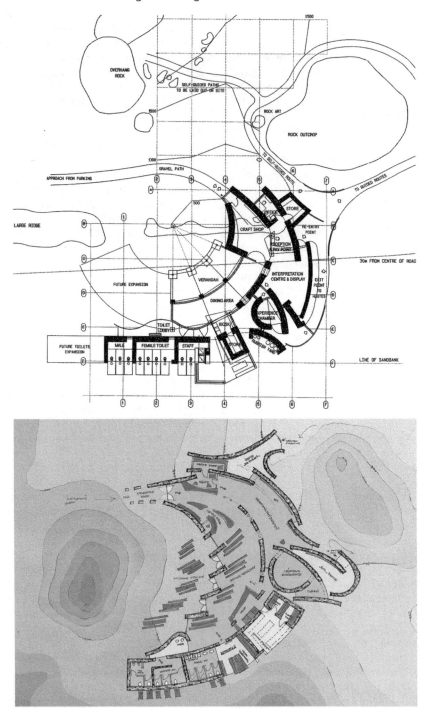

FIGURES 9.14 AND 9.15
Renderings of the second location of the Visitors' Interpretive Rock Art Centre overlaid onto the site; the rock outcrops are seen above (north is to the left). This new site plan is conceived as an organic spatial grouping that leads the groups of no more than eight people and their guide through the interpretive exhibits at ten-minute intervals. The exhibits introduce the visitor to the ethereal trance stages in preparation for viewing the rock engravings along the guided walking routes. Figure 9.15, below, is a final watercolor presentation drawing of the same site relationship. (Drawings courtesy of Dennis McDonald and Nina Maritz.)

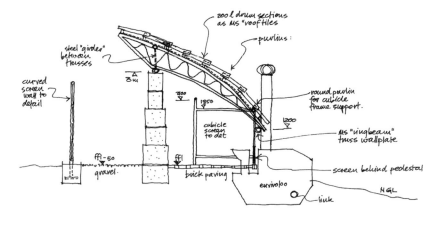

FIGURE 9.16
A sectional drawing through the toilet cubicle (dry toilets). Nine Enviroloo brand toilets were provided free from the funding agency. This detail drawing indicates rear access for cleaning out the large waste boxes. 'In the end,' Maritz notes, 'a modified double-vented pit latrine system would have been preferred.' (Drawing courtesy of Dennis McDonald and Nina Maritz.)

archeologist oversaw the project and ensured that the procedures, as outlined by the European Union, were followed for all contracts.

The original site selection by the consulting archeologist attempted to obscure the new building by shielding it behind existing rock outcroppings and away from the major collection of rock art. However, after a detailed site survey Maritz and architect Dennis McDonald realized that the clearing chosen had shallow rock beneath the sand, posing a problem for both the foundation and engravings that might be buried below thousands of years of erosion. The site footprint was also too small to accommodate the new building program. With the assistance of the resident archeologist, Dr John Kinahan, a second site was selected further down the slope and near the road (refer back to Figures 9.14 and 9.15). No undisturbed area for the site was used to limit any adverse effect. In addition, it was decided to demolish the visitors' kiosk and shade facilities in the valley below so that the visitor's sight lines were unobstructed by modern construction. The new site was out of visual range of the rock art, thereby enhancing the visitor's experience of imagining the prehistoric landscape as it was at the time that the artwork was conceived. Maritz summarizes these collective decisions as 'gently moving the tourist experience in the right direction.'[7] Previously, tourists used to climb over the sandstone carvings, and poured soft drinks over the carvings to enhance the contrast in their photographs which, in turn, eroded the stone. Maritz aimed at a more sustainable approach not only in her design decisions, but in the behavior of the visitors to ensure the integrity of the cultural resource.

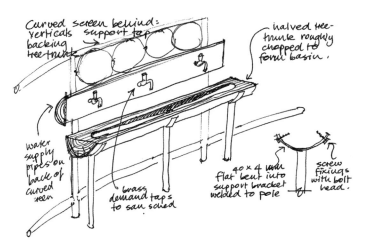

FIGURE 9.17
The visitors' toilet washbasin (detailed here) was to be made from a halved Leadwood tree trunk salvaged from a nearby river bed. Due to the experimental nature of the project, many details and design decisions were modified on site. 'Over elaborate details … were not always practical and had to be adapted to suit the realities of the projects.' The final washbasin design utilized a recycled galvanized drum with brass demand taps above to suggest a 'communal basin' in recognition of the precious offering of water. (Drawing courtesy of Dennis McDonald and Nina Maritz.)

138 Vernacular Architecture and Regional Design

Design development and interpretive program

Within these design parameters, Maritz developed the concept of transforming the original Visitors' Centre from its intended function as an observation area for viewing the works (Figures 9.18 and 9.19) into a communicative vessel that assisted the outside visitor in understanding the cultural and spiritual context out of which the rock art was produced. In turn, local inhabitants could recapture their heritage through the transmission of cultural information.

FIGURES 9.18 AND 9.19
The original observation platform with a view of rock-cut art below. The exposed soft sandstone erodes when people walk on it, requiring greater management and control of the historic site than was previously provided. (Photograph courtesy of Nina Maritz.)

Maritz, drawing upon historical evidence, focused her design concept and museum interpretation on the cultural meaning that the stone art held among the aborigines. The Visitors' Centre, Maritz believed, needed to evoke an understanding of the artwork as a cultural experience and expression. The project endeavored to relate to the visitor the creative *process* behind the artwork, rather than focusing exclusively on the *product*. Following the archeological evidence that supports the cultural practice of a trance dance (a cleansing ritual that preceded hunting and rain-making incantations),[8] the conceptual response utilized by the architect addressed three phenomena as part of the 'psychological preparation' for conducting the visitor through a series of walking routes leading to the rock engravings (Figures 9.20 and 9.21). These components related directly to the trance rituals that the rock artist (a healer or shaman) underwent during the creative process.

As Maritz explains it, 'Visitors approach the centre along a cleared gravel path edged with loose stones. The centre's round shape emerges from the landscape like a looming rock. Visitors enter through a narrow slit into a foyer occupied by the craft and souvenir shop. Just behind, the reception counter regulates movement through the building.'[9] Visitation through the exhibition areas – referred to by the architect as *experience chambers* – is limited to no more than eight people, led by guides at ten-minute intervals.

FIGURE 9.21
The third trance stage is transformation. The artist transforms and becomes the animal itself. Here, the 'dancing kudu' (part man, part animal) appears. Note the spiral phosphenes to the right of the image. (Photograph courtesy of Nina Maritz.)

The visitor is asked to enter the world of the supernatural. It is explained that during the first trance stage, images were induced by sensory deprivation (hunger and thirst, physical exhaustion, the use of hallucinogens, or chanting). Eventually, retinal images called *entoptics* or *phosphenes* appeared. These images generally took the form of spirals, circles, scrolls, and parallel lines creating abstract patterns. To evoke this phenomenon, Maritz designed a circular room whose only illumination is natural light emitting from the ceiling and filtered through metal cut-outs simulating entoptics or phosphenes.

The association or *little death* stage followed in the trance experience. Symptoms, akin to those of a wounded animal just prior to death, overtook the shaman. In addition to various physical responses, the brain associated the abstract patterns of the phosphenes with objects from daily experience; for example, parallel lines may become the markings of a zebra or the lines of an élan (see below). To capture this experience a network of wood framing, suspended from the ceiling, creates disorienting shadows over metal cut-out panels of animal figures.[10]

The third stage (the full trance) is *transformation*. This, according to Maritz, is 'strong magic.' The visualized animal and the shaman became one. The shaman, for example, was capable of taking on a lion form – possessing both animal and human characteristics. The transformed shaman, it was believed, not only moved through solid matter, but

FIGURE 9.20
During stage one of the trance ritual, images are induced by the shaman through sensory deprivation. The second stage is called association; visual patterns often appear at this time. The association stage is so named because the artist associates the visual patterns with the spirit of the animal that appears. (Photograph courtesy of Nina Maritz.)

FIGURE 9.22
Note the transmutation of the four-toed lion into the five-fingered captured lion spirit now possessed by the hunter during the transformation stage. (Photograph courtesy of Nina Maritz.)

also possessed supernatural powers to bring rain or to ensure a successful hunt (Figure 9.22). The visitor is now ready to embark on the site visit, the prehistoric artwork having been invested with cultural relevance critical to its interpretation.

Site response

Located in the northwest region of Namibia, the natural geography is defined by low rainfall, low humidity, high solar radiation and temperatures, high evaporation, and low wind speeds.[11] Soils are poor, vegetation fragile and easily damaged. The twenty-thousand-year-old red sandstone rock carvings emerge visually from amidst a dry landscape stripped of vegetation and surrounded by sand. Maritz immediately recognized the fragility of the site.

Exposed in this vast flat landscape, the soft sandstone rock carvings are vulnerable to both environmental and human impact. Visitors formerly climbed lookout towers to observe hundreds of thousands of years of geological succession spread before them. But, as Maritz notes, 'the environmental impact of a building is thus severe and visible.' In addition, not all tourist-related activities in the past have been respectful of the site. For example, some locally trained guides, seeking to promote tourist trade, defaced the works with spray paint. Their misguided efforts, effectively reducing cultural heritage to profiteering, will endure for generations to come (Figure 9.23).

Given the vulnerability of the site, the design imperative was to 'speak softly' with the new physical form. The Visitors' Centre is, in essence, invisible to the public upon arrival. Walking along the path, the rounded organic form blends into its physical setting. Not only did Maritz take her cues from natural features, landscape patterns and their intrinsic coloration, but animal skeletons and San (Bushman) shelters were evoked in the concept drawings (Figures 9.24 and 9.25). The plan itself

FIGURE 9.23
View of the defaced rock artwork. (Photograph courtesy of Nina Maritz.)

A poverty of resources/a richness of expression 141

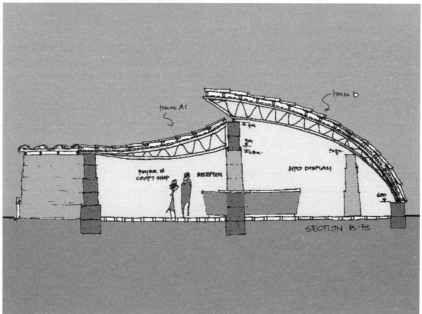

FIGURES 9.24 AND 9.25
Landscape features such as the San people's natural shelters, shown here without the original protective covering of bushes, served as form generators for the Visitors' Centre. This section drawing shows the information display area on the right with the craft shop on the left. (Photograph and drawing courtesy of Nina Maritz.)

emotes the shape of an animal curled in its death throws with its back arched. This metaphorical reference is overlaid onto the site (refer back to Figures 9.14 and 9.15), and reinforces the interpretive program regarding the second trance phase – *little death*. Spatially, the curved volume serves as a conduit for moving the maximum eight visitors and their guide sequentially through the *experience chambers* depicting the trance stages.

Building materials

Hardly any building materials are manufactured in Namibia. Most are imported from South Africa, adding to the transport energy load. In response to the shortages of standard building supplies, Maritz's design attempted to utilize both natural and recycled materials predominantly. Only sand and masonry were available, but getting water to the site was difficult and would have to have been trucked in for construction purposes. Maritz decided to make a 'waterless and reversible building.' The structure would be cement free. Instead, structural piers and load-bearing walls were bedded in gabion baskets – dry stack stone contained within a casing of chain-link mesh, hand made at the site out of standard galvanized diamond mesh (Figure 9.26). This decision addressed two local factors: there were no dry-stone masonry skills available to exploit the availability of sandstone as a structural material, and the country's affirmative action policy prompted a labor-intensive project that brought much needed employment to the remote setting.[12] In the process, the use of gabions introduced an alternative method of construction that was appropriate both to the surroundings and to the area's skill base.

In addition, caged gabion pebble paths replaced the original design of long lengths of concrete paths and steps, thus limiting the site intervention and avoiding the need for concrete. Stone (sandstone) was collected from sites outside the monument area as a heritage precaution and gathered from different areas around the site to avoid visibly scarring the land. One of the design adjustments made (regarding materials) related to the construction of the frame. A timber frame was rejected because of the short lifespan of timber due to extremely dry conditions and termite infestations. Recycled steel was decided upon, but the scrap merchant near Windhoek could not obtain the necessary sizes and quantity. It was decided to use new steel instead. One of the other imported components was the terracotta brick flooring made in Mariental (800

FIGURE 9.26
View of gabion wall baskets hand made on the site. The load-bearing tubular steel frame aided the laying out of the gabion baskets used as a free walling system. (Photograph courtesy of Nina Maritz.)

kilometers south of the site). The terracotta bricks were set in a herringbone pattern, leveled, and embedded in compacted sand, allowing for future reuse if necessary.[13]

Resolving sustainability challenges

Though partly in response to cost constraints, the principal motivating factor of such decisions was a commitment to a strong sustainability approach that was sensitive to the site and expressive of the need for others to respect the fragility of the environment. For example, believing that the embodied energy within building debris should be recaptured whenever possible, the rubble generated from the destruction of the semi-derelict visitors' kiosk foundation was originally intended for use as fill for the gabions and faced with local sandstone. Due to the labor-intensive nature of demolishing the concrete slabs, however, the demolition rubble was used

FIGURE 9.27
The materials, building form, coloration, and rhythms are consciously selected to camouflage the building in its desert context. Note the low, irregular form of the museum to the left of the taller rock outcropping. All building elements are completely reversible. (Photograph courtesy of Nina Maritz.)

instead for the foundation and for fill around the newly installed toilet boxes.[14]

Unskilled workers were trained at the site to construct gabion walls and piers, a relatively new construction technology in Namibia. The square gabion footings served as anchoring points for the tubular steel columns that supported the curved wall screens made from the recycled oil drum lids. All steel trusses for the two-directional curved roof, and screen frames were fabricated (including welding and bending) on site with considerable savings. The curved steel frame, for example, was manufactured on site by a 'farmer-builder' who made a jig on his pick-up truck and bent every curve by hand. In addition, rock obstructions prevented the contractor from excavating footings; therefore, the gabion walls were simply built over the layer of rock, allowing for an increased reversibility factor. Addressing the extreme heat-gain factors and the strong glare component prominent in this region, the building turns its back to the sun, uses the gabion walls as heat sinks, has a softening effect on the strong glare, and offers a physical effect on cooling the air by shading passageways and creating cross-ventilation.

Filled with loose boulders to allow easy drainage, the gabion baskets could easily be disassembled without scarring the land if attitudes regarding the conservation and interpretation of the cultural resource changed over time. This self-effacing recognition that architecture, like the landscape of which it is a part, is dynamic and ever changing restrains Maritz's work, in general, from being overly grand. Quite the opposite, it strives to be lost amidst the landscape like a camouflaged desert creature (Figure 9.27). It is completely reversible, and has an almost zero energy requirement.

Architect's reflection

'Architecture is not about the visual [for me],' Maritz maintains. 'Buildings are about blending in so totally they can handle rain and drought, and virtually disappear into their surroundings.' But, as flexible as the design is in terms of present use and planned obsolescence, its situated design response is tied very literally to the complexities and character of this site *alone*. Maritz admits, 'Architecture is not really an international skill.' If you emigrate to another setting different from your own local knowledge, 'you cannot come to grips with it unless you totally immerse yourself to understand its subtleties. Big societies can operate on the surface,' she suggests. 'You really have to get into [these smaller] communities. It is not just a design *in* a community. You need to get to know it; read ethnological studies; get to know the people; and understand the delicate nature of the environment.'

Architecture, of course, is not an exact science. Maritz confesses, 'Clients want certainty, but architecture is like gardening. You visualize results, but you are never certain how it's going to turn out …

You don't just stop and go away after a project is completed. You take the ideas you were working on and improve upon them.'

Author's summary

Similar to Howard Davis, Nina Maritz utilizes an eco-centric approach that is deferential to both the setting and its people. Her place-based designs draw not only from her familiarity with broad environmental and social factors evident to her as a long-time resident of Namibia, but also from an immersion into the subregional particularities of each place. Functioning as a vernacular scholar as much as an environmental designer, she observes, listens, researches, inquires, and confirms her findings before moving to design development. During the design development stage, she continues to weigh her decisions in light of the environmental impact each of her decisions will have; she stresses a commitment to reversibility, and assesses the fitness of her design to the situational context. All these components of design are addressed with thoughtfulness and rendered with an economy of means in recognition of limited resources – both financial and environmental.

Maritz strives in her work 'to design with meaning and to leave behind a positive, memorable impact,' Her impact is felt not only through her completed work, but through the training in appropriate materials and technologies that her collaborative projects bring about.

While Maritz is the first to admit that many of her sustainable strategies (from dry toilets to evaporative cooling systems) are not new, they are not widely practiced in Namibia. Maritz is often the first in Namibia to introduce engineers to new environmental design systems, and holds training workshops for clients to disseminate such fundamental knowledge as how to set up solar water heating systems. The challenge she faces is that it is not enough to introduce sustainable technologies (especially as they relate to energy, water, and sanitation) into a region; there has to be a willingness within the culture to adopt a *sustainability ethos* that alters the way people interact, on a daily basis, with newer or innovative building practices that depart from the norm.

The elemental philosophy Maritz has established does not distinguish between sustainable and conventional design when addressing a client. Instead, her firm 'considers sustainability in terms of the environmental, the social, and the economic contexts essential in the design of *any* project.'[15] As Michael Cockram puts it, 'Sustainability is a way of thinking about the world and not just a series of line items on a spreadsheet.'

Maritz cites George Orwell's earlier quote from *The Decline of the English Murders and Other Essays*, drawing attention to his fourth great motive for a creative endeavor: 'a desire to push the world in a certain direction, to alter other people's ideas of the kind of society they should strive for.' Nina Maritz has given us a set of principles to consider and is beginning to offer a built record for each of us to draw from in achieving that goal.

Suggested reading

Cockram, M. (2007). The sustainability of Nina Maritz. *Architecture Week*, 338 (June 13), 1–4.

Kwok, A. G. and Grondzik, W. T. (2007). *The Green Studio Handbook: Environmental Strategies for Schematic Design*, Architectural Press.

Maritz, N. (2005). Visitors' Interpretive Centre for a Prehistoric Rock Art Site at Twyfelfontein, Namibia, a paper presented at *Enabling Frameworks for Sustainability*, the Fourth South African Conference on Sustainable Built Environments, June 22–24, 2005.

—— (2006). Emerging architecture: a small practice in Namibia, a paper presented at *Sustainable Building: Mitigating Social and Environmental Poverty*, the Third South African Conference on Sustainable Built Environments, University of the Free State, Bloemfontein, South Africa, July 26–28, 2006.

——Visitors' Interpretive Rock Art Centre, Twyfelfontein, *Digest of Namibian Architecture* 2007 (edition 5), 68–71.

Marshal, S. and Kearney, B. (2000) *Opportunities for Relevance: Architecture in the New South Africa*. UNISA.

McDonald, D. and Maritz, N. (2006). Drums and stones – building with recycled materials: pitfalls and successes, a paper presented at *Renewable Energy: Key to Climate Recovery*, conference of the American Solar Energy Society, Denver, Colorado, July 7–13, 2006. Available in its *Proceedings*. American Solar Energy Society.

Mendelssohn, J., et al. (2002). *Atlas of Namibia, a Portrait of the Land and its People*. David Philip.

Notes

1. Nina Maritz was born in Pretoria. Her father was Namibian and her mother was South African. Ms Maritz grew up in Port Elizabeth on the south coast of South Africa. Her parents moved to Namibia in 1986, four years before Namibia's independence from South Africa. Maritz completed her architectural degree in 1991, and established her practice in Namibia in 1998 at the age of 31.
2. Unless otherwise indicated, all quotations are from a series of personal interviews between the architect and

author, and lecture comments quoted with permission by the architect during a conference at the University of Oregon, April 18–20, 2007, sponsored by the Historic Preservation Program and the Department of Architecture. Additional insights by the architect were provided in a lecture delivered in Canova, Italy, on July 10, 2008.
3. Maritz points out, however, that Namibia's 'transport and services infrastructure, health services, education system, judicial system and telecommunications are of the best in Africa.' Data compiled from Mendelssohn, J. et al. (2002), *Atlas of Namibia, a Portrait of the Land and its People*. Cited in Nina Maritz (2006), Emerging architecture: a small practice in Namibia.
4. In a follow-up essay on the modifications, challenges and performance of the project after completion, Maritz discusses that such second-hand drums are sought after in agriculture. Hence, the 600 drums needed had to be purchased in lots of ten to fifty at a time, because the air charter companies stockpile their supply and demand high prices. This item caused some time delay on the project. Nina Maritz (2006), Drums and stones – building with recycled materials: pitfalls and successes.
5. N. Maritz (2007), Visitors' Interpretive Rock Art Centre, Twyfelfontein, 71.
6. —— (2008), lecture delivered in Canova, Italy, July 10, 2008.
7. —— (2008), lecture delivered in Canova, Italy, July 10, 2008.
8. —— (2005),Visitors' Interpretive Centre for a Prehistoric Rock Art Site at Twyfelfontein, Namibia.
9. —— (2007), Visitors' Interpretive Rock Art Centre, Twyfelfontein, 70.
10. —— (2007), Visitors' Interpretive Rock Art Centre, Twyfelfontein, 71.
11. More specifically, 'Twyfelfontein has a median and average rainfall of 50 to 100 mm per annum (2 to 3 inches), with a 70 or 90 percent coefficient of variation. Temperatures are high throughout the year (averages of 34 to 36 degrees C maximum in the summer and 8 to 10 degrees C in winter), with relatively low humidity. The main environmental constraint is the extreme radiation and resultant heat and glare.' Quoted in Maritz, Visitors' Interpretive Centre for a Prehistoric Rock Site at Twyfelfontein, Namibia, 2.
12. N. Maritz (2008), lecture delivered in Canova, Italy, July 10, 2008.
13. With regard to the scarcity of water, it is delivered once a week from a nearby (20 km) commercial lodge by truck and placed in a high-tank, 5,500 liter, storage system; visitors' litter is removed on the return trip and taken to a landfill. Water usage is restricted to hand washing for the public; showers (cold) and drinking water are provided for the staff. The water drain into a hand-made French drainage system. Nine dry toilets are provided for the visitors and staff. Maritz, Visitors' Interpretive Centre for a Prehistoric Rock Site at Twyfelfontein, Namibia, 5. The discussion of the steel frame was cited in Maritz, Drums and stones.
14. Maritz, Drums and stones.
15. ——, Emerging architecture: a small practice in Namibia.

10

Celebrating and safeguarding the environment through residential design

People look at a gnarly tree and ledge and think Maine is rugged, but it's not. Just look at the lichens and mosses: it's easy for a person walking on them to destroy them. Architects should be looking that closely at a site before they do anything.[1]

Carol A. Wilson

Project: A Writer's Studio
Location: Mount Desert Island, Maine, USA
Architect: Carol A. Wilson
Time frame: One year of construction during 2003

Introduction

Wilson has earned a reputation as one of the most environmentally conscious architects practicing in Maine today. Recently elevated to the American Institute of Architects' College of Fellows (an honor bestowed previously upon only four Maine architects), Carol A. Wilson's work stresses an attention to place, whether in teaching a class at Bowdoin College's Coastal Studies Center, or siting a residence gently into an environmentally fragile coastal terrain. Winner of a 2004 AIA New England Design Award, and a 2004 AIA Maine Design Award, Carol Wilson's project for a Writer's Studio offers insights into a situated regional response by its sensitivity to the site conditions, its spatial economy, and its accommodation of the clients' highly particularized needs. Her design solutions yield sun-filled spaces, a merger of interior and exterior realms of experience, and elegant detailing that evoke the building's locale through the innate suitability of design elements. Though a native of North Carolina, after twenty-seven years of living in Maine, her work is Maine-internalized, accommodated, and revered.

The regional filter

Somes Sound (the only fjord in the USA) bifurcates Mt Desert Island. It defines a long, narrow, deep inlet of the sea between steep slopes, forming a natural fortress against the pounding force of the ocean. The island's regional character evolved from activities tied to granite quarrying and fishing economies into a summer resort area for *rusticators* by the end of the nineteenth century. As such, the area has a long fallow season when the summer residents and tourists are absent, and high seasonal demands on the area sites, particularly for water, during the summer and early fall. There is also a pattern of people from *away* 'buying up the island and those selling moving off.' The preservation of a regional culture, therefore, is one of the challenges that both locals and architects face. 'People come here to live in Acadia (National Park). They migrate to Maine in the summer to soothe their souls. With the locals now being displaced, it is quiet in winter.' Due to the shift in the economic base to tourism, the emphasis is, as Wilson put it, on the 'marketing of culture.' How, then, does an architect contribute to the essential characteristics that make a place unique without resorting to simply copying what is already there or, more to the point, what outsiders *expect to be there*? Carol Wilson's preference is to celebrate *where* the project is situated, and to address the needs of her clients so that they feel at one with the place (Figure 10.2).

Copyright © 2009 Elsevier Ltd. All rights reserved.

Celebrating and safeguarding the environment through residential design **147**

FIGURE 10.1
A Writer's Studio in Maine, one of four recipients of an Honor Award for Excellence in Architecture from the American Institute of Architects, New England Chapter. (Photograph courtesy of Brian Vanden Brink.)

Site demands

There is a sixty percent slope from the building site to the water's edge. The hillside land, comprised of many acres, originally was set amidst a stand of old conifer trees, offering filtered views of Somes Sound. 'A storm with hurricane force winds had caused a blow-down of trees, leaving a grove of tall, spindly eastern white pines (*Pinus strobes* – the only pine native to Maine) and eastern hemlock (*Tsuga canadensis*).' Site factors determined the tall, scaffold-like profile of the Writer's Studio that resulted. The tall steel framework was a necessity as an ecological measure. The topsoil is only a few inches deep, inhibiting the regeneration of the lichen and the under-story once disturbed. 'Excavating did not make sense. The point was not to disturb the little soil base that existed by building a basement and cutting into the earth.' What results is a lofty form that respects its site, allows for reversibility, and provides a thin structural profile of the foundation supports that mirrors the newly thinned trees (Figure 10.3).

Strong winds, such as those that accompanied the aforementioned storm, are commonplace,

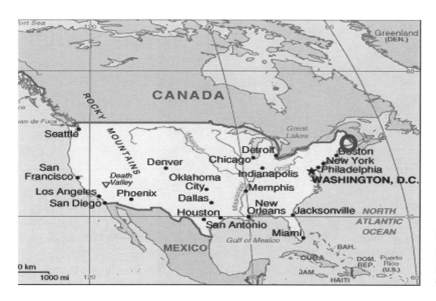

FIGURE 10.2
Mount Desert Island, Maine, USA, context map. (Map courtesy of CIA *World Fact Book*.)

FIGURE 10.3
View of the south-facing aspect of the Writer's Studio amidst the tree cover. (Photograph courtesy of Brian Vanden Brink.)

necessitating extra precautions against wind loading. Once the steel framework was constructed, cross bracing was added below the structure of the Writer's Studio; 'the frame is not completely rigid, so that it could move a bit. A second section of cable bracing was added later to resist movement and ease the clients' concerns' (Figure 10.4).

Architect's intent

The architect's intent was to address the issue of *place* by having the human intervention of a structure on a building site be as physically invisible as possible; do as little damage to the site in the process; avail itself to the beauty of the locale; and address the clients'

FIGURE 10.4
View of the studio footprint from below. (Photograph by the author.)

principal needs – not just wants. When viewed from the lower end of the site's topography, the structure stands as a built testimony to these premises. The entire footprint of the Writer's Studio is visible, allowing water drainage, the lay of the land, animal access, and site lines to permeate the area, which might normally be occupied by a structure.

Such commitment to the preservation of a site's integrity runs deep with Wilson. In a correspondence with the author on August 24, 2007, she stated, 'Having grown up in the South, Maine's image as a *North* land still holds quite an impression on me.' Wilson then quoted T.S. Eliot as if a mantra:

> It is not necessarily those lands which are the most fertile or most favored in climate that seem to me the happiest, but those in which a long struggle of adaptation between man and his environment has brought out the best qualities of both. (After Strange Gods)

Trained at North Carolina State University's School of Design when Henry Kamphoefner was the Dean, her commitment to the development of a skill base in industrial design and woodworking led to her appreciation of the act of *making*. During a 2007 interview with Carol Wilson at her studio in Falmouth, Maine, she referenced a lecture she was giving with regard to the role of the architect today who often stands aloof when it comes to the direct involvement with the construction process. Her premise was, 'architects don't *make* anything. We draw a cryptic set of instructions on large sheets of paper telling someone *else* how to make or construct a *thing* – a house, or a school, or a bridge – something that we have imagined and considered in sketches or in the miniature form of models, both substitutes for the actual architecture that fluctuate between reality and fiction. Architects operate in an abstract world. The work is almost entirely executed on paper and the irony is, that when the thing is constructed, the notation [citing the architect as the creator] becomes irrelevant and can be tossed out.'

The ultimate success of any project, Wilson insists, is one-third the influence of the architect, one-third the client, and one-third the builder. Hence, architecture is a collective social act. 'Between creating and making,' she states, 'is the interstitial role of the architect.' She smiles as she confides that her lecture disputes the Governor of the State of Maine's categorization of the architect's place in society as ' "part of the creative economy of the state" ', just another way of marketing culture, making a commodity of local artists, artisans, and craftspeople.'

FIGURE 10.5
View of the entrance of the Writer's Studio, facing southeast. (Photograph by the author.)

Given such premises, Wilson is careful to nuance the relationships among the client, the contractor, and herself. 'When people from "away" decide to build in Maine, they intuitively head toward home, seeking the familiar. Maine does not elicit suburban houses and grass lawns. My intent – as Landscape Architect Walter Hood states it – is "to mine and divine the soul of the place," [and be] careful not to destroy the thing that brought us here in the first place.'

The elevated site could have posed a problem for the client in this regard. 'It is a cultural need for some to touch the earth [the only direct ground contact was from the drive into the front hallway (see Figure 10.5)]. But, these clients live on the second and third floor of Seventy-Second Street in New York City.' Hence, they were preconditioned to inhabiting a lofty space situated above the ground level.

She added, 'The impact on a site that has had little human intervention in one hundred years can change overnight. Once, an excavator, thinking he was doing me a favor, removed all the trees within the building envelope.' She sees it as the role of the architect to sensitize the client and the contractor to the particular ecological determinants surrounding the project. 'My clients tend to be particularly well educated. They know issues of the environment, and resist excess. They can see value in a space that can serve many purposes, and [tend not] to spend or build in excess. We are learning to build only what we need.'

Design process

Unlike Glenn Murcutt (see the next case study), who takes his principal design cues from climate

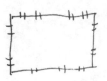 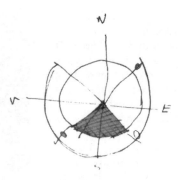

FIGURE 10.6
Diagram on the left is of a typical New England house with an equal number of windows on all sides. Diagram on the right indicates the circuit of December sunlight for the Writer's Studio. (Demonstration sketches drawn by Carol Wilson for the author.)

condition assessments (among just a few of the environmental determinants he responds to), Wilson's focus is primarily on the client. 'You have to understand the sensibilities of the client.' Will their residence be, metaphorically speaking, for 'a Cardinal in the woods, a Puritan in the woods,' or in this case, a writer in the woods? (The first two designations are how the clients characterized their homes.)

'It involves a mediation process. Understanding site issues and appropriate responses are not rocket science. The sun angles are fixed [Figure 10.6]; wind, for the most part, comes from the same direction; there is not a very diverse flora. What makes every project different is the client.' Sometimes the dialog between the client and Wilson takes over a year. '[I] survey the site and see the property on the map, because it gives me a better understanding [of the site] from which to develop a plan and section.'

Design concept

Originally conceived as part of a larger plan that included separate living quarters, Wilson's highly efficient plan for the Writer's Studio, precisely detailed fixtures, and elegantly designed built-in features resulted in a multi-use studio and summer living quarters for the New York-based clients – motion picture screenwriter Jay Cocks and his actress wife Verna Bloom. Simplicity was the goal throughout – a simple line of rooms that could extend (or close off) public and private spaces, as well as unite/separate interior and exterior activities.

By utilizing design strategies that she employed in a model modular housing project in Falmouth, Maine (the research and development phase of *House One* was undertaken with partner Susan Ruch and built by Burlington Homes of New England between 1990 and 1994), rational design principles were applied to a different topography, plant life,

FIGURE 10.7
View of the Writer's Studio illustrating reduced northern exposure. (Photograph courtesy of Brian Vanden Brink.)

Celebrating and safeguarding the environment through residential design

FIGURE 10.8
House One, Falmouth, Maine, was designed as a prototype for improved modular housing by Carol Wilson and Susan Ruch and built by Burlington Homes of New England in 1994. This highly flexibly open plan now serves as the home and studio (detached) for Carol Wilson. (Photograph by the author.)

and climate zone (Figure 10.8).² Soon the clients accepted the notion of living/dining in one room with the kitchen/bath wall as a barrier. Wilson maintains, 'Good design is not an issue of affordable design or million dollar design. It's the way you choose to live.' For Wilson, the difference in price often turns on the quality and durability of the materials selected, rather than shifting her design principles for each project.

Project description

Simplicity of form and space does not, however, translate into stark bareness in the Writer's Studio; simple elements are often used as foils to orchestrate the building in other ways – often by tapping into the wonders of the natural setting. The flexibility of an open plan is maintained throughout (Figure 10.9). It is perhaps worth noting that one of the books in her personal library is a monograph on Mies' Farnsworth House. Moving down the hallway from the entry (sheltered beneath a covered sun deck off the parking area) is a thirty-six foot band of sliding glass doors leading to a deck to its right (south). This route has built-in storage closets above (Figure 10.10). Immediately to the left of the hallway is the living/dining space, while the principal circulation path leads to the studio space: the generative space for the rest of the design.

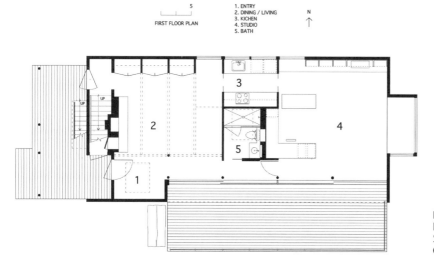

FIGURE 10.9
Plan view of the Writer's Studio. (Plan courtesy of Carol Wilson.)

FIGURE 10.10
View looking east along the passageway to the studio area. Note the thirty-six foot band of windows facing south (pictured on the right) and the revolving sunshades situated above. Additional storage is featured above the passageway (pictured upper left). (Photograph courtesy of Brian Vanden Brink.)

Film, art, and architecture critic (*Time, Rolling Stone*) and motion picture screenwriter Jay Cocks (*Age of Innocence*, 1993 and *Gangs of New York*, 2002) 'knows music, artists, and designers,' Wilson remarks. Opposite his custom-designed writing desk is a bank of cabinetry for his stereo, CD player, and audio videotape equipment. The cabinets are built in with adjustable drawers. 'The desk is made of continuous veneer "folded" at the vertical corner.' It wraps around an interior corner to provide an unobstructed work surface. Wilson designed the desk, all the cabinets, and the light fixtures. Part of the L-shaped desk space that accommodates his computer terminal is inserted into a wall alcove with recessed lights above. This hollowed-out space is answered in plan by the window seat/day bed area located directly behind the desk area that projects from the mass of the east-facing end of the studio. The other wing of the desk provides a southern prospect of the sound. Hence, the simple arrangement of the desk provides opportunities for concentrated work, and for visual relief (Figures 10.11–10.13). A well-designed work area is a way of honoring the work that is being done; and, for those individuals whose work defines much of who they are, having a work environment that also feeds their soul is a joy.

As Wilson points out, 'Maine gets wonderful warm days. They are rare, but when they occur they are nice and you want to avail yourself to them. You want windows and doors that open and close easily,

FIGURE 10.11
Photo of screenwriter Jay Cocks at his desk in the recessed work area. Note the M-Screen sun control roll-down shades to adjust light filtration in the studio work area (pictured upper left over the sliding window). (Photograph by the author.)

FIGURE 10.12
Interior view from the writer's desk looking east toward the window seat/day bed. Somes Sound is seen in the distance. To the right are the sliding glass doors and spinnaker cloth light/sun control curtains (not pictured here). The glass doors connect the studio with the south-facing deck looking out to the Sound, and offers varying degrees of enclosure. (Photograph courtesy of Brian Vanden Brink.)

for example. When the fog rolls in, a spinnaker cloth curtain is pulled along the thirty-six foot band of windows. The cloth is not an insulated fabric; it has a soft plastic quality. When the wind blows through the open sliding door units, it adds drama at the same time that it diffuses light and lends privacy.' Here is where Wilson's background in materials fabrication comes into play. It allows her to achieve the maximum effect by selecting (and sometimes crafting) the right material for the conditions desired. 'In addition to the spinnaker cloth curtains,' she continues 'the roll-down shades are made of a French material – M-Screen, a sun control fabric used for blinds and awnings. I use it to achieve a different percentage of light filtration. In addition we have room-darkening shades that allow for screening videos. You can fine tune the room environmentally: when you are working, when you leave, for temperature and light control.'

A coffee counter, efficiency kitchen, and the water closet are in close proximity immediately to the right of the desk. The galley kitchen and bath are

FIGURE 10.13
Interior view of the Writer's Studio looking west toward the writer's desk from the sleeping alcove. Note the public and private circulation paths on either side of the work area. (Photograph courtesy of Brian Vanden Brink.)

FIGURE 10.14
Interior view of the Writer's Studio looking west toward the living room's Rais Danish woodstove. Note the multiple circulation routes to the right and left. (Photograph by the author.)

FIGURE 10.15
Interior view looking west, showing the steel columns running through the interior space. (Photograph by the author.)

along the second circulation path to the right of the desk leading to the living/dining space (Figure 10.14). It can be closed off from traffic. A recessed door folds flush against the hallway circulation path to the left of the desk; it can also isolate this space from noise and traffic.

Moving down the north-facing hallway from the kitchen and bath zone toward the entry, multiple circulation routes are afforded to the right and left of the living room. To the left is the outdoor access from the driveway. Opposite this hallway is another corridor with built-in cabinets. This path provides access to the ground level, or up an interior set of stairs to a sky-lit loft, or outside to the tubular steel-framed catwalk (Figure 10.15).

Building materials

The long, rectangular, shed-roof form is raised on isolated footings. Its cedar shingle cladding softens its presence amidst the trees. In its construction, Wilson employed a steel framing system (a steel armature with SIPS Panels, structural insulated roof panels), as opposed to her earlier frames of clear recycled Douglas fir timbers shipped in from the northwest; steel was used in lieu of Douglas fir not only because the timbers were more expensive, but because the energy expended in long-distance delivery was a factor in the project's sustainable considerations. Round columns with inverted 'T' column caps and beams were painted and finished on the inside where they rise through the interior living spaces (refer back to Figure 10.15). On the roof, the structural insulated panels have cedar shingles placed over Cedar Breather and airspace. Wilson comments, 'Today I would use spray-in foam underneath instead of the sealed packets of fiberglass that were used.'

The floor has radiant heat, but in Maine, she points out 'it cannot respond quickly [enough] to differential heat and cold changes. Radiant heat is slow to raise the temperature. You need some type of heat back up (here is it hot air through a fan coil unit on the boiler), or you can light the Rais Danish woodstove in the living room space.'

As for other systems, the clients insisted that they did not want a propane tank for their gas cooking. They did not understand that unlike New York City, where natural gas is piped into their apartment, remote Maine has few underground utilities. Because this was a client-specific design project, the mechanics of the house had to be reconsidered in light of the design intent. Wilson buried the propane tank uphill, away from the water. This allowed an unobstructed view that preserved the shoreline and met the needs of the client.

'I insulated the core underneath the building where the mechanical systems were placed. Like an umbilical cord, this is the place where utilities come in and waste goes out.' The kitchen and bath are located directly above the core and stand freely between the studio and living room. Solar orientation was considered to maximize the exposure of

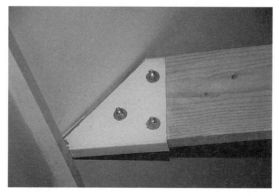

FIGURES 10.16 AND 10.17
Template designed by Wilson for a joist/rafter connection. This assembly ties the collar beam, top plate, and rafter on a twelve-by-twelve roof pitch together seamlessly. (Photographs by the author.)

the studio to the south (where the sliding glass door panels are), and minimize its exposure to the north.

Other materials and fixtures were selected for their durability and quality. 'The light fixtures are Italian. The Oslo window and doors (manufactured across the border in Canada by *Oslo Portes et Fenêtres ltée*) are equipped with German hardware so that the window units lift and roll. The nine feet by eighteen feet sliding door units were a special order. Most commercial manufacturers limit glass to sixty square feet in size. They are made of wind resistant, full one inch insulating glass – safety on one side and tempered on the other.' The lower glass panels measured nine feet by nine feet, while the upper panels were scaled down to seven feet by nine feet to subtly adjust the south elevation's compositional harmony. All wood cladding is 'harvested sustainable shingles of red cedar (unfortunately imported) from the Northwest.' She notes, 'Eastern white cedar is now grown so rapidly that it lacks the resin content that makes it durable without dipping and staining.'

As Wilson discusses her own joist hanger design for a seamless joist and wall connection, it becomes clear that material selection, detailing, and fabrication are her special joys and strengths. 'Architecture has a hands-on quality. This is why I like working at the residential scale. It allows me to understand the rules written in materials and detailing' (Figures 10.16 and 10.17).

FIGURE 10.18
Demonstration model of the modular units as viewed from behind House One looking toward the architect's studio (the studio is located to the upper right of this view and was a later addition, as was the study at the lower left). (Model by Carol Wilson; photograph by the author.)

But we might ask, 'how do the expensive design features in the Writer's Studio represent the principle of "living with less" and building "only what we need?"' Recall Carol Wilson's statement: 'Good design is not an issue of affordable design or million-dollar design. It's the way you choose to live … The difference in price often turns on the quality and durability of the materials selected, rather than shifting [my] design principles for each project.' A brief look at the design strategies for her *House One* project reinforces her point.

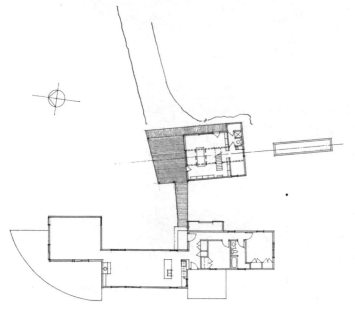

FIGURE 10.19
Plan view of House One with later additions. (Plan courtesy of Carol Wilson.)

Celebrating and safeguarding the environment through residential design

FIGURE 10.20
View of House One on site, looking from the studio deck space toward the interlocking cube of the bedroom/livingroom. (Photograph courtesy of Carol Wilson.)

House One

The design intent for *House One* was to provide an alternative product built in one of Maine's mobile home factories to fit the entry market for first-time homebuyers – housing that was sustainable and affordable. It was conceived within very tight and careful design parameters using the existing operations of the factory system geared to the manufactured house. As noted in the book *Building Tomorrow: The Mobile/Manufactured Housing Industry*, manufactured homes are the number one means of unsubsidized housing in the USA.

Wilson points out that *House One* components were largely determined by lending requirements for conventional mortgages at a lower rate of interest (as opposed to a chattel mortgage) by meeting the *BOCA National Building Code* rather than the HUD (US Department of Housing and Urban Development) Code that applies to factory-constructed manufactured homes. HUD Code modular housing, for the most part, depreciates in value. The house plan was conceived as an open-ended 1,100 square foot generic space. Measuring sixteen feet by seventy-two feet, the massing allowed for shifting boxes that could adjust to varying site conditions (Figures 10.18 and 10.19). The goal was to do as much work in the factory as possible. As Wilson stresses, 'prefab housing gets expensive when people depend on work to be done on site. We limited site work to minor patching and painting.'

The spaces were based on the dimension of a four by eight feet sheet of plywood. There was a standard twelve by twelve (45°) roof pitch. Specially designed collar tie connections accommodated painted and finished drywall-sheathed roof panels that were set in place on the site. Pine T-1-11 type plywood siding with 4-inch wide kerfs to look like vertical board siding was stained on the exterior.

In 1997, Wilson purchased the house, land, and private septic from the *House One: A Maine Corporation*; this was the corporation she and her partner set up for the design and manufacture of prefabricated housing. She later added a study, a deck facing the marsh, and a detached studio which allows her to work at home (Figures 10.20 and 10.21). Her rationale was: 'if you commute, you often turn your brain on and off. It was time consuming and disruptive to me in the creative process getting in my car. Continuum [of thought] is important in Architecture.' After five years of research and development of *House One* she admitted, 'I wanted to be an architect, not be a businesswoman. It was the pursuit and level of inquiry – a problem to solve – that motivated me.' The purchase of the model modular home by the architect stressed Wilson's own commitment to the principle of living with less. Those avenues of inquiry led directly to the design resolution of the Writer's Studio as well as other projects, where the needs of the clients – not just their wants – were achieved in the least amount of space.

Suggested reading by the architect

New England A.I.A. Awards (2005). *Architecture Week*, March 30, N2.1.
Cronon, W. (1983). *Changes in the Land: Indians, Colonists, and the Ecology of New England*. Hill and Wang.
Kreisler, H. (2004). *A Geographer's Perspective on the New American Imperialism: A Conversation with David Harvey, Distinguished Professor of Anthropology, City University of New York, March 2, 2004*. Available at http://globetrotter.berkeley.edu.people4/Harvey/Harvey-con1.html

FIGURE 10.21
View from House One looking toward the architect's detached studio. (Photograph by the author.)

Lippard, L. R. (1997). *The Lure of the Local: Senses of Place in a Multicentered Society*. New Press.

Lopez, B. (1998). The American geographies. In *About this Life: Journeys on the Threshold of Memory*. Knopf, 130–143.

Sandel, M. J. (1998). What money can't buy: the moral limits of markets – The Tanner Lectures on Human Values. Delivered at Brasenose College, University of Oxford, Oxford, UK (May 11–12, 1998). Available at www.tannerlectures.utah.edu/lectures/sandel00.pdf

Summer Guide (2005). *Portland Monthly Magazine*, 42–49.

Notes

1. Architect Carol Wilson finds new sense of place at CSC (2005). *Campus News*, Bowdoin College, October 27. Available at http://www.bowdoin.edu/news/archives/1bowdoincampus/oo2583.shtml
2. See House One (1994), *PA*, July, 34, for details.

11

Architecture of response rather than imposition

[The work of most architects] reflects no understanding of ecology or ecological process. Most tell its users that knowing where they are is unimportant. Most tell its users that energy is cheap and abundant and can be squandered. Most are provisioned with materials and water and dispose of their wastes in ways that tell its occupants that we are not part of the larger web of life. Most resonate with no part of our biology, evolutionary experience, or aesthetic sensibilities.

David Orr, quoted with permission from a letter dated September 7, 2005 to Glenn Murcutt from Stephen R. Kellert, Tweedy Ordway Professor of Social Ecology, Yale University.

Project: The House in Kangaroo Valley, New South Wales, Australia
Location: Latitude 34 degrees 44 minutes south, longitude 150 degrees 32 minutes, altitude about 30 meters
Architect: Glenn Murcutt, sole practitioner
Time frame: 2001–2003 – Design development
2003–2005 – Construction

Introduction

Born in London in 1936, but raised in the Morobe district of New Guinea, Murcutt learned in his early years the pragmatics that come with frontier living. He soon learned that being attuned to natural forces was a key to both survival and spiritual fulfillment.

Pritzker Prize Laureate (2002) Murcutt recently taught at the University of Washington (USA) as the Callison Distinguished Visiting Professor in the Department of Architecture.[1] His keynote lecture on May 18, 2007 entitled 'The Kangaroo Valley House: From Concept to Detail,' and a subsequent interview on May 19 with the author, provide insights into the process involved in moving from site schematics to final construction details by one of the world's leading environmental designers. Murcutt often collaborates with his wife, architect Wendy Lewin.

In the letter cited at the beginning of this chapter, Stephen Kellert goes on to describe Murcutt's design premises and practice as contributing positively to 'an emerging … movement to reform prevailing architectural practice by enhancing a largely low environmental impact design perspective, [and] enhancing beneficial human contact with natural systems and processes.' By focusing on the design process that Murcutt employs in his most recent residential project, it is hoped that this chapter will provide insights into his design approach that stress touching the earth lightly, and enhancing the occupant's connection with the forces and sensory attributes of nature. Murcutt offers a brand of regionalism that is situated in the specific environmental and phenomenological forces of a locale. This environmental awareness is coupled with a close examination of Australia's traditional building culture for insights into adaptive environmental response. This field data is filtered through his environmental principles and broad-ranging technical skills to produce a built symphony expressive of a residence that is at one with its natural setting (Figure 11.1).

Regional filter

Climatic extremes define much of the regional character of Australia. In Australia's Northern Territory, for example, are the monsoonal tropics where rain falls up to one foot an hour. High humidity and high temperatures accompany the heavy rainfall and underline the need for ventilation. Murcutt merges his awareness of the region's environmental

Copyright © 2009 Elsevier Ltd. All rights reserved.

FIGURE 11.1
View of the east façade of the House in Kangaroo Valley. (Photograph courtesy of Glenn Murcutt.)

dictates with his analysis of the indigenous Australian aboriginal huts and the way they address these natural forces. 'They are beautiful and often long. They use lightweight timber posts that raise the structure off of the ground level to protect against the heat, rain, and crocodiles. The frame is clad with bark that bends like corrugated iron. The bark is cured over the fire to flatten it and then turned in the other direction against the grain. The open ends are often oriented toward the prevailing cooling winds.'[2]

As an architect dedicated to working exclusively in Australia, such local knowledge of vernacular responses is not adopted literally; instead, it is reconsidered to address modern needs and opportunities (Figure 11.2). Perhaps Nihal Perera's term *critical vernacular* fits here (see Perera case study earlier in this text). Murcutt's design strategies, when deemed appropriate, look to indigenous architectural resources while implementing contemporary technological methods for improving ecological performance.

Accordingly, Murcutt's house designs in the Northern Territory, like the Marika-Alderton House, rely on long, open, adjustable walls that ventilate by way of cooling breezes. The walls can also be adjusted to insulate from heat while protecting the house from strong winds. Long, low, narrow forms occur frequently in Murcutt's designs as a way of manipulating drafts and facilitating heating and cooling demands. These signature elements are not mere design vocabulary; they are adjusted to the environmental specifics of each site (Figure 11.3).

For the practicing architect, such insights offer the true value of exploring the vernacular building process – in lieu of simply pilfering regional imagery for its pictorial appeal. Though visually less obvious to a casual observer, these place-based strategies provide a relevant continuation of a traditional building culture. As pointed out in the first section of this text, an area's regional filter is never static. Design professionals can introduce appropriate technologies that are responsive to issues of ecological performance and, at the same time, be in accord with prevailing cultural values. Collectively, such adjustments to the forces of nature and the sensibilities of place forge a situated regional response.

Project description

Q: 'How did you interview your clients to understand what their priorities were? Did you use a questionnaire, for example, as some architects do?'

A: 'We met at the site a number of times over the course of three years [2001–2003]. We discussed the size, their aspirations for the house, budget, and program. I don't use client questionnaires. The clients give answers to questionnaires that can be misleading and it can go horribly wrong. Informal discussions work. The clients become friends.'

This house, initially, will be used for weekend stays, since its location between Sydney and Canberra allows the family to attend to business and drive up on Fridays. Though the clients presently live in Sydney, they plan to live in Kangaroo Valley permanently upon retirement.

Architecture of response rather than imposition   161

FIGURE 11.2
Australia's regional divisions, indicating the location of Kangaroo Valley, near Canberra. (Map courtesy of US Central Intelligence Agency, *World Fact Book*, 1999.)

The setting for the House in Kangaroo Valley is within a dairying area with mountain views on the north, south, east, and west (Figure 11.4). The house site is also located at the base of a sacred mountain.

Climate context

Located slightly less than thirty-five degrees south of the equator, the Kangaroo Valley House has its own particularized site and climate conditions to

FIGURE 11.3
Marika-Alderton house in Yirrkala Community Eastern Arnhem Land, Northern Territory, Australia, 1991 to 1994. (Photograph courtesy of Glenn Murcutt.)

FIGURE 11.4
The setting for the house in Kangaroo Valley is characterized as a dairy farming area set within rolling meadows and mountain ridges. (Photograph courtesy of Glenn Murcutt.)

accommodate (Figure 11.5). 'Kangaroo Valley is not near any major city but between Sydney and Canberra; neither is representative of the climate of Kangaroo Valley.' Murcutt adds, 'Sydney, being coastal, is closest as it is on the east of the Great Dividing Range, the water shedding side. Canberra has a totally different climate, very hot summers – days of thirty to forty degrees centigrade. During the winter it can snow. The nearest town is Nowra. About eight kilometers inland from Nowra is Kangaroo Valley – on the coastal side of the Great Dividing Range. [Kangaroo Valley, therefore,] has a coastal climatic influence.'

Note the level of specificity (and the range of site considerations) that Murcutt brings to the predesign phase of the project: 'Temperatures vary daily throughout the year. The summer can see temperatures reach 38 degrees (rare) daytime, then drop to 15 degrees during the night maybe two days a year. Often, it is 20–26 degrees C for a month and during the equinox is 18–22 degrees C during the day with night temperatures falling to 15–20 degrees C. Humidity is not the issue here, although it can get to 80% very occasionally. [Also], there can be no N.E. breezes from the sea, so a floor fan is employed to get the air moving (up to 15 days/nights/year). We do not expect to have a constant internal thermal/humidity environment as do North Americans – we adjust our clothing.

'Winter days can reach 22 degrees C and, when there is no sun and S.W. winds come off of the snow fields some 200 km away, it can reach 10 degrees C.

Winter nights can drop to 3 degrees C. During the winter, the humidity is low (30%) with cool temperatures at night (3–10C), warming to 18–22C during the day. There is a beautiful thermal shift (diurnal) in temperature day/night. From the northeast come prevailing breezes. Sun in the winter comes over the mountains.'

The valley receives six feet of rain, often in heavy downpours. The environmental determinants

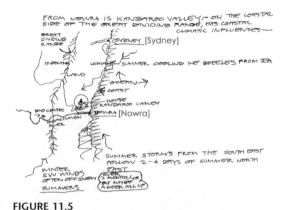

FIGURE 11.5
Detail of Kangaroo Valley within its environmental context. The ocean is to the right; the coastline is to the left. Note the coastal climatic influences. 'Summer cooling NE breezes from sea. Summer storms from the south east follow 2–4 days of summer north east. Winter SW winds often come off of the snow [fields] (over 2 months/yr., but maybe a week all up.' (Sketch and notations by Glenn Murcutt for the author.)

establish a need for rain catchments to harvest storm water in anticipation of the dry season, and site references are balanced with a desire to address seasonal sun angles.

Murcutt's brilliance as a designer, of course, lies in what he does with this data.

Design process

'In designing, my first move of course is to understand the site conditions.' In his lecture on the evening of May 18, 2007, Murcutt showed a 360-degree composite view photo of the building site (Figure 11.6).

Then, a contour plan is prepared by a registered land surveyor as required by law. 'From the contour plan, I generate sections of the site and beyond, taking into account mountain ranges, significant topographical features, trees, rocks, and water patterns.' The contour plan and panorama photograph are used as aids in deciding where to place the building between the points of the trees as spatial, visual, and environmental determinants (Figure 11.7).

These site notations are often followed by diagrams of sun angles with the section and plan together (Figure 11.8). The calculations prompt considerations such as solar gain, and air movements from positive to negative pressure. Roof strategies begin to be worked out in relation to sight lines (Figure 11.9). During these stages of the design, there are no elevations. He just focuses on the spaces rendered in section and plan as ideas to work through. He slowly builds up ideas to another level.

Once again, Murcutt references the design solutions of aboriginal cultures in his characterizations of regional response: 'Walls are open, yet slatted and used for privacy. From these traditional avenues of thought and behavior, Murcutt shifts quickly to how he precisely calculates the specific climatic demands affecting the site. 'I use a clinometer to determine the height of trees. I look up documents on a specific growth pattern for a tree and correct [for sun angles to the north in winter to avoid shade]. I'll calculate the angle of the mountains to determine to what degree they might block the sun, and get winter sun angles. I shoot an angle of the site's topography. Take dimensions for site conditions as opposed to surveyor's tools.'

Ideas are worked out for spaces that infer optimum breezes, light, and site references that reveal landscape features (Figure 11.10). Then, a fully drawn-up plan is presented to the client to respond to: 'captured light, filtered light, options for roof angles, a gallery is suggested – it's mad, but you suggest it.' The plan – a single loaded, narrow plan with details discussed earlier – generates a discussion of strategies for modifying spatial conditions with blinds, roof space, lighting, framing of views, slats. 'We hold onto the simple pitch of the roof. There is far less corridor space. There is a living room, dining room, kitchen, guest suite' – all designed with the spatial efficiency of a cabin on board a sailing skiff like the one built by Murcutt during his twenties. The interior corridor concept now yields to the decision to utilize a covered veranda, a characteristic Australian feature, between the sleeping quarters that is open at the sides. This longitudinal passage was employed at the Fletcher and Page House (also in Kangaroo Valley, built 1989 to 1994), and the Simpson-Lee House.

A series of preliminary plans (conceived between December 26, 2001 and February 25, 2002) begin to reveal Murcutt's design priorities as they relate to the client's essential needs and multiple site considerations. These are the principal programmatic concerns: to provide a narrow building section to optimize air flow; facilitate views and sun angles to the north from the bed locations of both the client and guests, as well as to the northeast from the kitchen/dining area through the verandah; develop an entry scheme that separates public and private zones and that ensures separate entries for family and guests; consider the guest area being totally self-contained. Murcutt's notations

FIGURE 11.6
View of the 360-degree composite photo of the site context. (Photograph courtesy of Glenn Murcutt.)

164 Vernacular Architecture and Regional Design

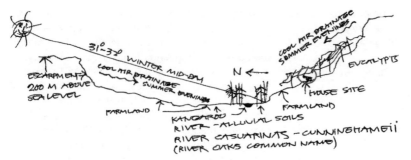

FIGURE 11.7
The House at Kangaroo Valley is on a north-facing hillside. The sun in Australia is in the northern sky – unlike the northern hemisphere, where it is the southern sky. (Demonstration sketch of site factors by Glenn Murcutt for the author.)

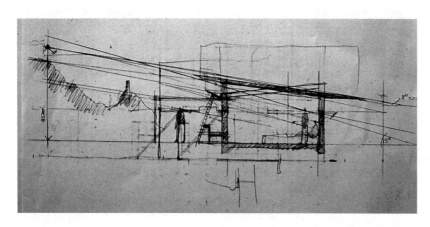

FIGURE 11.8
Drawing of sun angles related to the site's topography. The view angle faces north. (Drawing courtesy of Glenn Murcutt.)

read: 'kitchen sink-fry pan or future cooker/sofa/flap up table for 3…'. The design elements stress multiplicity of functions to provide spatial economy – 'note the single bed acts also as a sofa for 2 during the day and evening,' 'Lock this door and the shr/wc/bsn can be used by other than house guests' (Figures 11.11 to 11.13).

Murcutt's design concerns at this stage are: 'things that are good and things that need to be improved.' The client is concerned about cost. Murcutt replies, 'but do you like it? If you can't afford it as is, it is better that there is no fat in it.' This concern prompts design revisions, but it is clear that the environmental agenda directs the solutions. For example, 'the client wants a garage, but the cost is up; maybe, the roof can come out to the common area. Maybe there is an outside entry for the guest. Maybe we put a carport to the west to absorb the greatest amount of heat during the day [by blocking the low level sun from the west].'

Other considerations address the particularities of the site itself. They include research into 'geomorphology, hydrology, soil conditions, altitude, latitude, humidity, heat, and other climate factors.'

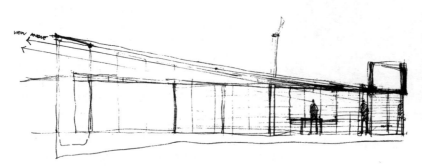

FIGURE 11.9
Preliminary sketch of the view angle facing north. Note the sun angle is from the north as well. The house is anchored into a hillside slope (see Figure 11.7). A stand of Eucalypts is situated above the house site and River Oaks are below. (Sketch courtesy of Glenn Murcutt.)

Architecture of response rather than imposition **165**

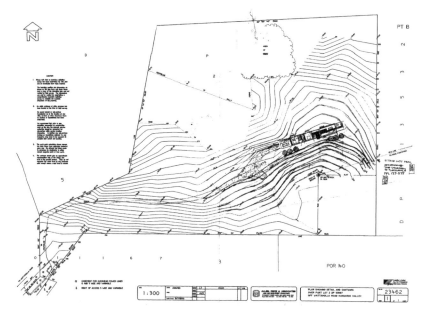

FIGURE 11.10
Plan showing detail, contours, and Murcutt's landform adjustments; comments on this drawing by Glenn Murcutt read, 'Siting not final. Reworking the land form to "natural" FFL 127–575,' March 24, 2002. (Plan courtesy of Allen, Price & Associates, Land and Development Consultants and Glenn Murcutt.)

Then Murcutt explores 'how to harness and exclude' these climatic factors. For example, he considers how to channel the 'cool northeast breeze' in his revised floor plans.

The revised plan is layered onto the contours (refer back to Figure 11.10 for the March 22, 2002 house plan and landscape layering). The plan is reworked to address environmental priorities. There is a continual evolutionary development.

He reconsiders the latest scheme with the client. 'I make the client work hard,' Murcutt concedes. 'Then they know you're serious.' He then goes back to the landscape and final drawings. He collaborates with the landscape architect to determine how the water tank encasment system will be resolved for storage.

Water sheds quickly during downpours in this region where an inch and a half of water in a half hour is not unusual. Accordingly, wide-mouth drain spouts are designed to collect water for later use and for fire protection in such remote areas. Brush and wild fires are legendary here. One of the west end steel storage tanks is designed to hold 10,000 liters of water with a valve connection for the fire brigade, and there is one in-house pump. On-site waste will be processed in a bio cycle unit, and the low

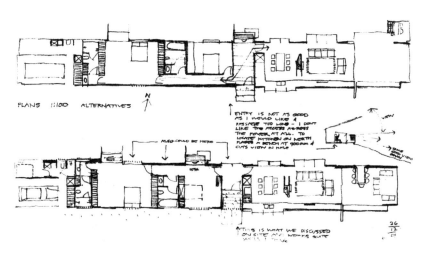

FIGURE 11.11
Sketch of plans 1:100 Alternatives: notations read: 'Entry is not as good as I would like & passage too long – I don't like the access across the foyer at all. To locate kitchen on north places a bench at 900 mm & cuts view in half.' (Sketch courtesy of Glenn Murcutt, December 26, 2001.)

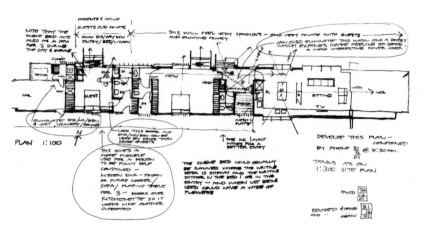

FIGURE 11.12
Refined plan solution with annotations by Murcutt for the client explaining the quality and flexibility of various spaces. 'Plan faxed to the client 26 December 2001; confirmed by client 31 December 2001; and revised and faxed again 31 December 2001.' (Plan courtesy of Glenn Murcutt.)

phosphate/nitrate (evaporated) effluent will be discharged by way of a drip system to trees and the garden (Figure 11.14).

Final design module

What results is a small two-bedroom house with an outdoor cooking area, verandah and reflecting pond along the east–west passageway (Figure 11.15). Fully opening sliding glass doors connect the verandah to the sitting area. The fireplace, located in the sitting area adjacent to the verandah, serves for heating in winter and, by opening the flue damper, allows for venting in the summer. The fireplace also is a room-divider for a smaller multiuse space to the west containing the writing desk, dining room, and kitchen. A foyer is situated to the west – directly behind the north–south entry; this entry also has a public/guest water closet. Continuing west off the foyer is *Bed 1*, offering a vantage point to the north from the bed. There is a private water closet, shower, and a built-in sitting/sleeping niche along the north-facing wall. A similarly appointed, but smaller, bedroom (*Bed 2*) is in the space to the west of this long, narrow house plan. Bed 2 has its bathroom facilities banked against those of Bed 1. Both bedrooms have private entrances. There is a garage/laundry area, in lieu of the carport, that terminates the plan to the west; its location is designed to serve as a thermal mass that absorbs the greatest amount of heat during the summer's late afternoon sun. There is thermal mass throughout the interior.

Structural details for trusses, lighting, and drainage are considered in plans and details. 'When you know when something is not good enough ... you continue to work through ideas in order to build up a complex understanding of how the building will perform, developing one part after another in layers ...' 'I lie in bed, thinking all the time, trying to reach the ideal solution – how the gutters work, how the roof works, certain climate zones, where water falls or discharges at the edge.' A gutter/roof detail,

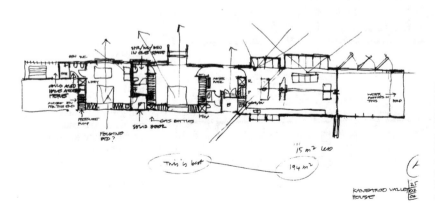

FIGURE 11.13
Refinement sketch dated February 25, 2002: 'This is best.' Sun and sight angles, circulation paths, basic program, and some operable window and door units have been ironed out. (Plan courtesy of Glenn Murcutt.)

Architecture of response rather than imposition   **167**

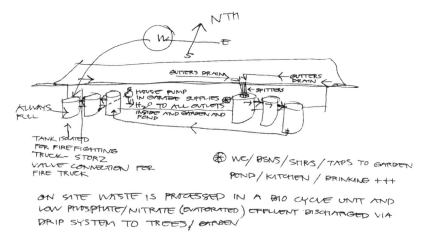

FIGURE 11.14
The Kangaroo Valley house's northern elevation maximizes its exposure to the sun, while the ten-degree shed or skillion roof slope facilitates rain encashment in several storage tanks fed by two large roof gutters. The large gutter to the south has two spitters that feed one tank. This tank supplies all others. The lines connect under ground. A house pump in the garage supplies water to all outlets inside as well as to the garden and pond. (Analytical sketch by Glenn Murcutt for the author.)

for example, provides a drainage solution that fits seamlessly between the steel I-beam roof plate and the projecting bed and writing desk bays (Figure 11.16), while the wide-mouth gutters are detailed to facilitate rain encashment (Figure 11.17). By this point 'the building is getting rich and is well on its way to development.'

Building envelope and climatic response

Though recognized for his stress on addressing the environmental particularities of a locale in his designs, like Carol Wilson (see the previous chapter),

it is in the practical response to design *discovery* that the essence of Murcutt's work seems to reside. Note his design for external aluminum blinds that take over for summer, the change of seasons and, occasionally, for winter climate demands. The blinds are fully adjustable; the blades are set between straps, fixed to ladder tapes and can tilt 85 degrees. The unit lifts up fully. 'The fixed blades on the roof set over glazing are set at the winter sun angle (noon, June 21, 32 degrees overlap – equinox sun noon, 55 degrees). As the sun gets higher than 55 degrees (up to 78 degrees in mid summer), no sun enters equinox/summer/equinox' (Figure 15.18).

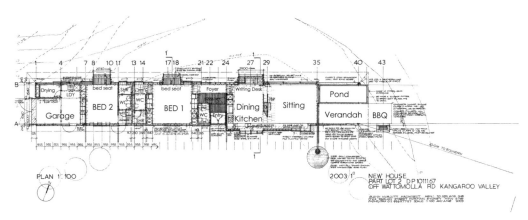

FIGURE 11.15
Augmented construction plan (dated 2003) with room designations highlighted by the author on the final scheme. (Drawing courtesy of Glenn Murcutt.)

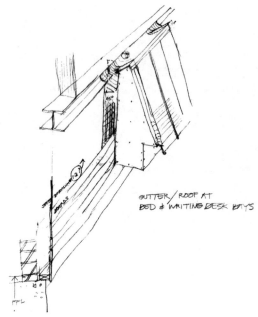

FIGURE 11.16
This sketch of the gutter/roof connection for the bed and writing desk bays clearly reflects the architect's concern for how design features are precisely detailed to function efficiently. (Sketch courtesy of Glenn Murcutt.)

hits the clerestory. On very hot days, it is *close-down* and a fan circulates the air. The clerestory windows have an internal drop-down roller blind – the back silvered and the face dark grey. These manually operated blinds are used in the winter, particularly, to reduce sunlight and to control warmth, as well as to exclude the light over the dining table. They also help in reducing heat loss in the winter. External Venetian blinds (lift/tilt) modify sun exclusion 100% – lift the blinds and there is full entry of the sun' (see photographic view in Figure 11.26). Above the clerestory windows over the roof glazing are sun screens to control lighting in the kitchen (Figure 11.19).

For the roof insulation: 'On u/s of the roof sheet, it is set on chicken mesh to keep it hard on u/s of the corrugated roof sheet. Roofing is silvered on both sides. 75 mm of Insulwool is laid over double sided reflective foil, and 50 mm Insulwool is set onto a 13 mm Gyprock ceiling that is sprung curved (see previous Figure 11.17).

Other heating and cooling strategies

'For cooling in the summer: first, no sun enters the house until equinox (greatly reducing the heat load) (Figure 11.20). The garage/laundry room is at the west end so as to "take up" the summer p.m. heat. [The western location of the garage mitigates] the impact of the late afternoon build up of heat in our summers.' In addition, 'There is a huge amount of thermal mass for not only winter heating but also summer cooling.

For additional light and shade control as well as ventilation, heating and cooling response, a favorite feature is the clerestory window. The north-facing windows are operable. During the 'summer, no sun

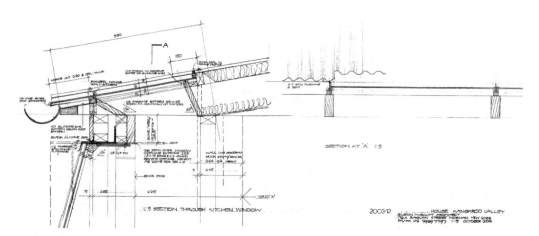

FIGURE 11.17
1:5 'Section through kitchen window,' dated October 2004. Note the oversized gutter that is connected to the wide-mouth drain spouts to facilitate the water tank encasement system. (Drawing courtesy of Glenn Murcutt.)

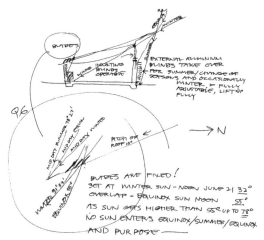

FIGURE 11.18
Analytical sketch of the internal insulating operable blinds and the external aluminum blinds with fixed blades. These features are detailed in relation to winter and summer sun angles. (Demonstration sketch by Glenn Murcutt for the author.)

Murcutt points out that 'Our wood is very hard hardwood and it burns at extremely high temperatures resulting in minimum pollution (zero carbon footprint). I think the fire would be lit for 1–1½ months/year around 4:30 p.m. The rock jacket and steel fire casing remain warm for the night after the fire has burned out … As a supplement to the fire, under-tile electric floor heat is installed in the sitting room and is used for up to fifteen times a year for three hours/day at most. The fireplace works well and is good psychologically.'

Detailing

Murcutt does from one to twenty section workups for key design features like the writing table to determine, for example, that air movement won't blow the paper on the desk and that proper lighting/shading controls are in place (for photo see Figure 11.25). 'I pursue ideals that I believe I have to achieve.' The smallest detail is considered. For Murcutt, the details are as important as the design itself. He displays a half-scale detail for a tracking system, sliding slatted timber screens, metal insect screens, and glazed doors – a tripartite system used since 1995 of various combinations and layer adjustments to meet varying environmental and human conditions from privacy to controlling air movement, solar gain, and 'the exclusion of native Australian biting insects' (Figure 11.23).

'All floors are concrete – stone mid-grey tiled – and *all* internal walls and *all* internal skins of external walls are of 110 mm clay-fired brickwork. All walls that do not have windows/vents/doors are constructed of brick, and are well insulated with reflective foil. 15 mm Caneite board and 75 mm Insulwood is used for double-sided reflective insulation with 20 mm board linings. This provides both convective and reflective insulation' (Figure 11.21).

'Winter mornings and nights require some supplementary heating, occasionally, but not daily.' The steel and rock fireplace in the Kangaroo Valley House accommodates this climate demand (Figures 11.15 and 11.22). Sun heats the floors/walls during the winter as well.

There are also 'insect screened louvred vent panels throughout; north and south sides of the house have timber slats externally, and twenty millimeter plywood doors are set on friction stays internally. Glass doors at the east end can slide to fully open the living space to the verandah. They

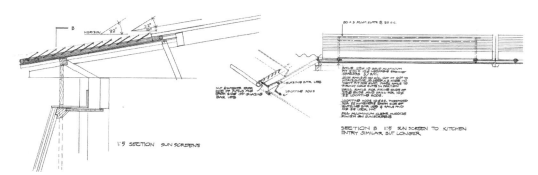

FIGURE 11.19
Drawing of the clerestory window design: 'Section B 1:5 sun screen to kitchen. Entry similar but longer,' dated October 2004. (Drawing courtesy of Glenn Murcutt.)

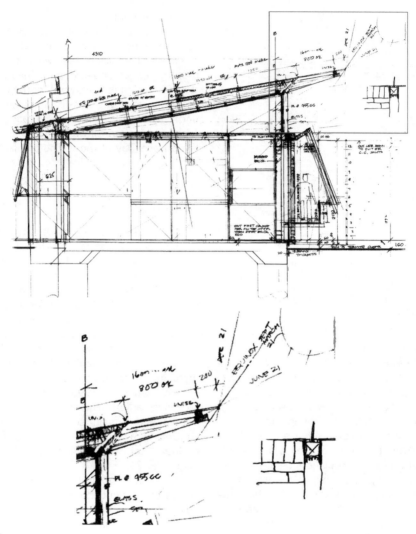

FIGURE 11.20
Sectional drawing (north is to the right) showing the sun angle during equinox. (Drawing courtesy of Glenn Murcutt.)

also have insect screens.' Hence, Murcutt designs 'windows and doors that slide, insect screens that slide, timber slatted screens that slide – any one can slide independent of another. Like sailing a yacht, one works these buildings to include/exclude light/sun/wind/insects/perfumes – nature.'

Murcutt produces between thirty and forty working drawings. 'The elevations are the very last thing, but I have thought of them all the way through.' He continues to present details of kitchen components, fireplace details, such as gravel around the hearth for greater heat efficiency.

It is the detailing stage – where carefully considered elements are finally resolved and integrated into the building itself – that defines much of the aesthetic character of Murcutt's work as well as its technical mastery. He delights in the pure act of *discovery* – as opposed to *invention* – wrestling with alternatives, and finally arriving at an ideal solution that celebrates a particular function and at the same moment is fabricated with the precision of a machinist. Notice Murcutt's consideration of a particular lighting strategy: 'The sun lights the southernmost wall which is usually cold in winter, but this way [the adjustable blinds] provide psychological warmth at the deepest part [that is] most removed from the light.' Through such considerations in all facets of the design scheme, the

Architecture of response rather than imposition **171**

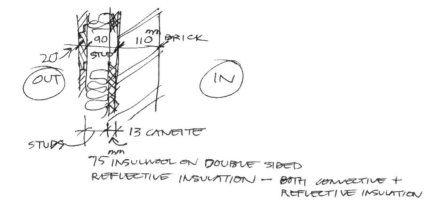

FIGURE 11.21
Drawing of the wall section. (Schematic drawing courtesy of Glenn Murcutt for the author.)

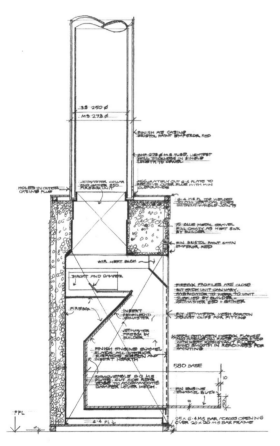

FIGURE 11.22
Sectional detail of the fireplace: the steel and rock fireplace has a heat exchange. The thermal rock jacket to the firebox (sides, back and top) has vents that move air. Adjustable vents move in the fire casing at the top and outer wall of the double flue chimney that are set near the firebox collar and on the underside of the ceiling. (Drawing courtesy of Glenn Murcutt.)

sun provides soothing warmth during the winter months at key locations such as the entry path, entry porch, and living/dining/kitchen spaces, while shading devices during the equinox/summer/equinox cycle provide sensory comfort for all aspects of the daily living experience.

Hence, the purpose behind such precise calculations is not limited to issues of human comfort in the pure technical sense. Murcutt is interested in controlling the *seasonal character* of the spaces as well. 'It is very green countryside.' But, Murcutt adds, 'When it comes to designing buildings, there is also a poverty of spirit – a bareness of the mind.' This future retirement house, therefore, must heighten the senses and embrace the spiritual uplift of the valley setting.

Though Murcutt is often cast as a rational modernist, his years at his father's side discussing Thoreau have left their mark. Murcutt fervently believes in the transcendent power of nature not only to instruct, but also to enlighten and to move. As a result, he offers a different proposition for environmental design. The entire ecosystem contributes to the pleasure of the human spirit, down to the scents of flowering plants.

Murcutt, for example, describes the environmental context of the Kangaroo Valley House as one of beautiful climate conditions, and discusses the setting of the house in anthropomorphic terms as though the house was a living organism. 'I designed the house with its back to the cold winter southwestern winds from the snow fields, and the front with the sun to the belly.' He then describes how he controls various material systems: 'I use the ground for insulating as a thermal mass. I bring light into the room up to the southern-located kitchen sink. Northeast breezes provide suction to the south and easterly breezes and [draw] cool air from the

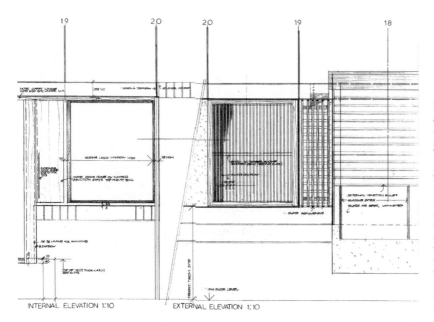

FIGURE 11.23
A section workup of a sliding slatted timber screen assembly unit. While such units are precisely detailed to function efficiently, Murcutt's concerns go beyond designing wall assemblies that meet code; the individual units are conceived within the framework of designing for human comfort and following sustainable practices. (Drawing courtesy of Glenn Murcutt.)

mountain behind to ventilate the house.' All natural forces come into play in the design. The color of the roof is calculated to radiate the heat. The trees in the surrounding forest have a type of feathering at the edge of the branches that offer delicate, near transparent, views through the forest when backlit.

Murcutt has designed the house so it can literally be *tuned* like an instrument to respond to seasonal cycles – slats for beautiful striated patterns of light, light slots over the front door to make the entrance enticing. It is as though the house is not just designed; it is choreographed to interpret the most beneficial characteristics of the natural environment. Patterns of water lilies, for instance, appear on the porch ceiling reflected from the pond. The pond, in turn, doubles as a holding pond for a built-in sprinkler system. This strategy appears at two other buildings: the Short House, Terrey Hills (where the roof holds the water), and the Simpson-Lee House in Mt Wilson. Far from being a statement of stark pragmatism, Murcutt's housing designs balance technological rationality with poetic sensitivity (Figures 11.24 and 11.25).

Some design features and technological strategies reappear in various projects like leitmotifs in a classical work – Murcutt did study piano after all. These include a predilection for long, low forms, slats set at various angles above the glass as screens for sun control and selected views of the sky; others combine a reflecting pool, such as those designed for both the Simpson-Lee House at Mt Wilson (1989 to 1994) and the Kangaroo Valley House. On these occasions, however, either such choices are prompted by similar climate conditions, or the variables are adjusted to the characteristics of a particular site. For example, while the pond in the Simpson-Lee house is used for fire protection, the House at Kangaroo Valley has a dedicated 10,000-liter storage tank for fire safety, allowing the pond to address other design issues: 'The pond reveals the pinnacle [of the sacred mountain 8 kilometers away] as one enters the living/dining room [areas]. It intensifies the sky colour and reveals wind/breeze patterns on the water surface.'

Philosophy on sustainability

Q: 'Your projects are so site specific and technologically sophisticated. Are there any rules that the general public in each region of Australia might take away with them from your projects that might improve environmental awareness more broadly?'

A: He answers succinctly and emphatically: 'Yes, all of the above!'

Murcutt adds, 'The problem with modernism is not with its ideals but with the practitioners [who use it] as dogma. You have to keep abreast of what's happening.' By 'what's happening,' Murcutt means technologically. He speaks of what he

FIGURE 11.24
Note the light reflecting from the lily pond onto the ceiling. (Photograph courtesy of Glenn Murcutt.)

phrases the *culture of components*. Just as he makes adjustments to the arrangement of spaces to manipulate climate factors, he consistently makes adjustments to standard factory-made components. He discusses, in particular, the tripartite window. Beginning around 1910–1914, 'the window was made in factories. It was clipped onto the outside using standard window technology.'

He believes in taking existing industrial components that are produced for different uses, and developing connecting elements to suit new needs. The augmented components and connections are reconsidered to produce some reasonably sophisticated, but affordable, details from standard industrial components. 'If you get both the details and design principles right, other things will follow that are not planned, such as the introduction of the phases of the moon to spaces.'

Murcutt then discusses the steel work system of construction (steel is procured locally). The house design utilizes a building module for a hybrid system of steel and wood with a brick skin. The wooden rafters are constructed of gang-nail connected off-cuts to reduce cost, but mainly to use good, short lengths of structural timber that would otherwise have been discarded. They are bolted to supporting members to enable disassembly later, if necessary, in keeping with the sustainable principle of reversibility and reuse.

By detailing connections carefully for assembly or reuse, little embodied energy is lost if the building elements need to be reworked in a subsequent building. For example, while the House in Kangaroo Valley utilizes concrete floors, brick is utilized in other projects; in such instances, the brick is laid in lime mortar, instead of Portland cement, so that the lime can be easily removed and both the lime and bricks can be reused. Similarly, wooden flooring, when used, is screwed to the joists, rather than nailed, for easy disassembly without destroying the integrity of the boards.

FIGURE 11.25
Natural lighting illuminates the writing table. View is looking west from the dining/kitchen/desk area, past the foyer, and terminating at Bed 1. (Photograph courtesy of Glenn Murcutt.)

With regard to the use of recycled materials in his projects, Murcutt notes, 'It is a personal choice and one's own level of [environmental] responsibility. If a supplier specializes in off cuts with strong connectors, it generally ends up costing the same as for a single-length timber member, but it is the way one uses off cuts, recycles bricks and timber, and other materials that contribute to a sustainable design process. This might mean acquiring a scavenging license for gaining access to timbers felled in the construction of new roads in forested areas, and then organizing the cutting, storing, and drying of the timbers in low energy black sheeted roof seasoning sheds with fan-forced air powered by solar energy.'

For calculating the size of a rafter or softwood timber, Murcutt purposefully uses the most durable hardwoods. He notes that five of the world's eight most durable hardwoods are found in Australia. Using inexpensive, readily available materials native to Australia is his preference. Murcutt details the timbers for shrinkage. He begins to list the properties of various native woods as they relate to framing. Eucalyptus, called *tallow wood* in Australia, has good natural preservative capabilities and has an incredibly high stress grade. Then there are many Eucalypts for flooring. Columns and beams are usually made from Australian hardwood and (these days where available) recycled timbers. Pine is used for lining boards internally. For cooler regions, Murcutt's buildings avoid open underfloor spaces, walls are of brick internally for thermal mass, and are stud-insulated externally.

Such a design stance often requires a shift in priorities on the part of the architect; in other words, the focus is redirected away from issues of cost, time, and expediency as *sole* determining factors in themselves, to one of enlightened resourcefulness whereby cost savings to the client are achieved by creative, practical, and environmentally sensitive means – either in the initial build or as part of lifecycle energy and maintenance costs. These same choices, informed by acute regional awareness, have far reaching implications related to energy consumption and resource depletion that can benefit many beyond the scope of the individual project.

Architect's reflections

'Most observers, I've found, don't get what I am attempting right. Yes, I get lots of positive feedback on the siting of the buildings, climate responsiveness, assembly principles, and finally "the buildings as objects" – as pristine elements in the landscape. But, think of a composer developing a superb musical score. Musicians/conductors interpret the music through various instruments [with] the recipients of the score being the audience.

'Now, think of nature offering us this score:

Climate – sun, shade, wind, stillness, heat, cold, rain, cloud, drought, flood, humidity, dryness.
Aspect – N[orth], S[outh], E[ast], W[est].
Nature – (above), plus geomorphology, geology, hydrology, topography, flora, fauna, acoustics, and so on.

'Add the above together, and one can capitalize on summer/flowering perfumed plants/wind direction/birds, etc. to be framed/introduced to the occupants of a building.

'Then, design a framework that captures the above, and introduce all those extraordinarily beautiful elements to an occupier/the audience of the building to have the building reveal/frame/heat/cool/sun/shade – be part of/with nature.

'[I see] the building as an instrument that captures the rhythms of nature within refuge. Nature writes the score; the building can reveal those elements most desired and reject [others] as not appropriate.

'There are so many issues that require consideration in the making of "an architecture that is responsive to place," such as (but not limited to):

- The geomorphology of a region: geology and hydrology – tones and eco-tones.
- The topography, which defines water flow and drainage.
- The latitude, which defines the relationship of the sun to our planet; influences temperature and the sun's position at a specific site.
- The altitude influences temperature and air pressure.
- The site's relationship to the coast/inland [and the] influences of humidity/moisture/temperature/rainfall/snow.
- Light – clarity or lack of clarity.
- Flora (all of the above is cited as an influence). Species respond to soil, drainage, climate (altitude and its relationship to heat, cold, sunlight hours, sunlight intensity or frailty, light/cloud cover).

- Fauna responds to flora and all the above conditions.
- Water – availability and lack of availability.
- Waste – appropriate management, responsibility to the environment.
- Materials – using those that are appropriate and available to the region; making responsible choices (ecologically); employing methods of assembly, so that the materials are easily retrieved and are able to be reused (bolt connections, screw fixings, etc.); understanding the energy that is being consumed [from harvesting to manufacture, to delivery of goods to the site, to construction, to lifecycle energy usage, to preventive maintenance].
- Structure/construction – appropriate to spans, technology and assembly.
- Space – quality of space/light/materials/temperature/ventilation naturally.
- Culture – working with diverse cultures within populations.
- Human – needs and aspirations [how the two can be achieved without confusing *needs* with *wants*].
- Contexts – urban, suburban, and rural.

'All of these issues must form a natural inclusion in our thinking about an architecture that is responsive to place, culture, and technology – the clarification of the essential – an architecture of response rather than imposition.'

Author's summary

The way Murcutt approaches his practice serves as a reminder that climate-oriented design (informed by the full spectrum of regional influences, constraints, and opportunities) provides a viable alternative within the profession of Architecture to dominating the natural world and consuming its resources. By embracing a low environmental impact design premise, Murcutt's work informs us that such *ecological functionalism* is critical to the fundamentals of *any* good design.

Murcutt's design strategies are neither the result of artistic self-indulgence, nor mere vernacular reminiscences of the Australian outback. Their uniqueness springs from the architect's experiential awareness of the region's natural forces; his masterful understanding of how to integrate natural systems into his designs; and his skill as an architectural technician that revels in celebrating practicality and precision. These collective strengths prompt lighting, shading, venting, heating, and cooling solutions that transcend bland pragmatics. Instead, they are often poetic, spark our imagination, and inspire us to 'give something back' in our own professional endeavors to enrich the world we live in through responsible design decisions (Figures 11.26 and 11.27).

FIGURE 11.26
View of clerestory, light louvers, and sliding screens. (Photograph courtesy of Glenn Murcutt.)

FIGURE 11.27
View of the completed house at Kangaroo Valley amidst its natural setting. (Photograph courtesy of Glenn Murcutt.)

As for aesthetics, one can speak of 'Miesian minimalism,' and the wonderful interior spatial experience that his *essential* designs offer. But, beyond his sophisticated contribution to the tradition of the modern movement, the true beauty inherent in his work is in the union of the building with its setting, the environmental premises that shape it, and the orchestration, in built form, of the cyclic rhythms of nature. This stress on the 'interrelationship among such factors as water, waste management, internal–external control of material collection, heating and cooling naturally' leads to an architecture of natural inclusion. In the process, his buildings conserve energy, work with nature, and cause as little damage as possible to the integrity of the site.

One may wonder if Murcutt's precision of execution and unique combination of acquired skills preclude duplication by others in the region. Can others benefit from his example in a way that would contribute to a broad-based, energy-responsive design tradition, or is this a case of the architect as individual performer? Murcutt's teaching in the master class at the University of Newcastle with Richard Leplastrier says otherwise. As one participant in the master class, Brook Muller, put it, 'the rigorous and sincere approach toward architecture we were encouraged to pursue in the master class [was] that architecture is to be investigated as a medium and not an object, distilled to its essence, to enhance our knowledge and joy of a particular place on earth.'[3]

Selected reading and websites

Beck, H. and Cooper, J., editors (2002). *Glenn Murcutt, a Singular Architectural Practice*. Images Publishing Group.
Davidson, C. (2006). Raised to observe: Glenn Murcutt. *Log 8,* Summer, 31–40.
Drew, P. (1991). *Leaves of Iron: Glenn Murcutt, Pioneer of an Australian Architectural Form*. Angus & Robertson.
Drew, P. (2001). *Touch the Earth Lightly: Glenn Murcutt in his Own Words*. Duffy & Snellgrove.
Farrelly, E. M. (2002). *Three Houses: Glenn Murcutt*. Phaidon.
Fromonot, F. (1995). *Glenn Murcutt: Works + Projects*. Whitney Library of Design.
—— (2003). *Glenn Murcutt: Works + Projects, 1962–2003*. Thames & Hudson.
Glenn Murcutt – Great buildings online. Available at http://www.greatbuildings.com/architects/Glenn_Murcutt.html
In the mind of the architect: Glenn Murcutt (Australian Broadcasting Corporation, 2000). Available at http://www.abc.net.au/arts/architecture/arch/ar_mur.htm
Muller, B. (2001). In the landscape of Murcutt. *Architecture Week*, September 15, 1–5.
Postiglione, G., Flora, N. and Giardiello, P. (1999). *Glenn Murcutt: Disegni per Otto Case*. Casalini Libri.
Pritzker Architecture Prize Laureate 2002. Pritzker Prize Jury Announcement. Available at http://www.pritzkerprize.com/2002annc.htm

Notes

1. Murcutt's appointment term at the University of Washington extends from 2003 to 2008. Once a year, he co-teaches a graduate studio (this year with Rick Mohler). He has also taught with Peter Cohan (2004/2005), and with Jim Nicholls (2007). Murcutt's involvement

consists of two intense periods lasting seven to eight teaching days, coupled with follow-up oversight instruction by the co-instructor. Students from other studios come to listen, observe, comment, and question. During these encounters, as noted by the Dean of the College of Architecture, 'Murcutt demonstrates a spirit and love for architecture that is contagious.'

2. Unless otherwise noted, all statements within quotation marks are from correspondence with the author, June 21, 2007.
3. Brook Muller, In the landscape of Murcutt. *Architecture Week*, September 15, 2001, 4.

Author's note: I would like to thank Glenn Murcutt not only for graciously consenting to an interview the day following his lecture at the University of Washington, May 19, 2007, but for his subsequent efforts to provide me with clarifications to this chapter by way of providing me with a full set of drawings (from preliminary sketches to fully developed plans and sections) for the House in Kangaroo Valley. In addition, Mr Murcutt sent me a twenty page faxed letter and five pages of attachments (mailed on June 21, 2007), and a disc of scanned images (mailed on September 13, 2007) for exclusive use in this chapter. Also, University of Oregon architecture professors Brook Muller, John Reynolds, Alison Kwok, and Nico Larco lent commentary on an earlier draft of the manuscript that led to the clarification of key design issues for the author.

Index

Abel, Chris, 20
Acadia National Park, Maine (USA), 146
Ackerman, James, 39, 59
Al Sayyad, Nezar, 4, 6, 32
Alexander, Christopher, 53–4
Allen, Stan, 111
Allen, Woody, 3
Amenity Infrastructure (Petrucci), 110–1
Annapolis (Maryland), 10–1
Anti-apartheid movement, 82–3
   artists, 77, 83
Apartheid, 48, 75, 77, 135
Architect:
   -client relationship, 134–5, 149, 160, 163, 165
   education *see* Architectural education
   role of the, xiv, 47–8, 51, 61–62, 72, 75–7, 93, 122–3, 129, 135, 143–4, 146, 149–50, 159–60, 175–6
Architectural blank, 22
Architectural education, xiv, 27–8, 47, 176–7
Architecture:
   as cultural/social production, xv (Note 2), 3–18, 22–32, 82, 149
   as symbolic image, 9–10, 82–3
   folk, high style, popular, 8-9
   vernacular *see* Vernacular architecture
Art *see* Public art
   see also Ornament
Australia, 159–61
Authenticity *see* Place, authenticity

Badt, Alfred E., 3, 5
Ball State University, 66
Bawa, Geoffrey, 63, 73–4
Bedrooms, *see* House: plans, sleeping spaces
Benjamin, Walter, 83
Bicycle to heaven (Martin), 9
Bloom, Verna, 150
Border postcard: chronicles from the edge (Cruz), 103
Border zones, 93–107
Bowdoin College Coastal Studies College, 146
Bratton, Denise, 98, 104
Bricker, Lauren Weiss, 19 (Note 3)
Brown, Denise Scott, 38, 40
Buggelin, Gretchen, 11

Building:
   codes, 102, 157
      see also Zoning
   components/units, standardized, 12, 157, 173
   earthship strategy (earth-filled tires), 98, 129
   envelope, 57, 114, 160, 167, 169–70, 173
   gabion baskets, 142–3
   materials,, 25, 142, 156
      adobe (mud bricks), 9, 43
      concrete/cement, 15, 57, 142, 169
      brick, 57-8
      discarded, 12, 95-6, 129–30, 142–3
      embodied energy, 35 (Note 10), 135, 142, 173
      local, 142, 174
      masonry, 11, 57, 134, 142, 169
      rammed earth, 134
      recycled/scavenged, 95, 129–31, 137, 174
      reeds, 7–8, 131
      shingles, 154, 156
      steel, 84, 116, 131, 142–3, 147–8, 154, 173
      steel drums, discarded, 12, 129, 145
      sustainable use of, 129, 142–3, 154, 156, 173
      tires, 98, 129
      water, 142
      wood, 156, 169, 173–4
   slipcovers (facades), 30
   windows, 131, 155–6, 167–70, 173
Building tomorrow: The mobile/manufactured housing industry (Hayden), 22, 157
Buildings:
   as social/political record, xiii–xv, 28, 75
   usable life, 16, 127
Bungalows, discarded, 95, 97
Burra Charter: the Australia ICOMOS charter for the conservation of places of cultural significance, 127, 135
Buyways: billboards, automobiles, and the American landscape (Gudis), 108

Cabarrus County (North Carolina), 24-6
Cardboard Architecture House II (Falk House, Hardwick, Vermont), 9
Caribbean islands, 12
Carson, Barbara and Cary, 87

Casa Familiar Organization, 93–4, 98
Casa Familiar – Mi Pueblo (San Ysidro, California), 93–107
Castagnola, Giacomo, 93
Castle as home, 9
CEDMA *see* Center for Development
Center for Development (CEDMA) (Tamil Nadu, India), 51, 53–4
Central business districts, *see* Town centers
Change, 3–4, 13–4, 30
  and cultural continuity, 53, 58
  threshold of, 14
  see also Cultural weathering
Charleston (South Carolina) single house, 7
Clifford, Sue, 39, 41, 47–8
Climate, design responses to, 22–5, 62, 127, 129, 143, 147, 155, 159, 165, 167, 171, 175
Cocks, Jay, 150, 152
Cockram, Michael, 129, 144
Collaboration in planning and design, 40–2, 54, 56–9, 69–71, 73, 87–8, 93–4, 99, 104, 108, 122–3, 134–5, 149
Colonialism:
  Dutch, 75, 78
  effects of on local architecture, 9–10, 18, 43, 62–3, 74
  post-colonial identity, 18, 63, 73–4, 93
Color *see* Design strategies, color
Commercial (re)development, 108, 110, 123–4
  linked to social empowerment, 53–4
Commercial space *see* Space, commercial
Common Ground (England), 39, 41
Community involvement, 56, 82, 108
Community planning *see* Urban Planning
Concentration camps (South Africa), 78–79
Concrete *see* Building materials, concrete
Construction:
  labor issues, 87, 135, 142–3
  on-the-job training, 87, 143
  phased *see* Phased development/construction
Context, 43–4, 47, 135
Contributive democracy (Cruz), 105
Council of South African Trade Union, 83
Critical vernacular (Perera), 61–3, 70, 73–4, 160
Cruz, Teddy, 4, 14, 35, 41–3, 48, 93–107, 108, 123
Cuellar, Adriana, 93
Cultural:
  cocoons, buildings as, 12, 26
  in South Africa, 79–80
  conservation movement, 5
  continuity, 53
  groups:
    Afrikaners (South Africa), 78–9
    Annamalais (India), 58,
    Filipino-Americans, 4
    Hindus, 54, 57
    Japanese-Americans, 4
    Jewish-Americans, 3
    Latino/Latina-Americans, 93–107

  Native-Americans (Pueblo), 9
  San (Bushman) (Namibia), 135, 138–41
  identity, 4, 35, 62, 75, 78, 94
  insiders/outsiders *see* Insider/outsider view of place
  revitalization, 38, 41
Cultural weathering, 6, 21, 22–6
  conceptual model, 3–21
  Montana case study, 22–4
  North Carolina case study, 24–6
Culture, commoditization of, 43–6, 78, 146
Culture of components (Murcutt), 12, 172
Cyprus, 106

Darrt-Newton, Deana, 9
Darwinian theory, 12
Davis, Howard, 16, 40, 42, 47–8, 51–60, 61, 135, 144
Davis, Robert, 46
Daycare, 101
Decline of the English murders and other essays (Orwell), 127, 144
Decoration *see* Ornament
Deetz, James, 12
Dehiattakandiya (Sri Lanka), 62, 68, 72
Delaney, Frank, 87
Design critiques, 58–60, 69–73, 87–90, 122–4, 143–4, 175–6
Design principles, 39, 53–4, 57, 98, 129, 148–51, 156, 174–6
  ethnicity and, 93
  collaboration *see* Collaboration in design
  role of nature *see* Nature, role of
  see also Situated regional design
Design development phase, 48
  Housing Initiative for Rickshaw Drivers, 54–7
  Kangaroo Valley House, 163–72
  Mahaweli Development Project, 66–71
  Museum at Red Location, 82–5
  Stripscape – 7th Avenue Urban Revitalization Project, 113–9
  Visitors' Interpretive Centre for Prehistoric Art, 138–40, 163
  Writer's Studio, 149–52
Design process *see* Design development phase
Design strategies 39, 51, 53–8, 60, 62, 66, 79, 85–7, 90, 98, 111–22, 171–2
  color, use of, 118, 120
  cost factors, 57, 157, 174
  graphics, 116–8, 120–1
  multi-use spaces, 95–6, 98
  pedestrains, 108, 113, 117
  phased *see* Phased development/construction
  place-based, 144, 148, 160, 174–5
    see also Situated regional design
  symbolism *see* Symbolism in design
  urban planning *see* Urban planning
  using standard industrial components, 157, 173
  ventilation, 160, 162–3, 171–2

Index **181**

water drainage *see* Water, drainage/collection/storage
  see also Situated regional design
De Sylva, Shenuka, 21
Diversity *see* Ethnicity/diversity
Doors:
  alignment of, 23, 57
  design, 156, 169–70
Downtown America: a history of the place and the people who made it, 31
Drive-in markets, movie theatres, and restaurants (extinct vernacular), 17
Drums *see* Building materials, steel drums

Economic redevelopment *see* Commercial (re)development
Ecological functionalism, 175
Eisenman, Peter, 9
Elliot, T. S., 149
El Vado Motor Court (Albuquerque, New Mexico), 17
Emergent typologies (Petrucci), 112
England in particular: a celebration of the common place, the local, the vernacular and the distinctive (Clifford), 39, 41
Entrances, 23, 59
  portico, 22, 25
  weather baffle, 23
  porch (veranda, gallery, piazza), 25, 163
Environmental issues, 5, 14, 22–5, 39, 41–2, 49, 56, 115, 63, 159–61, 165–9, 171–2, 174–6
Estudio Teddy Cruz, 93
Ethnicity/diversity issues, 19 (Note 3), 3–4, 40–1, 93–4, 123
  see also Cultural groups
European Union, 127
Extinct vernacular *see* Vernacular, extinct

Falk House (Hardwick, Vermont) *see* Cardboard architecture....
Falmouth (Maine), 149–50
Field guide to sprawl (Hayden), 108
Fletcher and Page House (Murcutt), 163
flooring/paving:
  brick, 173, 142
  passive solar, 169
  reversibility, 142, 173
  wood, 173
Functionality, 129

Gallatin County (Montana), 22–23
Galleting (masonry), 11
Gehry, Frank, 38
Gentleman in the Parlor: a record of a journey from Rangoon to Haiphong (Maugham), 59
Glassie, Henry, 16
Global sense of place (Massey), 4
Graphics *see* Design strategies, graphics
Graves, Michael, 43
Gudis, Catherine, 108

Habitat Research and Development Centre (Windhoek, Namibia), 129, 131, 134
Hardy, Holzman, Pfieffer Associates (New York), 44
Hayden, Dolores, 22, 108
Heating and cooling strategies, 24, 155, 160, 168–9
Heritage conservation *see* Historic preservation
Heritage development, sustainable *see* Sustainable heritage development
Heritage, intangible, 6, 8, 85–7
Heritage tourism, *see* Tourism
Hermitage (Tennessee), 27
Historic conservation, *see* Historic preservation
Historic Preservation Act (United States, 1966), 32
Historic preservation, 27–8, 32, 39, 41
  cultural diversity, 19
  education, 4, 28, 32
  policies, 7–8, 27–8, 30
  United States, 27
  see also Burra Charter and Venice Charter
  post-apartheid, 76
Historic sites, reconstituted, 32
Holocaust, 80
Hood, Walter, 149
House:
  plans, 21
  public/private spaces, 58, 101, 163
  sleeping spaces, 58, 166
  toilets, 57
  types (forms), 18, 25, 40
House, form and culture (Rapoport), 40
House in Kangaroo Valley (New South Wales, Australia), 159–77
  environmental factors, 159–61, 165, 167–9, 171–2
House One (Falmouth, Maine), 27, 150–1, 156–8
Housing, 39, 54
  aboriginal, 160, 163
  affordable, 22, 42
    Housing Initiative for Rickshaw Drivers and their Families, 51–60
    Casa Familiar – Mi Pueblo Project, 93–107
    Mahaweli Development Project, 66–71
    Stripscape–7th Avenue project, 108–24
  density, 99–101, 105
  discarded, 95
  government-built, 80, 105
  multi-family, 51–60, 61–74, 93–107
  new housing production, 22
  relocation, 79–80
  self-built, 54, 58, 77
  shacks, 79–81, 88, 130–3
  single-family:
    House in Kangaroo Valley, 159–77
    Writer's Studio, 146–56
  squatter, 98
  subdivisions, 98
  subsidized/unsubsidized *see* Housing, affordable
  temporary, 14–5

Housing Initiative for Rickshaw Drivers and their Families (Vellore, Tamil Nadu, India), 51–60
Hult Center for the Performing Arts (Eugene, Oregon), 44
Human behavior as a determinant of place
  see Patterns of use
  see also Place
Huyssen, Andreas, 84
hybridity, 6, 14, 70, 94
Hymes, Dell, 6

Identity
  community, 111, 120
  cultural see Cultural identity
  national, 63
Idiosyncrasy in art or architecture, 9, 104
I-house (Shenandoah Valley, Virginia), 16, 25, 35
Immigrants, 13–4, 35, 94, 99
  policies toward, 35
  Jewish, 3
  South African, 75
  Spanish-speaking, 99
Infrastructure, planning, 67–70, 110–111, 120
  amenity infrastructure, 113–4, 116
  electricity, illegal use, 98-9
Insider/outsider view of place, xiii, 39, 51, 57, 59–60, 62, 87, 93, 146
Intangible heritage, 85–7
  UNESCO, Convention for the safeguarding of, 8
Integrity, 7, 27–8, 32, 35
Ireland, a novel (Delaney), 87
Isenberg, Alison, 31–2
Izenour, Steven, 38, 40

Jameson, Frederick, xiii
Janz, Wes, 66
Japanese-Americans (Los Angeles, California), 19
Jencks, Charles,
Jokilehto, Jukka, 6–7
Jorn, Asgar, 110
Judd, Donald, 100

Kangaroo Valley (New South Wales, Australia), 159, 161–2
Kaufman Ned, 35
Kellert, Stephen R., 159
Kerr, Thomas, 51, 53, 56
Khon Kaen University (Thailand), 7
Kinahan, John, 137
Kitchens, 88-89
  as private space, 58
Kluge House (Helena, Montana), 9

LaGrange (Ohio), 4
Landscape, 39, 40, 47
  heritage, 19
  of contradiction (Cruz), 96
  see also Place
Landscaping, 116
Last Chance Gulch, Montana, 9

Laos, 7
Lee, Antoinette, 35
Leguia, Mariana, 93
Leplastrier, Richard, 176
Lewin, Wendy, 159
Libraries, 43, 80
Light in design, 128, 131, 139, 151, 153, 168, 170–2
  lampshades (illuminated canopies), 115, 116, 118
Liminal, definition of, 20–1
Little Manila (Stockton, California), 4
Living Rooms at the Border (San Diego), 100, 102, 105
Log buildings, 16, 25
Loose-fit planning strategy (Janz), 61, 66, 88
  in other design processes, 56
Los Angeles (California), 9

Mahaweli Development Project (also called Mahaweli Irrigation Project, Sri Lanka), 61–74
  effects of civil war on project outcomes, 71–2
Main Street Project (National Trust for Historic Preservation, United States), 29, 35
Maine (United States), 35, (Note 6), 42, 98, 146–7, 149–50, 152, 155
Make-believe State: governance, law and affect in a border territory (Navaro-Yashin), 106
Manufactured homes see Mobile/manufactured homes
Marika-Alderton House (Northern Territory, Australia), 160–1
Maritz, Nina, 8, 12, 42, 48–9, 127–45
Martin, John, 9
Mass culture, 16, 25
Massey, Doreen, 4, 45
Maugham, William Somerset, 59
McCleary, Ann, 16
McDonald, Dennis, 127, 137
Mda, Lizeka, 89
Memory, 43, 80, 83, 86
Memory boxes, 83–4
Merrill, Scott, 47
Methodologies, xiv, 51–3
  analysis, 8–18, 60, 112–4
  computer models, 112–5
  performance theory, 67
  social mapping, 53
  see also Structural models
Mies van der Rohe, Ludwig, 151, 176
Million Houses Program (Sri Lanka), 64
Minister of the Arts, Culture, Science and Technology (South Africa), 77, 80
Spanish missions, 9, 43
Mobile/manufactured homes, 9, 22–7
  building codes and financing, 157
Mockbee, Sam, 40, 42
Modernism, 44, 110, 172
Moe, Richard, 32, 35
Montana, 22-5
Morangyo, John, 78
Morphosis (Los Angeles, California), 38, 40

Moses, Paul, 51, 53, 56
Moss, Eric, 38, 40
Mount Airy Plantation (Richmond County, Virginia), 4
Mount Vernon (Virginia), 27
Mount Desert Island (Maine), 146–7
Muller, Brook, 176
Murali, Deepti, 21
Murcutt, Glenn, 12, 25, 41–2, 47–8, 149, 159–177
Museum at Red Location (Port Elizabeth, South Africa), 75–90
Museums, 8, 40, 48
   Museum at Red Location, 75–90
   Visitors' Interpretation Centre for Prehistoric Rock-cut Art, 127–45

Namibia, 12, 14, 42, 48–9, 127–33, 135, 140–4
   Tourism Development Program, 135
   National Monuments Council (NMC), 127, 135
National Historic Districts, 29,
National Historic Landmark criteria, 27
National Register for Historic Places (United States), 4, 27
   criteria, 4, 35
   integrity, 35
National Trust for Historic Preservation (United States), 32
National Trust Loan Fund, 29
Native-American culture, 9
Native versus non-native views of place *see* Znsider / outsider
Nature, role of, in design, 146–9, 151–3, 171–2, 174
Navaro-Yashin, Yael, 106
Neighborhoods, 32, 93, 120
   redevelopment, 94, 98, 108–123
Nelson, M., 51, 54, 57
New Brighton (South Africa), 75
New England (USA), 12
New South Wales (Australia), 40, 42
New Vernacular, 13, 15, 38, 40
New York City, 3, 149, 155
New York Times, 94
Noero, Jo, 8, 47–9, 75–90
North Carolina, 18, 22, 24–5, 146
Northern Territory (Australia), 159
Northwest Rock Art Visitors' Centre *see* Visitors' Interpretative Centre for Prehistoric Art (Namibia)
Nowra (Australia), 162

Oil drums *see* steel drums
Office of Neighborhood Involvement (Portland, Oregon), 32
Oral history, relevance of, 85, 87–8
Ornament:
   recycled materials as, 129–30
   paint, 133
   rice flour, 59
Orr, David, 159
Orwell, George, 127, 144
Ouroussoff, Nicolai, 94
Outsider art, 9, 20 (Note 16)

Outsider/insider *see* Insider/outsider
Outdoor rooms, 108, 116
Overpainting, strategic (Petrucci), 110

Pachwerbau construction, 9
Passive environmental responses, 115, 169
Pattern book designs, 11, 16
Pattern language, 51–3 *see* Place, patterns of use
Patterns of continuity/contradiction (Heath), 39, 39
Patterns of behavior, 51, 53–4, 56, 109, 112–3, 122
Patterns of effect (Jameson), 18
Patterns of use, *see* Patterns of behavior
Pavement dwellers *see* Street dwellers
Pedestrian, planning for, *see* Urban planning, pedestrians
Perera, Nihal, 18, 48, 61–74, 88, 95, 135, 160
Petrucci, Darren, 5, 31, 35, 108–23
Phased development/construction, 57–8, 66–7, 105
Philosophy of design *see* Design principles
Phoenix (Arizona), 5, 108–123
Piazza *see* Front porch
Pike Street Synagogue (New York), 3, 5
Pitera, Dan, 35
Place, xiii–xiv, 27–8, 30, 39, 43
   as a mental construct, 3–4, 43, 56, 122
   authenticity, 3–5, 35, 78
   determinants of, 41, 109, 112–3
   dynamics of, 3–5, 26, 30, 39, 58–9, 112–3, 121, 148
   ethnicity and, 6, 93
   native versus non-native view of *see* Insider/outsider view of place
   visual representations of, 43–4, 122
   perceptions of place, 51, 59, 96–8
   see also Patterns of behavior
Place and placelessness (Relph), xiii–xiv
Planning *see* Urban planning, Historic preservation planning,
Plan-types, 18, 57–8, 70
Plaza *see* Town centers
Plesner, Urlik, 61–3, 73
Plymouth Colony (Massachusetts), 12
Points & lines: diagrams and projects for the city (Allen), 111
Political unconsciousness (Jameson), xiii
Pon drums, 12
   see also Building materials, steel drums, discarded
Port Elizabeth (South Africa), 75, 79
Portland (Oregon), 32
Post-colonialism *see* Colonialism
Postmodernism, 47, 63
Privacy issues, 89
Public art, 113, 115, 119
Pueblo Indians, 9
Pyatok, Michael, 42

Quigley, Rob Wellington, 42, 45, 103

Rapoport, Amos, 38, 40, 47–8
Redevelopment *see* Urban revitalization

Regional design, 3, 5, 27, 63, 41, 434
  see also Situated regional design
Regional dynamics see Regional filter
Regional filter, 8–9, 13–4, 22, 26, 39, 40, 57, 73, 63, 109, 129, 146, 159–60
  Northern Territory, Australia, 159–60
  Namibia, 129
  Southern India, 57
Regional identity, xiii–xiv, 3–21,
  see also Identity
Regional Library (San Juan Capistrano, California), 43
Regionalism:
  defined, xiii–xiv, 11–13
  symbolic or personal, 43
Regionalism, critical see Forward, i
Regionalism, situated, xiii–xv, 39–40, 42, 46–8, 89, 94, 129, 146, 160
Relocation camps (South Africa), 79–80
Relph, Edward, 57
Resettlement, 77
Residential Hotel (Stockton, California), 4
Restorative Listening Project (Portland, Oregon), 89
Retail shops see Space, commercial
Reversibility, 129, 142–3, 147, 173
Ridout, Orlando, 10
Rocky Mountains (United States), 9, 22, 24–5
Rodia, Simon, 9
Roe, Kathleen, 93
Roof:
  design, 57, 131–3, 155, 167–8
  forms, 25
Rosenblum, Alan, 93
Route, 17, 66
Ruch, Susan, 150
Rules of thumb see Patterns of behavior
Rural Studio (Hale County, Alabama), 40, 42

Samper, Jota, 93
San Diego (California), 42–3, 93, 95, 98–9, 103, 105
San Ysidro (San Diego, California), 41, 43, 93, 98, 100
San Ysidro Affordable Housing Project, 103
Schlereth, Thomas J., 86
Seaside (Florida), 44–6
Second Boer War see South Africa, Boer War
Senior Gardens Project (San Diego), 101, 103–5
Seventh (7th) Avenue Merchants Association, 108, 111, 118, 122
Shacks see Housing, shacks
Shenandoah Valley, 16
Short House (Terry Hills, Australia), 172
Simpson-Lee House (Mt. Wilson, Australia), 163, 172
Single Resident Occupancy housing (SROs), 40
Site analysis/planning, 23–4, 53–7, 111, 129, 136–7, 140–2, 147–9, 163–4
Sites, endangered or fragile, 147–8
  effects of visitors, 127, 135, 140

Sleeping places, see House plans, sleeping spaces
Smith, Calvin, 5
Smith, Ted, 103
Snow load, 22
Social equity, 39
Social responsibility, 32–3
Social mapping, 53, see also Pattern language
Space:
  appropriation of, 98
  commercial, ad hoc/informal, 95, 98–9, 111–3
  economy of, 163
  flexibility of function, 98
  gender roles and, 58
  public/private spaces, 58, 85, 89, 98, 101, 121, 163
  social dynamics of, 57–9, 79
  social zones, 25, 57–9, 79, 85
Spielberg, Steven, 80
Square, public see Town centers
Squatters see Housing, squatters
Sri Lanka (Democratic Socialist Republic of), 15, 61, 64, 95
Stabilized vernacular architecture see Vernacular architecture, stabilized (folk)
Stripscape – 7th Avenue Urban Revitalization Project (Phoenix, Arizona), 108–23
Structural models, 8–9, 14, 39
  see also Methodologies
Sung Tak Buddhist Temple (New York), 3
Sustainability:
  as a design philosophy, 35–6, 129–33, 142–4, 172–5
  construction methods, 142, 173
  transportation of materials, 154
Sustainable heritage development, 32–3, 129
Sutthitham,Thada, 7–8
Symbolism in design, 25, 40–2, 44, 83, 85, 98

Tactical evaluation (Petrucci), 112
Tamil Nadu (India), 15, 21, 51–60
Technology see Building technology
Temple/shrine:
  Buddhist, 3–4, 8
  Hindu, 53, 57
  Sung Tak Buddhist (New York City), 3, 4
Thailand, 7–8
Theoretical model see Structural model
Thermal mass, 57, 166, 171, 174
Tijuana (Mexico), 94–100, 103–4
Tourism:
  as an economic base, 146
  effects of, 140, 127, 135, 146
  heritage, 3
Tower Apartments (Rohnert Park, California), 40
Town centers, 56, 66, 68, 70
  effects of civil war on, 71
  commercial growth and development, 108, 110
Towns, villages, hamlets, 68–69
Trailer homes see Mobile homes
Trance ritual, 138–40

Truth and Reconciliation Commission (South Africa), 89
Turner, John, 66
Tutu, Desmond, 82, 87
Twilight spaces (Noero), 84
Twyfelfontein (Namibia), 127, 130, 145

Union Station (LaGrange, Ohio), 4
University of Southern California, 80
University of Washington, 159, 176–7
Urban centers see Town centers
Urban Development Authority, 64
Urban planning, 61–3, 112, 122
   border zones and, 93–5
   Casa Familiar – Mi Pueblo Project (San Diego, CA), 93–107
   education, 27, 98
   ethnicity/diversity and, 93, 98
   Housing Project for Rickshaw Drivers, 51–60
   Mahaweli [Sri Lanka] Development Project, 66–71
   pedestrians, see Design Strategies pedestrians
   place-based strategies, 93, 160
   Rickshaw Drivers' Housing Project, 51–60
   San Ysidro [CA] Pilot Village, 93–107
   Stripscape-7th Avenue project [Phoenix, Arizona], 108–23
   suburbs, 94, 98
Urban revitalization, 29–32, 39, 93, 95, 104–5, 108–23
Urbanism/New Urbanism, 14, 46, 94–5, 101, 103

Vellore, India, 41, 43, 51
Venice Charter (1964), 8, 32
Ventilation, 160, 168–9, 171–2
Venturi, Robert, 40
Vernacular architecture in the Twenty-First Century (Davis), 49
Vernacular architecture, 8–21, 38, 40, 159–60
   and contemporary design, 61, 70, 141, 160, 163
   evolving, 6, 18, 32, 35 (Note 8)
   extinct, 16–8, 32
   high-style representations of, 10–1, 38, 40, 43
   stabilized (folk), 15–8
   traditional/local building practices, 4, 6–8, 10–2, 15–8, 38, 53, 57, 95–6, 159–60, 163
Vernacular, definition of, 6, 9–13, 16, 87
Villages see also Settlements, typology
Visitors' Interpretation Centre for Prehistoric Rock-cut Art (Namibia), 12, 48–9, 127–45
   scarcity of building materials, 129–32, 142–3
   effects of visitors on site, 127, 129, 135, 137, 140
   traditional influences on design, 141

Waste disposal, 137, 165–6
Water:
   as a design element, 172
   drainage/collection/storage, 132, 163, 165–7, 172
   scarcity, 137, 142, 145
Watts Towers (Los Angeles, California), 9
Weather baffle see Entrances
Weather see Climate
Weed, Andrew, 118, 122
Week, David, 51, 53, 56, 58
Weiss, Gregor, 26–8, 31
Wilson, Carol A., 27, 41–2, 98, 146–58, 167
   see also House One
Wind see Climate
Wright, Frank Lloyd, 39
Writer's Studio (Mount Desert, Maine), 146–56

Zoning/rezoning issues, 93–5, 103, 105, 113